PROVIDING FOR

INDIVIDUAL

DIFFERENCES

IN THE ELEMENTARY SCHOOL

Contributions from the editors and

J. RICHARD CHAMBERS, Ed.D.

Assistant Professor of Elementary Education
University of Miami, Florida

VIRGIL E. HERRICK, Ph.D.

Professor of Education
University of Wisconsin

EDWARD L. MATTIL, Ed.D.

Professor of Art Education
The Pennsylvania State University

ROBERT L. MORTON, Ph.D.

Professor of Education
Ohio University

ROBERT E. NYE, Ph.D.

Professor of Music Education, School of Music
University of Oregon

VERNICE TROUSDALE NYE, M.A.

Assistant Professor of Education
School of Education
University of Oregon

MARY E. SHECKLES, Ed.D.

Assistant Professor of Education
University of Florida

PROVIDING FOR
INDIVIDUAL
DIFFERENCES
IN THE ELEMENTARY SCHOOL

Edited by

NORMA E. CUTTS, Ph.D.
Professor of Education and Psychology
Southern Connecticut State College, and
Principal, Hillsboro Country Day School

NICHOLAS MOSELEY, Ph.D.
Educational Consultant

Prentice-Hall, Inc.   *Englewood Cliffs, N. J.*   1960

© 1960 BY

PRENTICE-HALL, INC.

ENGLEWOOD CLIFFS, N.J.

LIBRARY OF CONGRESS
CATALOG CARD NO.: 60-10353

PRINTED IN THE UNITED STATES OF AMERICA

73215-C

Preface

PROVIDING FOR INDIVIDUAL DIFFERENCES IS THE
key to superior teaching. Only when each pupil is taken where
he is and challenged to progress as far as he can go will his
achievement and the total achievement of the class approach
the maximum. And only if differences in physique, behavior,
background, needs, interests, and goals are considered can each
child be helped to attain the best possible adjustment.

Teachers have always been aware that great differences exist
between pupils. Knowing this, they want to know how to ascertain each pupil's status with regard to the major aspects
of development and how to provide instruction adapted to his
specific needs. This book has been written to help classroom
teachers in the elementary school and teachers in training
solve these problems.

*Providing for Individual Differences in the Elementary
School* is a highly practical book. Each chapter has been written
by a specialist in the field who has had extensive firsthand
experience in working with children and with teachers of

v

children. The classroom situation is always viewed through the teacher's eyes. First steps are emphasized first. Although there is much that is new in the recommendations, nothing is advocated that has not successfully met the test of actual trial in regular classrooms.

The chapters on art, music, the language arts, the social studies, science, and arithmetic are the work of separate contributors. The editors wrote the general chapters on studying the individual and adapting the program and procedures of the elementary school to provide for differences.

The contributors planned their chapters independently, and none of them is responsible for the contents of any chapter but his own. Various plans of organization and various techniques of instruction are suggested in the different chapters. This is as it should be. No one method is best for all subjects or for any one subject in all situations. Teachers as well as pupils differ, and a teacher may find that a technique applied in one field is exactly what he would like to try in another or in a situation where the pupils must integrate knowledge from different fields in order to achieve an objective. Furthermore, because a desire to serve the needs of individuals indicates a flexible attitude, there is cause to hope that many teachers will experiment with many of the proposed methods and then go on to create new methods of their own.

THE EDITORS

Contents

NORMA E. CUTTS *and* NICHOLAS MOSELEY

1. What teachers and pupils say . . 1

The nature and extent of individual differences. Problems of providing for differences. Rewards of individualization. Some general principles.

2. Studying the individual 13

An experienced teacher's recommendations. What to look for. Sources of information. Observation of day-by-day behavior and work. Conferences with pupils. Tests. Examinations by specialists. Conferences with parents.

3. The problem of method 34

Common practices. Finding time. Grouping. The use and abuse of basal texts, workbooks, and units. Ways of adapting methods to abilities. Vacation activities.

4. The teacher and administrative
policies 59

The teacher's role in establishing and implementing policies. Assignment of teachers. Age of admission. Promotion
and retardation. Cooperating with remedial teachers and
teacher assistants. Oversize classes. Ability grouping. Acceleration. Summer sessions.

EDWARD L. MATTIL

5. Art 79

Individual differences the source of creativity. Adapting
instruction and media to levels of development from preschool through adolescence. The gifted child. Suggested
materials.

ROBERT E. NYE and VERNICE TROUSDALE NYE

6. Music 104

Music the right of every child. The good teacher and music.
Identifying differences. Overcoming obstacles and capitalizing on abilities in singing, listening, rhythmic responses, and
in playing instruments. Music and personality development.

VIRGIL E. HERRICK

7. The language arts 128

Possible approaches to language instruction. The subject
matter of the language arts. The problem of standards. Materials and their limitations. Minimum essentials and the
pace of development. Effective ways to promote development in speaking and listening, writing and reading. Creativity. Some principles of instructional method.

J. RICHARD CHAMBERS

8. The social studies 152

The vastness of the field. The responsibility of the teacher. Pertinent differences in pupils. Cross-ability groups. Texts and supplementary materials. Graded study guides. Reference skills. Thinking. Pupil specialties. Units. An organizational pattern.

MARY E. SHECKLES

9. Science 179

Science for all. A framework of seven basic patterns. Planned content, special interests, and individualized work. Records and evaluation. Teaching materials.

ROBERT L. MORTON

10. Arithmetic 204

"Grouping in Depth" defined. How grouping in depth provides for slower, average, and excellent learners studying the same topic. Samples of exercises for each group in successive grades, with emphasis on exercises for those who excel.

NORMA E. CUTTS *and* NICHOLAS MOSELEY

11. Records, evaluation, and reports . 234

Theory and practice in record-keeping. A minimum program. Evaluation a continuous process. The pupil's self-evaluation. Group judgments. Standardized and teacher-made tests. Objectives of report cards. Forms of reporting. The parents' part.

12. Self-realization 254

Assistance from a friendly teacher. Meeting children's emotional needs. Toward self-discipline. Help for withdrawing and overaggressive children. Guidance. Self-responsibility and self-realization.

Index 269

*"The baby figure of the giant mass
Of things to come at large."*

1

What teachers and pupils say

NORMA E. CUTTS *and*
NICHOLAS MOSELEY

IF YOU TEACH A TYPICAL ELEMENTARY-SCHOOL class, you know that your pupils differ in a number of ways which affect their achievement and adjustment. You know, too, that the more help you can give each child, the better. But the differences are so great and so varied that the problem of organizing instruction to provide for individual differences may seem almost insoluble, although the opposite extreme, regimentation, is obviously absurd.

The Nature and Extent of Individual Differences

How great the differences are likely to be is shown by a survey of an actual class in the sixth grade in a well-run school system. This class is very similar to hundreds which we've visited in all parts of the United States. The twenty-nine pupils show a

1

range of more than $3\frac{1}{2}$ years in chronological age, 104 pounds in weight, 14 inches in height, 62 points in IQ, and 8 years 4 months in mental age. Their achievement, as measured by the Iowa Every-Pupil Tests of Basic Skills, ranges from 4.3 to 9.9 in grade average (that is, the average of a child's subtest scores expressed in terms of grade level), from 4.4 to 9.5 in reading, and from 3.5 to 11.4 in spelling. In general, the oldest children in this class are the lowest in IQ and have the poorest achievement records. The brightest are about average in age for the grade and have the best achievement records. But a study of the individuals shows the effects of other factors than intelligence. A girl whose parents are on a high socioeconomic level is seventh in intelligence (IQ 110) but first in the level of language usage (grade 9.9). A boy with the same IQ, whose family immigrated shortly before he was born, has a grade level of 5.7 in usage but 7.1 in reading and 6.7 in arithmetic problems. The pupil, a girl, who has the next-to-highest IQ (124) now ranks sixth on the grade average. Last year she ranked third and the year before, second—not a bad record, but her teacher knows she is bothered by her father's financial difficulties and that she has taken on heavy household duties because her mother is working.

If you teach in an early grade, there will still be great differences in intelligence, physical development, and emotional adjustment, though the range in CA, MA, and achievement will be narrower. (The records show that in May of their second-grade year the class we have been describing had a range of 2.5 grades—from 2.0 to 4.5—on the Metropolitan Achievement Test, Primary Battery.)

Even if you teach a class grouped by ability, you must be prepared for a wide range of differences and, such is the effect of the multitude of influences on learning and adjustment, for variety in achievement and attitudes. One school in a system that prides itself on its skill in ability grouping had five fifth-grade classes grouped according to ability. In May, the twenty-six pupils in the top class had a range on the battery median of the Stanford Achievement Test from 7.5 to 11.1. In the following October, when they had started sixth grade, the range was from 7.9 to 11.6. One boy *dropped* from 9.2 in May to 7.9 in October; but the one with 7.5 in May jumped to 8.6 in October. The boy with the big drop held an illegal summer job that was too much for his physique. The one whose score jumped reports, "I took a two-week fishing trip with my father, who had just come back from service in Germany, but the rest of the time I played ball, went swimming, and read."

As your pupils come into your room on the first day of school, you begin to sense their separate personalities. There is the prim little girl in her new dress who looks like a doll just out of its box, the boy in rather ragged jeans who drags his feet and looks sidewise at you, and the cheerful redhead who is having difficulty balancing a goldfish bowl in his hands because he has a catcher's mitt clasped under one arm.

If you have taught in the same school for some time, you already know a good deal about these children and are alert to help them. Alice, the prim little girl, is living with an aunt. Her father and mother went through an unsavory divorce during the summer. You see how fearful and self-conscious she is and you greet her with a remark about her pretty dress—a first effort to give her the affection and reassurance you know she needs. Alf, the boy in the jeans, has a reputation of being a holy terror. You give him a friendly smile, but you keep your eye on him. Ben has been experimenting for two years with breeding goldfish. His father is a famous research scientist, and Ben himself has an IQ of 145. You're glad to see the catcher's mitt because you believe in all-round development for bright youngsters. And as the days and weeks speed or creep toward the time when you complete the last syllable of the records and pass your children on to the next teacher, you become better and better friends with each of them. They are both a class and a group of individuals.

Teachers' Doubts

You may agree wholeheartedly that the ideal system of education would take each child where he is and carry him from there as fast and as far as he is capable of going. But when you are faced with the problem of how to do this with your own pupils, you may be troubled by many doubts. For example, here are some remarks of teachers with whom we have talked about ways of providing for individual differences:

If I take each child where I find him, what do I do about the required curriculum? What would my principal and superintendent say?

Wouldn't I need an awful lot of books and materials? Our budget is pared to the bone. How would I get them?

What about discipline? If each pupil is working separately, they are sure to work at cross-purposes. They'll be tripping each other up, literally and figuratively.

I believe in drill on the fundamentals and I must say it helps my children. But if I drilled each child separately, I'd do nothing else. Besides, group drill adds snap and interest.

If you let each pupil go ahead at his own rate, won't he go as slowly as possible? That's human nature. But it's also human to try to measure up to a high group standard. Why sacrifice that?

Youngsters need to learn to work together and to feel part of the group. If I teach them as individuals, they'll become a bunch of prima donnas.

Frankly, I don't know enough to break away from the text in science. Charlie knows more chemistry than I'll ever learn. How could I help him?

The teacher in the grade after mine is a stickler for standards. He expects every pupil I promote to be up to grade in every subject, and I really don't blame him. On the other hand, he's upset if he finds a pupil has already finished the reader for that grade. So, if I were to let pupils work at their own level, I'd be in hot water every September.

Our board of education has a policy of "basic education." They've prescribed a return to numerical marking and to fixed standards for promotion. The superintendent has forbidden us to use units of work. He has bought basal texts for every subject, and he has received some very favorable publicity in newspapers all over the United States. A return to yesterday is the order of today.

Whatever your situation, this book is designed to give you practical help on how to discover and provide for the needs of each of your pupils. We hope that as you read you will become convinced not only of the desirability of trying to provide for individual differences but also of the great satisfaction that will reward your efforts.

The Values of the Traditional

One point needs immediate emphasis: we are not suggesting that you sacrifice values in which you believe or abandon methods whose worth you have tested and proved. Providing for individual differences does not entail scanting the fundamentals, omitting drill, deserting the curriculum to pursue ephemeral fancies, or lowering standards. On the contrary, it means knowing when a child has not learned something you think he should learn, and helping him rectify the omission as promptly and as surely as possible. A major result should be that all your pupils will do relatively better in the three R's than they would have under mass instruction, and some will do enormously better.

Nor does providing for individual differences call for complete individualization of instruction. Teaching the whole class as a class will always have a place in education, not only because of the necessities of time and personnel but also because of its inherent values. When a class of pupils work together, they learn give and take. Their knowledge of one another affords them a basis for self-evaluation. Class routines, including a weekly schedule, increase a child's sense of security and so give him the confidence which enables him to undertake new adventures in growth. And the whole class must engage as a group in many activities if it is to acquire the high morale, the *esprit de corps,* which makes every pupil strive to do his best. As Viktor Lowenfeld says, in his *Creative and Mental Growth,* "Every sensitive teacher feels when his group is keyed up to one experience through which his whole group has just gone.

At that time it would not only be quite out of place but superficial to divide the group into smaller groups." And again, "Satisfaction through group work [is] a very important part of creative activities." But, he adds, this does not mean regimentation.[1]

Automatic Adjustments

You will feel more secure as you consider new ways of providing for individual differences if you will also consider the many ways in which you and your pupils are already meeting the problem. For example, you are probably careful to ask a slow child a question you feel sure he can answer, thus giving him confidence. You challenge a bright child with a brain-teaser. You draw out the shy child who has special knowledge or a special interest. You anticipate the trouble you think some children will have with a problem and explain things for their benefit. You tactfully avoid topics that might hurt the feelings of a child who belongs to a minority or who is upset by some condition in his home. You are careful to match chairs and desks to the children's heights, to give a child with poor vision a seat with a good light, and to give a hard-of-hearing child a seat near you.

The children themselves adjust their work to their own abilities. This is often evident in their written work. For example, we asked a class to write papers on "The Nicest Talk I Ever Had with a Teacher." In the fifteen minutes allowed, one youngster covered two sides of a sheet of theme paper with passable verses, while another laboriously finished five lines. Both were sincere efforts. You accept as a matter of course similar differences in book reviews, oral reports, and speed in finishing an assignment. You know that homework which takes one child half an hour is done by another in ten minutes. All the children may be absorbed in a film which the class watches or a story which you read aloud—but each concentrates on parts that interest him and each takes away his own idea of what he has seen or heard. And if you remember your own school days, you know that some children read ahead and finish a book before others are through the first chapter.

Casualties of Casualness

No matter how sympathetic a person you are and how keen your intuition, you run the risk of overlooking many of the individual needs of your pupils if you do not make deliberate, systematic, and determined efforts to discover and provide for them. You cannot fail to notice the extremes: the very slow child, the very brilliant child, the behavior problem, and the handicapped child who peers at you through thick lenses. They call themselves to your attention. But it's easy to overlook the needs of the many boys and girls who never thrill you by an achievement or cause you any trouble. The children so carelessly and mistakenly lumped together as average are the forgotten children of American education.

The way some of these neglected children feel is shown by papers pupils wrote for us on the topic "Last year in school I didn't learn as much as I should have liked because . . . ." Three replies are particularly to the point: "My teacher just gave full directions to the whole class"; "I was never pick to answer"; "I just sat and daydreamed."

The same papers show what happens when classwork is too hard for some children and too easy for others, either because the teacher has not correctly gauged the range of his pupils' abilities or because he is bound by an inflexible curriculum. Pupils write: "I didn't have much time. Most of the smarter kids learned as much as they wanted. But I think I learned enough to pass." "Some of the kids in our class were good in arithmetic but I wasn't too good and the teacher didn't give us much of it." "I didn't know what the teacher was talking about." But others write: "Most of the stuff I already knew." "I didn't get quite enough arithmetic and it was too easy and I like arithmetic very much." "The books were too easy and not much good."

Sometimes teachers slight a subject a child wants to study, even though it is required by the curriculum. Children write: "I like music but our teacher didn't like music. He even admitted it. So we listened to records." "We had a lady teacher and they don't know much about machines anyway." "I want to be a nurse but he always had health last thing and then the busses came."

The Rewards of Individualization

Perhaps the teacher's major hesitation about trying to adapt his instruction to a wide range of abilities centers on the question, "How can I find the time?" One teacher, writing early in October, said:

Our school certainly did a marvelous job last year—I know I did. My children did research on all the latest missiles—I didn't understand much of it—atomic power, etc. But this year I haven't a very inspiring class—and we have a new principal. Renewed emphasis on numerical marks means plugging away every minute. The new cumulative records are driving me frantic. Correcting papers takes hours each day. Meetings—committee meetings, P.T.A. meetings, faculty meetings. I'm in charge of the committee on health and I'm to write the report to the county office. We weigh, test eyes, measure heights. I'm supposed to have a detailed daily plan written out and on my desk each morning. Now I have to make out exams, give them, correct them, and make out report cards—and that will come each six weeks all year. And you ask me how I provide for individual differences. At least, I don't have time to interfere much with what my pupils are learning.

This same teacher reported in February:

You know, when we settled down, my children proved grand, and the principal is not such a dragon after all. Come see our room setup: each corner equipped to cater to different interests and abilities in different subjects—a library corner filled with books; a science corner with shelves crowded with children's collections; a music corner with bells, a record player, and a tape recorder; and art cupboards with all the materials I've always wanted.

The classroom would be a dull place if every child were a blank cut from the same strip of metal and you were a power press stamping out containers, each finished in exact detail according to the specifications of the curriculum. And the world would be an automated home of robots. So even when you feel overwhelmed, as our teacher did in October, and wish that all you had to do was to twirl a dial or change a disc, take courage.

Whenever you help a child individually, you earn his immediate good will and his lasting gratitude. Consider some of the papers that junior-high-school pupils wrote for us on "The Best Teacher I Had in Elementary School." The papers again and again use the words "understanding" and "helpful," and they leave no doubt that each pupil was thinking of the way a teacher treated him personally. For example:

On understanding.

He was understanding and helped me solve my problems not as a teacher but as a friend.

She was patient with me and she was very nice. I wish I could go to see her again just one time.

He made me do things to try and overcome my shyness. I'd never danced with a boy before, and he had dancing and taught me how. He was very understandable about my being shy. He was very nice.

On helpfulness.

I think she is the best because she helped me with my lessons and other things and I thank her for helping me and I think she is a wonderful teacher.

He gave me easy words.

She helped me more than any teacher in spelling and reading which I am not to good in.

I like Science very much and in his room we did a lot of it.

The papers show that pupils are as keen as any critic of education on the importance of subject matter, but that they have a better insight than many critics do into the influence which human nature has on learning. They stress interest: "She was strict but very understanding and taught in such a way that it was interesting and fun." They value having a part in planning: "We studied and made projects as friend to friend not teacher to pupil." They approve field trips and work on projects and units: "She took us to the U.N. and we learned lots"; "I think she was the best teacher I ever had because of the good job she undertook, to run the workshop class I was in through Grades V and VI. She taught me most of my better work habits and helped me more in my studies than any other teacher."

If you are alert and helpful, your pupils will remember the little things you do for them. Sometimes, unwittingly, you may come to a child's aid in a crisis in his life, and later he will know what he owes to your intervention and your firm guidance. You may, like many of your unassuming predecessors, become famous when a great man pays tribute to you in his autobiography! But your real reward for being a sensitive teacher is in the inarticulate good will of the children you are teaching now.

Some General Principles

In our democracy all children are equally worthy of our care and concern, and all should have equality of opportunity. But, as the Rockefeller Report on Education says, equality of opportunity recognizes differences in endowment and motivation, and therefore each child, according to his ability, should have "the freedom to excel which counts for so much in terms of individual aspirations, and has produced so much of mankind's greatness." [2]

The basic problem in dealing with individual differences is one of learning and of the ways by which the teacher can facilitate learning. Children differ not only in endowment and motivation but also in many other respects which affect both achievement and adjustment. And in school, children learn not only subject matter but also ways of behaving. If a child is to have the freedom to make the most of himself, he must be helped to gain the strength that will free him from adverse influences and enable him to capitalize on his assets.

Learning is not like watching a bad movie. One can't start at any point and leave when he realizes, "This is where I came in." Sound new knowledge is built on a firm foundation of accurate old knowledge, and, when this is the case, there is no end to learning. Any plan of education which tries to fit every child into a predetermined program is extremely inefficient. The child who is not ready will learn little and soon forget that, because he lacks the right foundation. The child who already knows what he is being taught is at best bored—and he may learn to hate school.

A program that takes each child where he is and challenges him to do his best gives each an opportunity to progress. This is an essential condition of education because continued efforts to learn depend on the feeling that progress is being made and success is possible. Moreover, a program which provides for individual differences allows each child to earn his teachers' sincere praise, in itself a powerful motivating force.

Providing for individual differences is not to be thought of as a means of bringing all pupils in a class to the same level. In fact, if you do a good job of teaching, you may expect the range of achievement in your class to increase. True, the children who have been behind will gain greatly and come nearer to "making the grade." But bright children, because they learn faster than slow children, will pull relatively further ahead. This is as it should be, for one of the dangerous results of regimentation is the killing of intellectual curiosity and initiative in learning.

Individual differences are the source of creative contributions to our society. Every teacher, whether he teaches all subjects or a single subject, should give his pupils experiences which show how often the efforts of many individuals in many fields must be combined to solve a problem or to achieve a goal.

NOTES

[1] Viktor Lowenfeld, *Creative and Mental Growth,* 3rd ed. (New York: The Macmillan Company, 1957), pp. 3, 57, 58. By permission of The Macmillan Company.

[2] *The Pursuit of Excellence: Education and the Future of America,* Special Studies Project Report V, © 1958 Rockefeller Brothers Fund, Inc. (New York: Doubleday & Company, Inc., 1958), p. 16. Reprinted by permission of Doubleday & Company, Inc.

2

Studying the individual

NORMA E. CUTTS *and*
NICHOLAS MOSELEY

A LARGE NUMBER OF SUPERIOR TEACHERS HAVE
told us how they form opinions of the development, intellectual
ability, achievement, attitudes, and adjustment of their pupils.
One teacher, who has taught for twenty-five years, writes:

I have 35 pupils—I have had as many as 48 in one class—so I have to
organize my efforts. Before school opens I read over the records, not just
of last year but of all the years to date, to see which pupils have been progressing steadily, which losing out a little, which forging ahead. Our "life
packets" contain results of tests, notes on classwork, on health, and on
social contacts. Our pupils are given standardized tests before October 1
each year. I immediately compare results with each child's past record and
with the results of all the members of the class. This helps me divide my
class into separate groups for various subjects, and gives me clues on teaching each group. I retest at intervals myself—sometimes using weekly
tests printed in the books and sometimes tests I make myself, and I regroup as necessary to give help to those who need it and to allow others to
work faster or at extra activities. I take into account each child's oral and

13

written work. I observe the children on the playground and in the class-room—their friendliness to me and to their classmates, their facial expressions, their enthusiasm.

A Professional Attitude

One mental hazard which may interfere with gathering information about children is the fear that you will discover something which will prejudice you against a child. Teachers say, "Every child is entitled to a fresh start every year"; "A bad pupil should have a chance to turn over a new leaf"; and, "I believe in letting bygones be bygones." These statements are all sound in themselves. But the idea that knowing what a child has done and what sort of person he is will prevent you from helping him to the best of your ability affronts your professional standing. It is like saying that a doctor should not know that a new patient, come to consult him about a pain in the chest, has had a heart attack. Leaving aside the probability that a child's reputation casts a very visible shadow over the grade ahead so that you are generally aware when a storm is coming, ignorance of an adverse condition may very well result in your aggravating it. Instead of helping the child to a new start, you get off to a bad start with him. For example, instead of putting forth an extra effort to win the immediate and continued cooperation of a pupil who is inclined to misbehave, you may, out of ignorance or a false first impression, let him drift until he commits some offense. Then your reprimand or punishment makes him think, "What's the use? All teachers have it in for me!" The slow pupil has a similar reaction if you start the year by expecting him to do work beyond his ability. And the bright pupil, given a book he has already read, settles back into boredom.

The sooner you ascertain the facts, good and not so good, on which you must chart your course, the happier the year's voyage will be for you and for each of your pupils. You have a definite point of departure from which you can calculate your progress. Knowing a child you are teaching is very much like knowing a subject you are teaching—it gives you a sense of security. But in each case you must, like a good mariner, keep eyes, ears, and mind open and be ever ready to avoid dangers and to take advantage of favorable currents and winds.

Early knowledge of a pupil's good points is even more important than awareness of potential difficulties. It lets you begin the year by giving the pupil an opportunity to earn praise from you and recognition from his classmates. This lessens the strain of the opening days for him and for you. If you can arrange for a considerable number of your pupils to start immediately on work they like and do well, you create the favorable emotional tone which is so important to good morale and high achievement.

Of course, you can never know all about a child. The most thoroughgoing case study misses some facts, and perhaps important facts. Sometimes, because you are a good teacher and a child knows you like him and are trying to help him, he gains the strength to solve a problem of which you were never aware. And certainly your efforts to inform yourself about him as well as the facts you discover will increase your sympathy and your objectivity.

What to Look for

A multitude of influences, good and bad, work to create differences between children. There are so many factors in the behavior of any child, and they operate in such a complexity of patterns, that you cannot hope to associate every effect with its cause. But if you organize your thinking concerning causes, you increase the possibility of avoiding an oversight and you acquire a framework for your efforts at guidance.

A sevenfold classification has proved very useful to us in our own study of children. The major heads are: (1) Family, Home, and Neighborhood, (2) Physical Development and Health, (3) Social Development and Status, (4) Emotional Development and Mental Health, (5) Mental Development, (6) Motivation, and (7) Achievement.

Your experience with children of the age you are teaching, your professional preparation, and your common sense all serve to let you know when there is something unusual about a child in any of these respects, *if you think how each child stands in each classification.* If you trust to intuition or wait until a child forces himself on your attention, you are quite likely to do one or both of two things. First, you may ignore a child's assets and concentrate on adverse influences. Second, among the adverse influences, you may fasten on one and fail to explore the others, though they might be more nearly the cause of difficulty.

For example, when you know a child comes from a cracked or broken home, it's easy to think that nothing can be done to ameliorate the situation, though there may be grandparents who stand ready to satisfy his needs for love and security. Or the child himself may have a goal which he is so eager to achieve that, by helping him to make progress which he can see, you will give him the strength to hold up under the strain of the home situation. It's easy, too, to accept the poor emotional tone of a home as the sole source of trouble, when actually poor health or a low IQ or some other cause may be equally important.

Sources of Information

The principal methods of studying children are examination of cumulative records, conferences with prior teachers, direct observation, analysis of day-by-day oral and written work, papers written by the pupils on special topics or in response to questions, conferences with the children themselves, standardized tests, reports from specialists, conferences with parents, and case conferences. Which of these you use depends on the grade you teach, the time of year, the custom in your school and community, and the help you receive from the principal and other members of the staff. Though you may use several of these methods simultaneously, some are particularly adapted to securing certain kinds of information. And there are special cautions to be observed in the use of each method.

One general warning is in order. You will be tempted not to use all the resources at your command unless a child presents a serious problem. Remember that the average child is the forgotten child, and try to apply every appropriate method in the attempt to compile as much accurate information as you can about each and every child in your room. To do this, you must be systematic. One guarantee against overlooking a child is to set up a check list. Take a blank page from an old register or classbook. Enter your pupils' names alphabetically. Write at the head of the columns each of the methods you think you use in determining a child's status or needs. Opposite each name under each heading enter the date when you use that method to study that particular child.

Cumulative Records

The contents of cumulative records vary greatly from school to school. Within a school, one teacher will do a good conscientious job and another be neglectful. Chapter 11 takes up what a good record should contain, how it should be kept, and how to ensure its being kept. Here we are concerned with how to use it.

Teachers report that they depend heavily on the cumulative record for information about health, physical condition, and family background, and to set up initial intraclass groups in the various subjects. They also use the records as a guide to what books and materials should be on hand at the beginning of the year and to the children's special interests and hobbies.

You'll have to judge for yourself the value of the records available to you. No matter how good the record form and how well it has been filled out by previous teachers, remember the probability that the child has changed since the last entry was made. Moreover, vital information may be missing. One teacher writes: "I was new in the school and read the records carefully. But I didn't know Dick was deaf until after I had scolded him for not answering when I spoke to him. I was very much ashamed of myself."

In using records you should first read *in order of entry* the year-by-year results of standardized tests, dated samples of work, and anecdotes of behavior. In this way you are able to see both the extent and the direction of a child's progress and to tell whether his earlier teachers, each of whom has probably studied him for ten months, agree in their opinions. Reading the entries in order frequently gives you insight into the causes which account for a child's present attitudes, good or bad. Next, study as a whole the latest entries to see not only what each indicates but also the *pattern* of achievement and adjustment. Finally, compare the data listed for each child with the data for the other children in the room. This guards against judging him by national norms or even by your own expectation of what the children in your room will be like. A child's background, behavior, and achievement may be commonplace in one group and exceptional in another. The standard illustration of this is the recent immigrant in a class of immigrants and the one in an "old neighborhood." Moreover, when a whole class has done relatively poorly or well on one test, the results for a given child must be considered with this in mind. A score lower or higher than a previous score means little if the other children are in like case, especially if there is no marked change in the rank order.

The secret of using records well lies in your mental set. Cultivate an eye for any discrepancy. Ask yourself, "Why?" Why did he do better year before last than last year? In study skills than in social studies? Ask yourself, "How can I help Ed?" Recall your successes with children who exhibited similar patterns of achievement and behavior. Let your imagination run. Above all, make a deliberate effort to note and remember each child's good points.

Conferences with Prior Teachers

Some schools very wisely stress continuity of instruction. In June they arrange for each teacher to discuss all the children in his class with their next teacher. Then the teacher-to-be has a brief conference with each child, and perhaps the whole class visits the new room. In September everyone feels friendly and ready to start work at once.

If you can talk with the teacher of the children who will be in your room next year, by all means do so. You will get off-the-record anecdotes, opinions about strong and weak points, and suggestions as to what works with one child but not another.

When anything in a record strikes you as a discrepancy or when, at any time of the year, you are doubtful about your approach to a particular child, don't stand on ceremony. Make a point of seeing his former teachers as quickly as you can and asking for their help. The teacher of the deaf child mentioned above had already noticed that Dick seemed inattentive, and he might have saved himself a feeling of shame if he had made inquiries. One third-grade teacher, on the basis of the record, put a boy in the top reading group. There was an appalling silence when his turn to read came. Not until she asked his previous teacher did she discover that the boy had an emotional block against oral reading and was under a psychiatrist's care.

Direct Observation

Children do thousands of little things which give you clues to their needs. The problem is how to be sure that you see what a child does. You can't sit and watch one child when thirty others are clamoring for your attention. But when children are busy with their own concerns in study periods, free-work periods, and recess, you have some time for observation, and you can tell a great deal by concentrating on a particular child for a minute or two. If you take the children in alphabetical order and make a written note of what you see, you'll be sure that you are not missing any child. The note can be jotted down immediately and slipped into your desk drawer, or written up from memory later. You'll probably have some notes on each child by the end of two or three weeks. Read them over and repeat the process.

Once you have made note of a specific type of behavior, you'll be on the alert for it even when you're not concentrating observation on that child. If it does not recur, you can attribute it to some temporary mood or condition.

Many techniques have been worked out for observing children in a group, and many lists compiled of what you should look for.[1] Matters worthy of note certainly include whether or not a child voluntarily speaks to others, whether they speak to him and their attitudes as they do, whether he has close friends and who they are, whether he volunteers remarks in a discussion, how he answers when you speak to him informally or call upon him in class, how he behaves in study periods—whether he keeps at work, stares vacantly at the same spot on the page, finishes early, finishes late, checks over his own work, asks help unnecessarily, or interferes with others—how he reacts to praise and to frustration and disappointment, and whether he tends in general to be withdrawing or overaggressive, excessively quiet or a "perpetual-motion machine." You learn much about a child by watching the expression on his face in different situations— when you give back a paper, when the class is choosing sides for a game, or when he is reading to himself.

When you think a child should learn to behave differently, you can list things that you'd like to see him do or avoid, and watch for these. If he shares your feeling that he should change, suggest that he keep a diary of his failures and successes. For example, if a child boasts so much that others ridicule him or ostracize him, he probably knows this and wants to reform. You and he can chart his lapses. They will almost surely diminish in frequency.

Oral Work

Vocabulary, sentence structure and grammar, and organization of ideas are means of estimating concentration, memory of facts, maturity, and ability to think abstractly. Oral work offers the main evidence of growth in these aspects of language when a child is too young to write, and much evidence at all levels. In many ways oral work is more difficult than written work. Even lawyers, accustomed to speaking in court, mispronounce words and fail to complete sentences. A reporter, describing one president's news conferences, said, "He always has difficulty in bringing subject and verb into focus." So if a pupil speaks accurately and well, you can be fairly sure he is bright, and you can regard progress as a sign of real achievement.

When you have a large class, you may find that you are allowing a few eager hand-wavers to monopolize the oral work. Remember the boy who wrote, "Last year in school I didn't learn as much as I should have liked because I was never pick to answer." A good remedy is to think over your class one by one, perhaps when you are preparing your daily work or when you are reviewing the progress of the past week, and try to remember when each child last participated, what he said, and how well he said it. One teacher, who found that some of his pupils were not taking much part, writes:

I've made what I call a "participation chart" of my class. The names are listed alphabetically in the lefthand column. There are four other columns, headed "Volunteers," "Answers," "Thinks," and "Cooperates." I put a plus mark opposite a child's name when he does well in any of these, a minus when I'm aware that he has missed an opportunity. Sometimes I can make entries right in class. Usually I do it when the children are studying. The chart certainly shows up my failures as a teacher as well as theirs as pupils.

There are at least two dangers in estimating abilities on the basis of oral work. The naturally quiet child may not participate enough to give you any basis for judgment, but he may be learning well as he listens and criticizes mentally. The second danger is the "halo effect," overestimation of the abilities of the cooperative, nice-looking, well-dressed, and well-spoken child. He probably comes from a good home, and his assets, great and welcome as they are, may be the result of his parents' example. One teacher of a reading-readiness room writes, "He appeared bright and alert, but tests indicated that he was low-average."

Written Work

Written work is the traditional evidence of a pupil's achievement, and it remains one of the best grounds for judging. When all the pupils in the class have written compositions or reports for social studies, or done their arithmetic papers, or taken a test you have set them, you are sure of samples from each child. You can study these at your own convenience and take time to analyze them and to compare them with each other and with samples of each child's previous work. They serve as objective records. Corrected by you, with or without comments, they help a child see his own mistakes. They are useful as a guide in conferences with the child about his work and as a routine occasion for a conference which you hope to extend to other matters.

Probably there would be much more written work assigned in class and as homework if it did not place so great a burden on the teacher. When children correct their own work or each other's work, you lose a certain amount of direct information and you lose that opportunity to focus your thinking on the particular child which comes when you correct his paper personally. The same criticisms hold when a "teacher's helper" does the correcting, especially if you cannot save enough time to confer with the child about a series of papers.[2] But employing either or both of these devices is better than drastically reducing the amount of written work that pupils turn in.

Written work is not an infallible guide for judging a pupil's knowledge and abilities. Essays and essay-type examinations are notoriously difficult to grade. Neatness, good writing, and even good spelling may constitute a halo effect. Individual deficiencies in these items may obscure ability and achievement, as may a habit of carelessness. On the other hand, the bright, slow, careful worker who likes to check and double check each example or the spelling of each word may accomplish so little that you think him stupid. (The same child may be very quick in oral work, if you can get him to take part.) We're not suggesting that you condone any of these shortcomings, but you should keep them in mind as you try to determine a child's true worth.

Papers on Special Topics

You can get an immense amount of direct information if you ask a child to talk or write about such things as his out-of-school experiences, his relations with his classmates, his special interests, or his feelings. We are thinking here not of the general conference or interview with a pupil but of finding out about some specific point which will help you understand the child and plan for him. Kindergarten and first-grade children will have to dictate answers to questions, but some second- and third-graders can write well enough to set down the needed facts. Older children can answer questionnaires, fill in forms, and write brief papers.

In our own work with children, we have found replies to direct questions very productive. Experience shows that the more specific and concrete the question is, the more reliable the answer is likely to be. For example, we have better success when we ask pupils, "What is the last thing you did in school which you should not have done?" than when we ask them to write about discipline. You will probably want to experiment with formulating questions which will help fill gaps in the records and in your personal knowledge of your pupils. Here are some of the questions we have found most useful.

What do you like to do most out of school? With your parents? In school?
What do you dislike most in school? Out of school?
What do you worry about most at home? In school?
What was the last book you read at home? Magazine? Newspaper?
What would you have liked to learn more about in school last year? Why?
What do you most want to learn in school this year? Why?
What do you want to be when you grow up?

Some schools make it a regular practice on the first day of the year to have each child fill in a form designed to bring the record up to date. This saves labor and gives you some idea of the child's ability to follow directions and to express himself in writing. You might well ask him to use a separate sheet of paper to describe his summer vacation. Give him a list of the points you think important—trips taken, books read, unusual experiences.

Sometimes good strategy requires that you ask the whole class to answer a question which you are actually aiming at one individual but which you think he would evade if you asked it of him face to face. Questions about worries are an example.

The possibilities of securing information by written answers to questions and by essays on revealing topics are almost endless. If you are accustomed to have your pupils write papers as part of their work in the language arts, you can save time by using exploratory questions and topics as subjects.

Sociometric techniques are helpful in exploring the status of a child in the group.[3] You can, for example, ask all the children to name the three others with whom they would most like to sit, play, or work, and then chart the replies graphically. Some children may prove to be "isolates," that is, entirely left out, and others, more or less popular. Children's opinions of each other —probably more valid in many ways than your opinions—can be revealed by the "guess-who" method. A typical cooperator, boaster, or talker is described, and the children write down the names of the members of the class they think fit the description. Naming "the person I'd most like to be like" reveals the child's own aspirations.

Conferences with Pupils

When you talk informally with a pupil in private or in company with two or three other children, you have the opportunity to fulfill three of the important functions of a teacher: to learn to know him better, to help him correct his mistakes, academic and social, and to encourage him to plan for the future. The three functions are closely interrelated. Here we are mainly concerned with the first.

If you are a good listener—and, says *Guidance in the Curriculum*,[4] skillful listening is more than not talking—you can learn a great deal about a pupil in the multitude of casual contacts with him during the day: a minute before school, an extra few seconds when he has come to your desk for special help, the times when he joins you as you supervise the playground at recess, when he meets you on the street and walks a block or two with you, or when you are both waiting for a bus. Much depends on your attitude. You must show that you like him, that you are interested in what he says, that you think his ideas are worth serious consideration.

One boy, describing the nicest talk he ever had with a teacher in elementary school, says that one snowy day at recess he and his teacher "talked about the different places to go skiing. We could ski about the same. I think this talk helped me to understand my teacher. It helped the teacher to understand me, too. You see it worked both ways." And a girl, going back to Grade II, tells of helping clean erasers after school and talking about the teacher's cats: "She talked like a friend." Another boy, with a talent for art, tells of "A Colorful Chat" with his teacher about some water colors and of how "this helped me to know what he liked and why he liked art. It gives us a better understanding of each other."

The pupils' papers show that part of being a good listener is a willingness to tell something about yourself. You can do this without monopolizing the conversation, and certainly without imposing your opinion on the child. The purpose is to get away from academic topics. The child feels at a disadvantage when talking about school subjects, and he is inclined to play a role, to act the way he thinks you think a pupil should act—all respectful attention.

Sometimes, in order to start a pupil talking about himself, you may have to ask a leading question. This is very different from the question of fact which can be answered "Yes" or "No" or otherwise briefly and specifically. (Even in these, too many questions and too much pressing are less productive than listening. One sixth-grade friend of ours, whom we were asking about how he had used school subjects during vacation, said, "One more question and I'll plead the Fifth Amendment.") You can often start children talking by asking about a brother or sister, about a hobby, or about what they want to be when they grow up.

A child who talks freely to you will sooner or later reveal much of his picture of himself: how he feels about things, why he thinks as he does, what his present purposes are and what his goals in life, his hobbies, and the values he places on different types of behavior and achievement—in brief, his "level of aspiration." He'll tell you, too, much about his family, his feelings for them and theirs for him, about his friends, and about the group he generally plays with. Little of this information is available to you from any other source, and it forms the base of the best guidance.

Our papers from pupils show that very often they took the initiative in starting a conversation. This is desirable, but if you depend on the pupils' coming to you, you'll probably miss the withdrawing child and the antagonistic child, both of whom need help that you can best give only if you know how they feel. One system that ensures an occasional talk with every pupil is to make brief conferences a routine part of instruction. When the class is studying, the children take turns coming to your desk, ostensibly to talk over their work. If you can talk for five minutes with, say, eight pupils a week, you'll meet with each child in your room several times a year. If the child feels the meeting is worth while, he'll respond to a suggestion that he might come in for an extra talk before school or that he might remain after school to help you clean up the room. You may be pleasantly surprised by a difficult child's making such a suggestion himself.

Standardized Tests

Standardized tests have proved their worth beyond question. They have revealed the wide range of abilities and achievement present in most classrooms. Frequently they show a teacher that his subjective judgment of a pupil has been wrong, that he has been unfairly underrating a pupil or unfairly demanding too much of him. They are an important tool of guidance, one that can be used by teachers, counselors, and the individual himself. Wisely interpreted, they so generally predict the subsequent academic achievement of pupils that they are more and more used at all levels of education. They are the nearest approach researchers have to the measurements necessary to create a science of education.

If you teach a class like that described in the last chapter, the sixth grade in which twenty-nine pupils showed a range of more than eight years in mental age and more than five years in achievement, you will want the results of standardized tests as a means of verifying your judgment, selecting materials adapted to abilities, planning work, and measuring progress. But you ought to be constantly aware of the possibilities of error. These are so great that we are stressing them in what follows.

No test is proof against mistakes in the giving and the scoring, to say nothing of the copying of scores from the blank to the record. Again and again in scanning records of classes to determine the extent of individual differences we have been struck by some discrepancy which proved to be a clerical error. Even so, we have caught ourselves making mistakes in taking off the figures. When your mental set alerts you to question the unusual, ask yourself first of all, can it be a clerical error?

The way a child feels when he is taking a test may have an adverse effect on his score. If he is sick or angry or frightened or just plain bored, he may do badly. For this reason, when one test shows a sudden drop from earlier tests, you should not assume that it indicates a permanent downward trend. Sometimes a pupil has out-of-school experiences—for example, a summer spent reading or working on a hobby—that will cause sudden increases in his scores. This is all to the good. There are a few children who rarely do themselves justice on group tests. One teacher tells of a pupil who did so unexpectedly badly on a group achievement test that the teacher gave him a separate diagnostic test: "This was given in regular class time under little pressure and he proved to be well ahead in achievement. Now I know him better I know that his emotions play a large part when he's taking a formal test. He's high-strung and never does as well as he should."

Standardized group intelligence tests are supposed to yield comparable scores and generally do, but the scores obtained by an individual on successive tests may fluctuate wildly. For example, 25 children were given the Kuhlmann-Anderson Intelligence Test in Grade IV and the Otis Quick-Scoring Mental Ability Test, Beta, in Grade VI. Of these children, 18 varied less than 5 points in their IQ's according to the two tests—a good argument for the concept of the intelligence quotient—but of the other 7 children, 4 lost (7, 8, 8, and 19 points) and 3 gained (10, 13, and 19 points).

If you were reading the records of these children, which IQ would you pick? If only one IQ was available, what guarantee would you have that it was correct?

Many errors of interpretation creep in if you do not check and double check yourself as you read test results. Common errors are the confusion of total scores with percentiles or intelligence quotients; failure to note the date when a test was given and mistaking an MA calculated as of that date for the MA as of the present; and noting the grade level without noting the chronological age of the pupil. (A pupil aged 8 years 11 months who makes a score of 4.3 is presumably brighter than one of 10 years 6 months who makes a score of 4.5 on the same test.) And remember that a battery median, which is often the only result entered on the record, is made up by averaging all the subtests, and the scores on these frequently differ from each other by two or more grade levels.

Whenever possible you should read the test manuals for each of the tests given through the years to your pupils. Most publishers of tests provide a copy of the manual with each packet of test blanks, and extra copies can be purchased for a few cents. A copy should be filed in the record drawer. If you will read it carefully, you will be on your guard against mistakes.

If the cumulative records of the children in your room contain the results of several standardized achievement tests, you can be pretty sure that a pupil whose scores show a steady rate of progress has actually made the progress indicated. Similarly, when several group intelligence tests give a pupil about the same IQ, this is probably approximately correct. If most of the children have taken the same tests, you have a further check by seeing whether the progress of the class as a whole has fluctuated along the same lines. For example, the records of the pupils in one class show that they all did badly on a spelling test in Grade IV, though the class averages on tests in Grades III and V were above the national norms for those grades. The results for Grade IV were probably due to some fault in the way that test was constructed, given, or scored. Scores on different forms of a test or on tests constructed by different authors may consistently run relatively higher or lower. Here again, the performance of the class as a whole offers a clue to what to expect in the case of a particular pupil.

You facilitate your interpretation of test scores if you make a chart showing all the scores of all the children in your room. If only battery medians are entered, this can be done in less than an hour for a sixth grade of thirty children who have had a total of six tests. Separate charts of the results of the reading and arithmetic subtests are generally worth the effort of making. A further refinement is to indicate each child's rank order on each test.

Rank order is a particularly valuable safeguard when few test results are available, either because you teach in an early grade or because few tests have been given. The rank of the pupil in the class is readily comparable with his rank on tests which you devise yourself and on any written work to which you assign a numerical grade. And when a pupil's rank surprises you, take pains to reconsider your judgment. Your judgment has probably been correct, but you may have been misled by a halo effect, the quietness of the child, or even an unsuspected prejudice.

Test experts are well aware of the fallibility of tests and of possible mistakes in scoring and interpretation but still consider them one of the best sources of information about a pupil. Robert D. North says: "Great care should be taken to avoid placing excessive emphasis on a single test score. It should be understood that no test is perfectly reliable or completely valid, and that temporary conditions, such as ill health or emotional disturbances, may cause a child to work below his ability level on some occasions. It is desirable, therefore, to interpret the test scores in the light of all the information that is available about the pupil on his cumulative record card whenever possible." [5] Arthur E. Traxler says: "Used with proper perspective and caution, test results form one of the most important sources of personal data basic to the process of individualizing education." [6] And Ben D. Wood says: "Comprehensive spring and fall testing programs . . . are suited to multiple purposes . . . and . . . a cumulative record based in part upon year-to-year test results is one of the most valid selective procedures yet devised." [7]

Examinations by Specialists

An individual psychological examination by a school psychologist or qualified psychological examiner is more likely to yield valid results than even a long series of group tests. The psychologist is trained to notice a child's behavior during a test and to know when it affects results. He has a variety of tests in his repertoire, including tests which do not depend on a child's ability to read. He may also use various projective techniques, including the Rorschach Test, which help him gain insight into the child's personality and emotional adjustment. You are lucky if your school has a psychologist on its staff or if there is a child-guidance clinic to which you can refer puzzling or difficult cases. You are doubly lucky if you receive complete reports and continuing guidance in handling the child.

Other specialists have similar special resources. Subject-matter specialists command a knowledge of diagnostic tests beyond that of the usual classroom teacher. Nurses are better judges than you are of a child's health, the regular doctor is better than the nurse, and the specialist best of all. Oculists[8] and otologists[9] locate defects in vision and hearing that would almost surely escape examiners with less training.

When you are referring a case to a specialist, you will protect yourself and help him by giving him an anecdotal record or diary of the incidents of behavior which made referral necessary. Complete objectivity is a must. If you interpret at all you sound as though you were arguing for your opinion, and the specialist may think you are usurping his function.

You should familiarize yourself with the resources for special examinations in your school system, your community, and your state. Know where you can get help, how long it takes, and how well the different agencies cooperate with teachers. Know the proper means of referral—and if there are any short cuts that won't get you into trouble, know these, too.

Conferences with Parents[10]

The time to catch a parent is when the parent and the child are both eager to see you. Too often this strategic opportunity exists only while the child is starting school. Descriptions entered in the record by kindergarten and first-grade teachers often remain the sole source of information about home backgrounds. In many schools teachers never see the parents of a pupil unless the child is in difficulty and the parents are summoned.

In contrast, some schools and some individual teachers make a point of the teacher's knowing the parents of each pupil. One good method is to have, at stated intervals, group meetings of the parents of the children in each class. The children engage in supervised play in the gym or on the playground while the teacher and the parents meet. Some parents will stay after the meeting for private conferences. Even better is for the administration to work out a plan that gives teachers time to visit the homes of their pupils. A few school systems do this by paying the teachers extra money to take the school census.

Whether your meeting with a parent is a prearranged conference or a fleeting moment at a P.T.A. meeting, you should have in mind what useful information about the family you might expect the parents to give you. Presumably the facts about address, marital status of the parents, and number and ages of siblings will be correct in the record. Perhaps the most important influence on the child is the emotional atmosphere of the home. Your best chance of sensing this is to encourage the parent to talk freely. You may have to ask a question or two as a starter. Begin by praising something a child does well and ask if he has mentioned it at home. Plans for the child's future are another productive topic. Even when you are aware of some problem, for example spoiling or overharsh discipline, the indirect approach is best, though once rapport is established, you can ask direct questions. Parents are likely to be your best source of information about a child's relations with his siblings, about any unusual experiences he has had, about his health history, and about the economic and cultural status of the home.

If you acquire any significant knowledge that is not obviously of a confidential nature, be sure to make a note of it in the record. Be sure, too, to describe the parents' general attitude toward teachers and toward education.

GENERAL REFERENCE

Strang, Ruth, *The Role of the Teacher in Personnel Work* (4th ed.), Part III. New York: Bureau of Publications, Teachers College, Columbia University, 1953.

NOTES

[1] Gertrude P. Driscoll, *How to Study the Behavior of Children*, 8th ptg. (New York: Bureau of Publications, Teachers College, Columbia University, 1956).

[2] *Educational Testing Service, Annual Report 1957-1958* (Princeton, N.J.: Educational Testing Service, n.d.), pp. 34-35.

[3] Helen H. Jennings, *Sociometry in Group Relations*, 2nd ed. (Washington, D.C.: American Council on Education, 1959).

[4] *Guidance in the Curriculum*, 1955 Yearbook of the Association for Supervision and Curriculum Development, a Department of the National Education Association (Washington, D.C.: 1955).

[5] *1957 Fall Testing Program in Independent Schools and Supplementary Studies*, Educational Records Bulletin No. 71 (New York: Educational Records Bureau, 1958), p. 64.

[6] Arthur E. Traxler, Robert Jacobs, Margaret Selover, and Agatha Townsend, *Introduction to Testing and the Use of Test Results in Public Schools* (New York: Harper & Brothers, 1953), p. 12.

[7] *1957 Fall Testing Program in Independent Schools and Supplementary Studies*, p. xii.

[8] Anthony J. Pelone, *Helping the Visually Handicapped Child in a Regular Class* (New York: Bureau of Publications, Teachers College, Columbia University, 1957).

[9] Norton Canfield, *Hearing: A Handbook for Laymen* (New York: Doubleday & Company, Inc., 1959).

[10] Grace Langdon and Irving W. Stout, *Teacher-Parent Interviews* (Englewood Cliffs, N.J.: Prentice-Hall, Inc., 1954).

3

The problem of method

NORMA E. CUTTS *and*
NICHOLAS MOSELEY

THEORETICALLY THERE ARE TWO EXTREMES IN methods. At one end, a teacher tutors each child individually in an attempt to make him letter-perfect on an assigned lesson. At the other end, the pupil himself is permitted to follow his own interests and is made responsible for his own progress. Probably no classroom today exemplifies either extreme, but elements of each can be found in the methods of most teachers. For example, the following quotations from children's papers are about the same teacher: "When I didn't know something he would help me until I knew it"; "He always gave those who were ready for more advanced work more advanced work."

Current Compromises

Our reports from teachers on the ways in which they provide for individual differences show that many teachers have arrived at some sort of compromise. They use basal texts, but in connection with these they arrange for their pupils to carry on various projects or units of work. Sometimes these activities are suggested by the text, sometimes by the teacher, sometimes by the pupils. Usually the pupils have at least a minor part in the choice of a unit, and they often plan much of their own work. There is a schedule, approved by the principal, which allots specific periods to each study but also allots time for individual pursuits—a "show and share" period, or an "activity hour." Study periods are usual, either as a part of a subject-matter period or scheduled separately, and teachers regularly tutor individuals in these minutes. Most teachers use some form of intraclass grouping which lets them concentrate their attention on a few pupils while the others study assignments or carry on their work on units.

Because the distribution of the limited amount of time available is a controlling factor in every effort to teach individuals, let us discuss scheduling first.

Scheduling

Whenever a critic cites the case of a child who has not learned to read in school but has been successfully taught at home, we wonder what a trained teacher could have done if he had had the same amount of time to give this particular child. Even if you devoted your whole day to individual instruction, the fair allotment to each of thirty pupils would be less than ten minutes, with less than three minutes for each major subject. Some combination of group work and independent work is obviously necessary.

Almost every classroom we visit has a detailed daily schedule neatly written on the board. Few classes, when we visit, are actually engaged in the work scheduled for that time. This is all to the good if it means a teacher is exercising judgment and shifting the schedule to accommodate the needs of the class or of individuals. For example, a teacher may feel that a project provides at least as much practice in reading and arithmetic as would the regular period, and additional values besides. Or a teacher may know that his class as a whole excels in arithmetic but that only a few are good readers. He can well let these few work independently while he takes time from arithmetic to help the slower readers.

In a flexible schedule, the teacher must guard against slighting some part of the curriculum, either because he inadvertently devotes too much time to a project or to a subject in which students are deficient or because his own tastes and limitations incline him to favor one subject as against the others. Art, music, health, and science are most vulnerable, both because many teachers doubt their own knowledge in these fields and because these subjects may be allotted only a period or two a week and any encroachment would leave little time. One safeguard is to think back over a week's work, figure the time actually spent on each subject, and compare the results with the schedule. Putting a neglected subject first in the day is one way to correct the situation. If the class holds daily or weekly planning sessions, consideration of when a neglected subject is to be studied should be part of the agenda.

Long periods and "block schedules" have several advantages. They reduce the amount of time lost in shifting from subject to subject, not only in getting out and putting away books and materials but also in redirecting attention. They facilitate grouping by giving the teacher more time to work with each group while the remaining pupils work independently. They encourage pupil planning and pupil responsibility.

Grouping

Treating a whole class as a single group would be the most efficient form of instruction if it were not for individual differences. But it is in fact the most wasteful. Pupils who do not understand what the teacher is saying are wasting their time; so are the pupils who already understand it. When the teacher takes time to repeat and elaborate an explanation for the slower pupils or to propound ideas which only the better pupils can grasp, the loss of time is compounded.

Intraclass ability grouping is designed to solve the problem. The practice is common in reading in all elementary grades and very frequently used in arithmetic and other subjects. Teachers, however, still raise several questions in connection with it. What size of group is best? What is the best basis for grouping? How much time should be allotted to work with each group? What do the other pupils do while a small group is working separately with the teacher?

These questions are interlocked; perhaps the key issue is the basis of grouping. The usual base is a combination of ability and achievement as determined by teacher opinion and test results. If you follow this system, there are some points to which you should be sure to pay attention.

A distribution of your pupils according to their test scores will give you an idea of how many groups you must set up to limit each group to any given range of scores. It will also demonstrate a fact often overlooked: separating a class into groups of equal size may not be as efficient as separating them into the same number of groups of different sizes. For example, 25 pupils in one fourth grade have arithmetic computation scores (grade equivalents) ranging from 3.6 to 5.8. If they were divided into three nearly equal groups of 9, 8, and 8 pupils, there would be considerable overlapping—because several pupils have the same scores—and the widest range would be in the slowest group. The bottom group would have a range of 3.6-4.5, the middle of 4.5-5.0, and the top of 5.0-5.8. But it is possible by shifting numbers to have a bottom group of 5 pupils, range 3.6-4.2, a middle group of 11 pupils, range 4.4-4.8, and a top group of 9 pupils, range 5.0-5.8. This puts the biggest number in the group with the smallest range and the smallest number in the lowest group.

Presumably you do not divide your class on the basis of the results from one test but exercise your best judgment in view of all the information available, including your experience with children. No matter how you originally choose the members of groups, shifts from one to another may be advisable on very short notice. *Flexibility is essential.* This applies to the membership of the groups, the size of the groups, the number of groups, and the amount of time allowed for each group to work with you. Be alert for pupils who learn quickly or slowly, who remember well or forget easily, who need the challenge of hard work or a force-ful reminder that they are not doing well, who have had special experiences or have read a book the group is studying—such pupils should generally be shifted as the occasion indicates. Sometimes a pupil in a top group may be put in a lower group for a day or two while it is studying something he has missed. Sometimes you will find it helpful to increase temporarily the number of groups, even to the point of taking separately a single slow or very bright pupil or one who has missed work the rest of the class has had, and even though this means cutting down the time available for others. Frequently you will want to forgo group work altogether so that the class as a whole will have extra time for a general discussion, or to see a film or an unusual TV program.

There is no set number of groups that is best for any subject. Try to be sure that each group is small enough and has enough time with you to let each member take an active part in the work, preferably every day and certainly several times a week. Only then can you form a sound opinion of each pupil's strengths and weaknesses and give each the immediate help he needs.

You cannot automatically put your brightest pupil in the top group in every subject or your slowest pupil in the lowest group. In the fourth grade described above, the distribution of scores on the subtests shows that of the top eight in spelling, two are in the middle eight in arithmetic computation and one in the bot-tom nine, and of the middle eight in spelling, three are in the top eight in arithmetic computation.

Bear in mind the many possible bases for grouping in addition to ability and achievement. A common interest makes a group work well together. A pupil who is slow in making friends might well be placed in a group with a good mixer, even when this means stretching the academic range. A pupil who speaks with a foreign accent should be for at least part of the time with children who speak correctly. On the other hand, several children with faulty speech might be grouped for special drills. A committee working on a class newspaper needs a writer, a speller, a typist, an artist, and perhaps a business manager—and while they work together they learn from each other. The variations in basis and purpose offer you the opportunity to vary each child's experiences in work and in friendships.

When you arrange for a child to work with several groups, each of which has a different membership, you minimize the chance that grouping may make him conceited or give him a feeling of inferiority. But actually, children accept grouping very matter-of-factly. And they are never misled by teachers' attempts to disguise the ranking of groups, for example by designating them in reverse order, the least able as Group A or Group 1. One child writes:

In arithmetic we had three groups. The third group was the highest, they got up to desmels. The second was the middle group and they got up to fractions. The first was the lowest group. I don't know what they got up to. In reading there were three groups also. All groups did work in their own book and the highest group wrote book reports.

Pupils who have not been used to the class's working in small groups have to learn to plan, to work without interfering with others, to get out books and materials for themselves, and to seek out answers to their questions rather than always turning to the teacher. They need time to learn these things and to become accustomed to independence. One teacher describes how he manages with his class:

The teacher who has the grade before mine in our school is one of the best in the city, but he is very formal and old-fashioned, and I've learned that if I put the pupils much on their own when they first come into my room they tend to break loose rather violently. So I start them all together on a text. After a day or two I divide the group in half, arbitrarily picking alternate children from the class list but balancing boys and girls. Then while one half is discussing the last lesson with me, the other studies the next assignment. Within a week I add reference work to the assignment— use of the dictionary and encyclopedia. By that time I know the children pretty well and I try them out on brief reports on the same topic. They give these orally to the whole class, and I try to get everyone into a discussion of how the reporter used his materials. This introduces the class to planning and evaluation. Finally I regroup the pupils on the basis of ability, setting up three or four groups, and begin to differentiate the work. In about a month or six weeks everything is running smoothly. The children know how to use reference materials, and they work quietly and steadily. Then I have the groups try committee work, planning and discussing by themselves. The acid test of success comes when a group or an individual suggests shifting a pupil from one group to another, either because of some special interest of his, or because he has some talent which he can contribute.

Pupil Teams

An experiment with groups of two or three pupils working as teams has been conducted in Dedham, Massachusetts, under the direction of Dr. Donald Durrell of Boston University.[1] The 1,200 pupils and 45 teachers who have participated are reported to be enthusiastic about the system. Discipline problems are practically nonexistent. Before the system was adopted only about 50 per cent of the pupils made a full year's growth or more during the school year, whereas 74 per cent are now advancing at least this far. About one-third of the pupils have done two years of arithmetic in a single year. One of the limitations of the technique, according to Durrell, is that the subject matter must be broken down and reprocessed into specific tasks. (An application of the pupil-team plan to the social studies and some of the techniques which are involved will be described in Chapter 8.)

The Use and Abuse of Basal Texts

If you are using basal texts in most or all of the subjects in your curriculum—and a vast majority of teachers are—much of the work of organization is done for you by experts. Facts and concepts to be taught are selected and arranged in sequence, topics for discussion suggested, and supplementary books and desirable equipment and materials listed. In a field in which you yourself are not thoroughly at home, a basal text has special value. You must, however, be careful lest the convenience be bought at the expense of ignoring the best development of the individuals in your class.

Most texts are designed to have one volume or set of volumes cover a year's work. By implication this is *the* work for that grade. The temptation is to accept the implication and to try to have all the pupils progress through the book at the same rate, beginning the first page together in September and together finishing the last page in June. The results can be disastrous. A considerable number of pupils will always be left here and there by the wayside, bogged down in ignorance and misunderstanding. Many will be bored, some because the facts and concepts and vocabulary are meaningless to them. Equally bored are the children who know the content of the books already and those who grasp it quickly and quickly tire of hearing the slow children's discussion. All tend to consider finishing the book as the main objective, and when the task is accomplished, their minds discard much of the knowledge as no longer useful.

The subject matter of a text is set, and unless provision is made to take up current events and topics of special interest to individuals, an immense amount of natural motivation is lost. Children, writing on what they would like to have learned more about, complain again and again that the class was studying South America when they wanted to know about Alaska.

Grouping solves some of the problems that arise when pupils of different abilities use the same text. The groups can go at different speeds. You can adapt your contributions and comments to the abilities and interests of individuals in the group. You can elicit responses from each child and, in the light of your knowledge of a child's needs, direct the discussion so that he feels satisfaction in what he has learned and sees how he can use it in the future. You can assign him independent work, to be done when his group's turn is over, that will help him overcome his particular deficiencies or develop his particular interests.

But trouble arises when the official text for your grade is too hard for the bottom group and so easy that the top group gallops through it. Many teachers meet this situation by substituting earlier or later volumes from the same series, but there are drawbacks in either case. The slow pupil, if he has already studied the earlier text, recognizes it and dislikes the idea of repeating. The subject matter is probably not suited to his chronological age, and he will consider it babyish. He may not recall the facts, but he recognizes them as he meets them, and boredom is added to resentment. The fast pupil anticipates the work of the next grade, and so the problem recurs for the next teacher. The question of the bright pupil's using advanced texts ought to be thrashed out in faculty meeting. Studying the texts of later grades is a good solution, provided all the teachers are willing to take each pupil where he is and carry on from there. Another solution is to have in every room a wealth of supplementary books and materials adapted to various levels and catering to special interests. Then, if you are familiar with all the basal texts in use in your school, you can select books that supplement the present text without duplicating the work of the next grade. This use of the infinite wealth stored in books is a major means of enriching the basic curriculum. True enrichment involves the pupils in studies that broaden and deepen and advance their knowledge. Requiring a pupil just to do more of something he already does well bores him to distraction or at least to the point where he distracts others.

As long as you expect a whole class or the smallest practical group from a class to cover the same amount of a text, there will be some who cannot finish in the allotted time, and so miss part of the work, and some who finish ahead of others. Among our materials is a set of pupils' papers written to complete the sentence, "When I cannot finish my work before the end of the period I feel . . . ," and another set beginning, "When I finish my work before the rest of the class I like to . . . ." Some of the papers give a vivid picture of futility. Others show how the spare time can be used constructively.

A slow pupil writes, "I never finish before the rest of the class they whatch me and some others suffer." Another writes, "I feel like giving up. Sometimes when I can do the work it still takes me longer than the rest of the class. Because of my natural slownest."

A bright pupil says, "I like to read a book or draw pictures on scrap paper because there is not much to do. It would be better if the teachers had something that we could do while the others were still working. Else the people that are finished will bother the other people while they are still working on their subject." Other pupils who idle when they finish early mention talking, fooling around, playing ticktacktoe, playing chess, and daydreaming. A perhaps precocious girl writes, "I stare at my man teacher and daydream of Boys. Who doesn't?"

Less wasteful occupations described by the pupils include checking work, doing homework, drawing and modeling, reading, writing letters, cleaning the blackboard, and doing errands for the teacher.

A class discussion will disclose endless possibilities for making constructive use of even small bits of time. The pupils ought to agree that each is to be responsible for himself and that, though he may work with others, for example on a committee, he will never interfere with anyone who is busy. Even so, you would be well-advised to observe your class as they work on an assignment. Note who is suffering and who is playing ticktacktoe.

Some textbooks incorporate suggestions for the use of spare

time. If you serve on a textbook committee, suggest that the members study Robert Lee Morton's excellent statement of what a text should contain to provide for individual differences.[2] Though he is writing about arithmetic, the criteria are valid for all subjects. According to Morton, texts should include attainment tests that are diagnostic in character, specific directions for reteaching, supplementary materials for fast learners, and suggestions for establishing groups, for equipping an arithmetic "table," and for relating arithmetic to home, community, and play.

A good text should also suggest many units and projects related to a wide variety of interests and capable of being carried on without elaborate resources. The text or the teacher's manual should make suggestions for both correlation and integration with other subjects. The manual should discuss in detail stages of development over a wide range. This discussion should include a graded list of concepts which students of different mental ages may be expected to grasp.

Workbooks

Theorists disagree about the value of workbooks. Some advocate them. Some think workbooks kill all interest in learning. Administrators, however, continue to provide them and teachers to use them. A well-designed workbook saves the teacher much time and effort that would otherwise be taken up in organizing practice and drill. But any workbook is a poor substitute for a text, and great harm may be done when time is given to a workbook that otherwise might have been used for direct instruction or for the pupil's own efforts to work out answers to questions he himself has raised. In brief, it kills creativity. Lowenfeld, in *Creative and Mental Growth,*[3] shows how children's sensitivity is inhibited by copying and coloring stereotyped figures in workbooks that are meant to teach young children vocabulary or arithmetic. For a questionable advantage in one field, such workbooks do positive harm in another. A workbook should not be used just to keep a pupil busy. It should not require him to do more of something he already knows. The legitimate purpose is for needed practice and drill. To accomplish this the workbook must be interesting.

Workbooks are cheap enough to make experimenting with them relatively inexpensive. The workbooks written to accompany the text you are using may not be the best available in the subject and may not provide a range of materials suitable for all the pupils in your class. If you try out several, you'll soon learn which are suited to pupils on one level and which to those on another. The good workbook is arranged for the pupil to correct his own work and measure his own progress— both factors in successful drill—but you have to check on results fairly frequently. Even an honest child finds it easy to cheat himself.

Units

There are many definitions of "unit." In general, teachers and children speak of a unit as the study of a particular topic over a period of days or weeks, using a variety of resources. Usually, but not always, the procedures include discussion of the topic, planning, gathering data, organizing data, a summary or "culminating activity," and evaluation of results.[4] Each step affords opportunities for the whole class to work together and for small groups and individuals to work independently. In theory, units are one of the best methods for providing for individual differences in ability, for capitalizing on separate interests, and for helping each child integrate his knowledge.

A broad view of the actual results of units is presented in 129 papers written for us by pupils in Grades III-VI of a summer session in a teachers-college training school. The 74 boys and 55 girls were drawn from 22 schools. All degrees of ability were represented. Some of the pupils attended the summer school to satisfy a condition of promotion, some because the school seemed to offer pleasanter occupation than they would otherwise have, and some because they were already hoping to skip a grade and enter college early. The papers were written to answer the questions: "Did your class take part in any units of work last year? If so, what were they about? What part did you take? What did you learn?"

All of these pupils, including all the third-graders, said they took part in at least one unit, and some gifted sixth-graders from a special class for the bright and gifted listed 17 apiece— 8 in science, 5 in social studies, and 4 "major topics," namely, United States Government, United Nations, Water Conservation, and Playwriting and Acting. The topics varied from the broadest, "The Universe," to the rather limited, for example, "The Liver." The replies show that the schools which were represented are aware of the different types of curriculum described in the professional literature but do not adhere to any one. The same class may within a few months center first on some phase of a subject and then on some community problem, or vice versa. The replies show that most of these schools use units in connection with basal texts. One pupil writes: "We studied Indonesia. First we had to make a scrapbook and put in it every detail. When we finished we had to work on Indonesia in the social studies book. That's the most I ever learned."

The activities described by the pupils show the possibilities which units afford for all kinds of learning on the level of the individual who is reporting—reading, writing reports, book reviews, and letters, making oral reports, keeping accounts, making graphs, making maps, conducting experiments in science, modeling, drawing and painting, writing plays and acting, singing, writing songs and music, serving as secretary, reporter, and chairman of a committee, taking trips, seeing movies, following educational TV programs, and "social learning."

The pupils' evaluations of what they had done and learned reflect great enthusiasm on the part of some and great skepticism and dissatisfaction on the part of others. Examples of favorable opinions are:

We did research, wrote reports, gathered news articles, made murals, spelled countries and words, drew maps, made a plaster-of-paris map, made exhibits, sent away for material, gave programs on our work, went on trips. We learned quite a bit more, which helped us with our regular studies.

We had a pleasant and quite fascinating trip to the U.N. We read over 300 U.N. publications. We all read over 1200 newspaper articles. We had a Commentators' Club in which the people who contributed the most in news were unanimously voted to be in the Club. In the Club you rated commentators. And we went to the College to hear William Shirer the great commentator give a speech. In our classroom we believed in democracy. Everyone had an equal chance to be a leader and a follower.

On the unfavorable side are comments like:

A unit on space. Junk.

We spent all of our time on a mural on Greece.

I just observed. I didn't learn very much.

I watched the experiments.

We put on a play about litterbugs. I was in the play. I didn't learn anything with the play.

Adapting Methods to Abilities

The pupils' papers on units show the need to adapt methods to abilities. The brighter children report ranging far and wide in their search for information, retrieving a vast array of facts and organizing them well, and growing in both fundamental knowledge and in knowledge of how to find and apply what they need to know when trying to solve a problem. Slower pupils, on the other hand, often seem to have been lost sight of and to have wandered in a daze, unguided and uncomprehending.

These pupils' experiences with units illustrate what J. Wayne Wrightstone, in *Class Organization for Instruction,* says about adapting instruction to pupils of high and low ability. Bright pupils, according to Wrightstone, analyze and reason well, are original, resourceful, have initiative, and can interpret abstract ideas. Therefore they can engage in long-range assignments, recognize related materials, organize materials, and criticize their own results. They need opportunities which "challenge their skill in organizing ideas and in integrating related ideas into basic but systematic generalizations." Slow pupils, on the other hand, learn by simple mental processes, are confused by complex associations with a topic, prefer the concrete to the abstract, the specific to the general, and have little power of self-criticism. The wise teacher gives them specific assignments or short-time units and organizes their work so that they can proceed with order and certainty. Much use should be made of current events, real-life applications of knowledge, and visual aids.[5] Elsewhere Wrightstone stresses "the needs for differentiated curricula . . . materials that will challenge the abilities of the relatively brighter pupils . . . and curricular materials and instructional methods . . . which will meet the abilities and needs" of pupils with lower IQ's.[6]

You can adapt the unit method of teaching to a class with a considerable range in IQ if you plan carefully to provide for each individual. Here are some recommendations.

1. You must be well acquainted with the abilities, interests, and work habits of each pupil and suggest activities in line with these.

2. You should observe each pupil systematically to be sure that he is taking an active part in the unit and that this part meets his needs and does not exclude other desirable learning activities.

3. You should not expect that any pupil, and particularly not that any slow pupil, will learn much from the oral reports of other pupils or from any demonstration or experiment in which he does not take active part.

4. You must try hard to introduce novel and exciting activities, because these impress themselves on children and so make them learn more and remember longer. Well-planned trips are very productive, as are many forms of visual aids and interviews with adult experts.

5. Periodic tests in the fundamentals are essential, and pupils who are not progressing in line with their ability should be given special instruction, including drill, when this seems advisable.

6. You as the teacher and the pupils as learners should evaluate results individually and collectively. Try to devise objective criteria by which you can judge progress and, ultimately, how well the goals of the unit have been achieved.

7. When any of the goals implied by the curriculum or set up at the time the unit was inaugurated concern social development ("sharing," "learning democratic procedures"), help the pupils generalize from what has happened in the unit to what ought to happen in real life. The principle that there is little transfer of training without generalization, without recognition of common elements in two situations, is as true of social learning as it is of other kinds of learning.

The Individual Project

Pupils of all abilities in all grades can carry out individual projects of their own. These may be undertaken as part of a unit or to develop a topic of special interest or as an experience suggested by the teacher. A pupil who has a project under way can work on it when he has finished required work in less than the allotted time, when you are working with a group in which he is not included, and in periods set aside for all the children to work independently. He may become so interested that he will voluntarily spend a considerable amount of out-of-school time on it.

Young children profit from experiences with a variety of materials and objects. (See Chapters 5, 6, and 9.) Children who can read and write can collect their own materials, make notes, organize the information, write and rewrite their conclusions— all processes they will use more and more as they continue their education.

A written report is useful in several ways. It helps you gauge how a pupil thinks and works and gives you a chance to correct mistakes in fact and procedure. It makes an excellent focal point for a talk with the pupil. Kept in the pupil's file, it serves as a base of comparison for evaluating his later work and his progress.

You will have no doubt of the value of this type of project if you will think back to your own school and college days and remember how much you learned when you worked hard on a term paper.

Tutoring

The pressure to try to bring backward pupils up to grade is tremendous. It springs from tradition, parental opinion, anticipation of what the next teacher will think, your own pride in your skill as a teacher, and your natural sympathy for children who are slow. Moreover, the satisfaction that you feel when you succeed increases your interest in similar cases. Many teachers are so eager to help slow children that they devote to them almost all the time they can find during regular periods and are willing to work overtime.

Before you expend much intensive effort in the attempt to bring an individual up to grade, ask yourself several questions. *What are the chances for success?* One mother told a teacher, "You've been awfully good to Fred, but you can't do what God didn't do. You can't give him brains." If a child is making progress in line with his ability, any speed-up resulting from tutoring is sure to be temporary. *What are the reasons for his backwardness?* If his progress isn't in line with his ability, why not? Pay special attention to his attendance record in your grade and earlier grades to see what fundamentals he may have missed. Use all the diagnostic techniques at your command. *Do I know his special interests? Does he make any connection between the subject and his present outside interests and future goals?* Lack of progress often results from lack of foresight. *Is there any way he can secure individual help other than by working with me?*

If your school has remedial teachers, you will of course try to secure their help. Perhaps a parent can act as a tutor. Perhaps a bright child in your class or a member of the Future Teachers Club from Grade VI can help.

When a brighter or older child helps a pupil, the tutor must know what he is to do and how to do it. You can't just say, "George, please help Harry," and leave it at that. Mutual respect is important. The pupils should like each other, and, if they are classmates, the slower should have opportunity to help the brighter in some way, perhaps in a sport, perhaps when they are working together on some chore. No pupil should be asked to take much time from a vital pursuit of his own in order to help a slower or younger pupil. Probably the most legitimate occasion for one pupil's tutoring another is when the slower needs drill and the brighter knows that he himself will profit from overlearning. A bright pupil who is impatient with drill for his own sake may gladly work hard on it for the sake of a friend.

Automation

Education is still only on the threshold of the world of automation. Even such long-time favorites as filmstrips, motion pictures, and record players offer possibilities for individualizing instruction that have been little explored. Tape recorders are being tried in many fields. TV has barely made its debut in the classroom. In today's classroom one child may be viewing stereopticon slides, another child listening through earphones to a tape recording of his own speech, and a small group using filmstrips, the while the teacher works with a fairly large group using a basal text. Tomorrow we may see classrooms with whole libraries of recorded materials more easily displayed than a silent 16-mm. film today. Then, when the teacher or the group wants a special demonstration or a snappy form of drill or a lesson in the language of the Martians, the bill can be filled by turning a switch.

Automation, including TV, already makes it possible for the curriculum to include subjects, like foreign languages, music, and science, in which the classroom teacher may not be an expert. Moreover, by this means instruction can be adapted to meet the needs of one pupil or a small group of pupils in a large class. Techniques of organization, planning, and evaluation are still being developed, but they will probably be much like those now used in a unit. Your local telephone company may have materials it can give you on educational television, both closed-circuit and broadcast. Newspapers carry full programs of broadcasts, including many that are suitable for use in the classroom.

Mechanical visual and, might we say, oral aids to instruction have the great advantage of novelty. They catch the children's attention and create a feeling of excitement, and thus promote quick learning and good retention. For this reason it is difficult to assess the relative effectiveness of older and newer methods. There will always be pupils who learn better by seeing and hearing demonstrations than they do by reading. But no one now knows whether in the long run automation will increase the effectiveness of classroom instruction. Certainly there is little ground for the fears some have expressed that the wide use of TV programs and other new media will regiment the new generation. The greater probability is that the curriculum will be broadened and the individual needs of pupils better met. You may well take part in work toward this goal.

Games

"Play is the child's business." Games, social, mental, and athletic, afford the child a chance to try out his growing body and his growing mind. They may simulate adult conditions and bring the vicarious experiences of books closer to reality. Robert J. Havighurst has pointed out that action with a child's peers and their reaction to what he does are a principal agency for teaching him values and giving him a sound conception of his skills as he contributes his share in achieving a common purpose. Moreover, Havighurst says, when a child in play has an adult role and other children accept him in this role, he matures.[7]

If you observe children as they play, whether at "store" in connection with a unit or kickball on the playground, you will soon discover who takes little or no active part; who always tries to dominate; who is the weakling; who, the athlete; who, afraid. You cannot manage children's games for them without cutting down the values which depend on give and take. You can, however, be sure that games have a real share in the school's program, and you can occasionally suggest a role for a particular child which will help him develop.

Homework

One obvious way to gain more time for the study of academic subjects is to require children to do homework. Moreover, because there are many hours between dismissal time and bedtime, even a slow child, by working long and hard, can complete an assignment. Opponents of homework, both among parents and among teachers, point out that it is hardly fair to assign tasks that take one child a few minutes and another many hours. They think that the school day is already long enough and that the children need the free hours for play and rest and to be with their families. Continual controversies prove that the question of whether there should be homework is not simple.

If your school has regularly required homework, you can do much to make what the child does at home satisfy his particular needs without working him overtime. The blanket assignment given to all pupils is rarely wise. Better results come when you and the pupil and one or both of his parents can discuss the need he may have for extra help and the possibility that he may profit from going into a subject more deeply than he can in school. By picking books to be used at home and by showing parents how these are to be used (so that the same methods will be followed at home and in school), you can often arrange for a child to receive more individual attention than you yourself can ever give him.

The narrow concept of homework as a specific assignment of so many examples or pages tends to fix the idea that schoolwork and playtime are antipathetic. It prevents children from realizing that what they learn in school can be useful here and now and not just in some remote future, and it leads parents to ignore thousands of situations where they could teach their children how to apply "book learning" in practical ways. One of the great arguments for units and for the community-centered curriculum is that they help break down the barrier between life in school and life out of school. Whatever system you follow, try to discuss with your pupils how they and their parents and other members of the community use the facts and techniques presented in the curriculum. Encourage the children to bring to school ideas as well as objects met in their daily experience. This broad concept that life and learning are one ought to permeate all the child's activities. We don't mean that when a child goes to the store he ought to think, "Now I'm using my arithmetic," but he ought to realize that being good at arithmetic serves more purposes than getting a "100" on a paper. Parental example, always a potent factor in the child's learning, becomes doubly effective if the parents help the child generalize by showing him that they are using knowledge he is gaining in school.

Summer Activities

Knowledge which is not used is easily forgotten. This is evident in the way many pupils fail to remember in the fall facts that they knew in the spring. Research shows that, on the average, pupils lose ground in arithmetic, language usage, and spelling during the summer months, though they may make minor gains in reading.[8]

Here, as always, there are great differences between individuals. We compared scores made by 120 pupils in May of their fifth-grade year on a Stanford Achievement Test with their scores on the same test in the following October. A gain of four months or more on the battery median was registered by 46 per cent of the pupils, less than four months by 37 per cent, and actual losses by 17 per cent. In the subtest scores there were many surprising gains by individual pupils. One girl jumped 2.3 years in science, a boy 1.8 years in social studies.

These 120 pupils had been taught in five groups formed on the basis of ability. The high and high-average groups had larger losses in arithmetic than the other groups. This is in line with Elizabeth Bruene's finding that bright children lose more than the average in arithmetic fundamentals.[9] But, contrary to Bruene's finding that bright children gain in reading more than slow children do, the low-average group showed the best over-all gain on the reading subtest. Of the 24 pupils in this group, 19 made gains of four months or more and only 1 retrogressed. Investigation showed that they had had a fifth-grade teacher who was very fond of reading and of teaching reading and who inspired a liking for literature in his pupils. We have reports from all the 120 pupils on the books they read during the summer. Those in the low-average group, the group that did so well, had a better record in quantity and quality than that reported by the average and high-average groups.

The influence of summer activities on achievement is also evident in the cases, cited above, of the girl who progressed so far in science and the boy who advanced so much in social studies. The girl had been to a camp that specialized in nature study. The boy had been on a long motor trip with his parents. Obviously, the pupil who reads, thinks, and applies his school knowledge during the long vacation stands to gain, and the one whose mind estivates loses valuable learning time.

Of course the longer hours for play and the relative freedom of vacation time promote physical growth and growth in independence and responsibility. But these gains are not reduced by a considerable amount of intellectual activity. In truth, the summer days are days of golden opportunity for individual pupils to remedy their shortcomings and advance their special interests.

Class discussion and planning are of great strategic value here. Children can readily grasp the probability of summer forgetting, and if the group adopts the view that everyone should give some time every day to reading and to hobbies, there will be a higher percentage of individuals who carry out the program. You will also want to plan with individual pupils to make sure that each child knows what he needs to do and to help him see that he can have fun doing it. The slow child in particular needs specific suggestions. Perhaps lending him or giving him a paperback book would be a good idea. You must count on the children rather than the parents to take responsibility for summer activities. If the children show initiative, their parents will be pleasantly surprised and almost sure to cooperate. But most parents, left to themselves, maintain the attitude that a vacation is a vacation and all intellectual activity is unpleasant work.

Here is a brief check list of some possibilities. It can serve to start the discussion in your class. The class will add to it, and some pupils may go much further. You yourself ought to be familiar with local resources for summer activities, ready with information about programs and hours, and glad to act as liaison officer in any moments you can spare before school closes.

Reading. Has each child a library card? Does he know how to get to the library? The summer hours? Are there any special summer programs in the library, for example storytelling, suitable for any member of your class? Paperbacks children might own.

Spelling. Classmates on vacation, even in the same town, can have good fun as pen pals.

Language usage. (Twenty-nine per cent of our total group and 50 per cent of our low group showed summer losses here.) What TV programs which interest children have literate dialogue? Encourage attempts at analysis and imitation. Are there "barn circuit" or "starlight" theaters in the neighborhood? Pen pals, again.

Arithmetic. Budgeting allowances. Serving as "treasurer" on family trips. Hobbies involving mathematics.

Social studies. Travel and the use of maps. Stories to be read in connection with trips. Excursions nearby, through the state, to a city.

Science. Nature study in park groups, playground classes, summer camp, the Scouts. Hobby clubs and personal hobbies. TV programs. Science fiction and other science books.

Arts and crafts. Playground groups. Art exhibits. Camp and Scouts. Hobbies.

Music. Playground groups. Special programs in the community or a neighboring city. TV. Records.

In Conclusion

Later chapters elaborate and apply the methods that have been discussed in this chapter. You will find different opinions expressed about, for example, grouping, texts, and workbooks. This is as it should be. No one method suits every teacher in every subject or even in a specific subject. You serve your pupils best when you use the methods which are adapted to your qualities and theirs in the varying situations in which you find yourselves. To discover when to follow one method and when another and when a combination of methods, you must exercise ingenuity and initiative and be willing to give the possibilities a fair trial. Keep your principal and supervisors informed of your problems and your experiments. They know that teachers differ as much as pupils, and they'll want to help.

NOTES

[1] *The New York Times,* June 14, 1959, sec. 1, p. 57.

[2] Robert Lee Morton, *Teaching Children Arithmetic* (New York: Silver Burdett Company, 1953), p. 6.

[3] Viktor Lowenfeld, *Creative and Mental Growth,* 3rd ed. (New York: The

Macmillan Company, 1957), pp. 16-18. By permission of The Macmillan Company.

[4] John V. Michaelis, *Social Studies for Children in a Democracy,* 2nd ed. (Englewood Cliffs, N.J.: Prentice-Hall, Inc., 1956), p. 129.

[5] J. Wayne Wrightstone, *Class Organization for Instruction,* What Research Says Series, No. 13 (Washington, D.C.: National Education Association, 1957), pp. 21-24.

[6] J. Wayne Wrightstone, *Survey of Intelligence, Reading, and Arithmetic Ability—Sixth Grade Classes—October-November 1956 and January 1957—Summary Report* (New York City Board of Education, Bureau of Educational Research, Division of Tests and Measurements, P.N. 22-231, typewritten), p. 47.

[7] Robert J. Havighurst, *Human Development and Education* (New York: Longmans, Green & Co., Inc., 1953), chap. v.

[8] May V. Seagoe, *A Teacher's Guide to the Learning Process* (Dubuque, Iowa: Wm. C. Brown Company, 1956), pp. 233-37.

[9] Elizabeth Bruene, "Effect of the Summer Vacation on the Achievement of Pupils in the Fourth, Fifth and Sixth Grades," *Journal of Educational Research,* XVIII, No. 4 (November 1928), 309-14.

4

The teacher and administrative policies

NORMA E. CUTTS *and*
NICHOLAS MOSELEY

WHETHER OR NOT YOU AS A CLASSROOM TEACHER have much voice in the formulation of educational policies, the way the policies are carried out depends very largely on your attitude and your skill. Wise principals and superintendents know this and try to be sure that teachers are consulted before a policy is determined and that all policies are flexible enough to allow a teacher freedom to manage his own classroom as he thinks best.

We've already mentioned the way many teachers alter official schedules. Many also, on their own initiative and with at least the tacit approval of their principals, adapt the published curriculum to the different needs of individual pupils and, by begging, borrowing, and buying, provide a wealth of books, materials, and equipment to supplement prescribed basal texts. A principal of a rather formal school described the one room in his building where this kind of "extracurricular" activity was

59

the order of the day as a place where "really interesting things are happening."

Moreover, when official policy lays down principles about such things as promotion, retardation, ability grouping, remedial teaching, and teacher's helpers, your judgment and your suggestions are usually the controlling factors in what happens to a pupil. This chapter is planned to discuss some major matters of policy from the point of view of the classroom teacher who is trying to provide for the individual differences of his pupils.

Organization for Instruction

Your assignment to a classroom or to other academic duties should be made on the basis of your special qualifications. But too often the so-called "good jobs" are allotted on the basis of seniority and the "difficult schools" are staffed by new and inexperienced teachers. State certification regulations offer some protection to you and the pupils—a teacher of the mentally retarded, for example, must earn a special certificate by taking special training—but the idea that anyone can teach all subjects in any elementary grade, regardless of his training, dies hard. You are most likely to be happy if you assess your own abilities and disabilities and volunteer for a position in which you think you can give the best service.

If you are given a chance to choose among classes grouped by ability, try to ignore the question of prestige. The temptation is to work with the bright and gifted, but your particular qualifications and interests may be better suited to a slow or average group. The slow group may offer the greatest challenge. The children are frequently handicapped by their backgrounds. They need a teacher who is a warm, friendly, objective person. Work with them offers great rewards in human values and in a sense of solid achievement. Average groups are in some ways the hardest to help because they represent such a mixture in the way of backgrounds and of goals. You'll be in tune with them if you think of yourself, as many teachers sincerely do, as "just a good average person" with a fondness for variety—"I like teaching because there's never a dull minute. Something new is happening all of the time." The teacher of the bright and gifted is happiest when he believes that grouping them together is in their best interest and that of the community. He should habitually write and speak excellent English and have a broad cultural background. He must be willing to take each pupil where he is and plan and learn with him, improvising and experimenting to satisfy individual needs.

The Teaching of Special Subjects

Itinerant teachers or supervisors of music, art, and physical education are often used in the endeavor to provide instruction in subjects in which the classroom teacher may not be competent. If they are superior teachers as well as specialists, both pupils and regular classroom teachers welcome their visits. However, they are rarely scheduled for more than a period or two a week, and many of these periods may be lost during the school year. The classroom teacher who feels weak in these subjects tends to leave all instruction in them to the specialists. The specialist, who may visit twenty classes a week—a total of six hundred or more children—is unable to give any considerable amount of individual instruction. At best, he notices only a few children with outstanding talent. His time would probably be more profitably employed if he devoted most of it to counseling the classroom teacher on methods and materials and confined his own teaching to an occasional demonstration. If a specialist customarily takes over your class, you cannot tell him he is wrong. But if you are aware of your need to improve your knowledge of a subject and your skill in teaching it, you can ask him for advice about books to study and methods to use. He will be glad to help. If you have a pupil who seems to you really talented, the specialist will be particularly glad to help you gauge the pupil's ability and to advise you on how to guide him.

Music and art are sometimes provided for in club or activity periods which cut across class lines. In these periods children from two or three grades who share a special interest meet with a teacher who is himself an enthusiast. Pupils are so keen about their club activity that in between the meetings they do a great deal of voluntary work. One school tried to have a group of gifted children work together at their regular subjects during the club period, but the bright boys and girls rebelled. They preferred the clubs.[1]

"Teacher teams" is a relatively new term used to describe an adaptation to the elementary school of the secondary-school system under which each subject is taught by a separate teacher. A team may consist of two or three or, rarely, more teachers. Each teacher is in charge of a home room. The children in his room spend the major part of their time with him but go to other teachers for instruction in one or several subjects, for example, in mathematics, science, or music. Each home-room teacher specializes in one of these subjects and exchanges services with the other teachers. This setup differs from the old platoon system in limiting the number of teachers whom the pupils meet and in emphasizing teamwork by the teachers so that various types of integration are possible.

If all subjects are scheduled at the same time in different classrooms, the pupil who does not fit into any group in his own room can go to a higher or lower grade or to a higher or lower ability group for his work in a particular subject. This system presumes a very rigid observance of the schedule. A possible variation is to allot regular periods only to art, music, and science and have the classes in each draw from several grades.

Special Arrangements

Despite the other possibilities, most school systems still expect an elementary teacher to teach the whole curriculum of his grade. When you feel ignorant in a required subject, and if you believe that, in Emerson's words, "None can teach more than he knows," you should ask your principal to explore the feasibility of a one-period exchange. For example, if your talents supplement those of another teacher, if you are particularly interested and knowledgeable in art and he in music, you can exchange classes for these subjects. When you teach just one extra group of children, and that in a subject you know and like, you may find the break stimulating. You and the children get to know each other very well. You can plan with individuals and the group so that they can use the subject you teach in their other work, including any units they are carrying on.

If you have a gifted or talented pupil whose knowledge of a subject greatly exceeds yours, you may be able to arrange out-of-school instruction for him. This could be given by a private teacher or by an expert who lives or works in your community. Some states officially approve releasing pupils from school for a period or more for such instruction, but it may have to come in out-of-school hours. In this case the pupil can use the regularly scheduled school period for other work, perhaps for homework.

In the last analysis, you cannot know everything about every topic that may come up in your class. Older boys and girls in particular have such diversified interests and knowledge that only a battalion of experts could provide all the specialized instruction from which they might profit. Under these circumstances your first step is to confess ignorance. You may then set out to learn with the child, or you may merely discuss with him where he can get the information he needs. Books and records in the school or public library, a "sunrise seminar" on TV, and a hobby club in the community are possibilities. The pupil will think no less of you for admitting you do not know as much as he does, and he will be grateful to you for your guidance.

The Age of Admission

Most schools require that a child should be at least 5 years 8 months old on the first of September if he is to enter first grade. This traditional age of admission was arrived at empirically. Experience showed that most 6-year-olds could learn to read. Of course, many bright 5- and even 4-year-olds learn to read before they come to school. On the other hand, some bright children and many slow children do not learn until they are 7, but then learn well and make·normal or rapid progress. Similar differences in readiness to learn prevail in other subjects, but reading, as the principal tool of academic learning, has always been a major concern of primary instruction.

The advent of intelligence testing made possible the determination of mental ages and so afforded a method of singling out children who might do satisfactory work in the first grade (or in kindergarten) even though they had not reached the chronological age ordinarily required for admission. One of the present editors instituted a program of Binet testing for preschool children in New Haven, Connecticut, in 1922. Children who had an MA of 5 years 8 months were admitted to Grade I if they seemed physically and emotionally mature enough to get along with other first-graders. Careful follow-up studies showed that practically all these children did well throughout elementary school and high school. Studies by other investigators have confirmed these findings.[2]

Unfortunately, few school systems even today have sufficient psychological personnel to examine all candidates for early admission. If the authorities succumb to parental pressure and admit children who are not qualified, tragedy may result. If they are unyielding, many children just too young chronologically yet mentally well-advanced suffer heartbreaking loneliness when their playmates start school and may be misfits when they themselves enter school a year later.

One solution to this problem is the two-year kindergarten. The alert kindergarten teacher, with ample opportunity to observe the children, may judge some capable of admission to first grade after one year. If psychological examinations are not obtainable, reading-readiness tests can be used to supplement the teacher's judgment.

Another possibility is the "primary unit." This, in most cases, groups together all children in their first three years of school. (Some primary units are for two years rather than three.) Grade designations are avoided. Children progress at their own best speed. Some are reading when they enter; some require two years of reading-readiness work and do not actually learn to read until the third year. A few may enter the fourth grade after less than the normal time in the primary unit, but, because the fourth-graders are children whom they knew before, there is no problem of adjustment. Very few are kept in the unit an extra year. One supervisor of an outstanding rural school system reports:

> Unfortunately we have no kindergarten, but our primary unit goes a long way to make up for the lack. We admit children who are 5 years 5 months old by September first. Normally they stay in the unit three years. We assign our best teachers to these units and generally we keep the children with the same teacher throughout the period. The teachers are not only expert in work with young children, but also have ample time to learn to know each individual, his ability, temperament, and background, very thoroughly. As a result the great majority of children enter fourth grade able to do the work of that grade.

Retardation

You will presumably be the person mainly responsible for deciding if a child is to repeat a grade. A few years ago you would rarely have been faced with the problem. "Social promotion," that is, the automatic promotion of a child with his age mates regardless of the quality of his achievement, was almost universal. Today some critics of the public schools and some parents are insisting that no child should be promoted if he has not "passed" in every subject. They are convinced that most children who have failed to meet the standards of a given grade in one year could "make the grade" by repeating.

Actually, the research on the subject indicates that most repeaters make little gain in the extra year and that many retrogress. Wrightstone, after reviewing the findings of numerous studies, says: "In sum, the results of nonpromotion are shown to be not greater mastery of subjectmatter, but less; not greater homogeneity of mental ability in the grades, but greater diversity; not the building up of personality, but an undermining of it." [3]

Our own materials afford a specific illustration of how ineffective retardation is in bringing pupils up to grade. We surveyed the records from Grade I through Grade VI of the children in one class who were promoted regularly, and compared these records with those of five children who started with the class but were kept back, and with the records of four who joined the class because they were repeating a grade. All five who were kept back were relatively further below grade in Grade V than they were in the year before they repeated. For example, at the end of Grade II one boy was reading on the first-grade level and was kept back; at the end of Grade V he was reading on the third-grade level—that is, he made only two years' progress in four years. (A pupil who closely matched this boy in CA, IQ, and Grade-II reading score was for some reason promoted then and regularly thereafter. He made better than normal progress and was up to grade by the end of Grade VI. However, not all the repeaters, had they been promoted, would necessarily have done this well.) The four pupils who dropped back into the original class from the class ahead were aged 12 years 4 months, 12 years 7 months, 13 years 5 months, and 13 years 8 months in October of sixth-grade year and were the oldest four pupils in the class. All four were below grade level in achievement, and the oldest two were the lowest two in the class.

When retardation causes a pupil to be overage in his new class, several bad results are probable. The overage pupil resents being placed with the younger children. He often bullies them. He finds the books normally studied in the grade childish and beneath him, even if he is unable to read them well. Resentment and boredom keep him from applying himself. He is more than likely to play truant, fall in with bad companions, and become delinquent. A severe but not unusual case is described by a fourth-grade teacher:

> Ike stayed two years in Grade I, two in Grade II, and one in Grade III. The third-grade teacher threatened to resign if he repeated her grade. He was 11 years old when he came to me, and big for his age. He had an IQ of 87, but was barely able to read second-grade texts. In class he was surly and impudent. On the playground he took pleasure in bullying the boys in the class, particularly in twisting their arms. They were too small to fight back, and afraid of what he'd do to them if they reported it. One day he followed a third-grade girl into the girls' toilet and forced the door of the cubicle she was in. She screamed and a passing teacher luckily heard her. The next day, while we were asking the central office for advice on what to do with him, he played hooky with a gang of older boys who staged a mass robbery of a candy store. The police caught him and he was sent to the State School for Boys.

Of course there are some children who profit from repeating.[4] Retardation may benefit a pupil who is underage for his grade, physically smaller than most of his classmates, and socially immature. (A liking for play with younger children is a sign of immaturity.) Before deciding not to promote a child, you should be sure that he and his parents understand and agree with your reasons and that the parents know how they can help him improve. But the child who should repeat is certainly an exception. Generally, regular promotion is the best policy. And if you have an overage misfit in your class, you might well urge that he be transferred to a grade with children of his own age.

Remedial Teaching

You can probably do as much as a remedial teacher could for a child who is making progress in line with his ability, even if his IQ is low and his progress correspondingly slow. This assumes that you are willing to take him where he is, provide books and materials that he can master but that are suitable for his chronological age, and give him at least his share of individual attention. However, when a child's slow progress is due not to lack of ability but to excessive absences, some deficiency in the fundamentals, a special subject-matter disability, or an emotional block, he may profit greatly from remedial work. Even a short period of tutoring by a specialist may result in remarkable and permanent advances. Remedial teaching is far cheaper than retardation (taking into account the cost of delinquency) and is constructive rather than destructive.

Before you recommend a pupil for remedial work, you should study him and his record very thoroughly. If possible you should arrange for him to be given an individual psychological examination and for you to secure the recommendations of the psychologist. If a psychologist's services are not available, you should give the child the diagnostic and other tests at your disposal to be sure that the difficulty is not one you can correct quickly by yourself. Consult with the remedial teacher and give him all the information you have. Do your best to make the child see that remedial work offers him an opportunity and that he should try hard to benefit from it.

Scheduling remedial work may be a problem. The special teacher has to work with several classes and perhaps in several schools. Before- or after-school sessions are inconvenient, especially when bus schedules must be met, and they may make the child and his parents resentful. Evening work in the home is rarely practicable. Under these circumstances you will do well to try to suit the convenience of the remedial teacher and help the child make up any regular activities that he misses.

Unfortunately, there is a great shortage of trained remedial teachers. This situation could be quickly corrected if more retired teachers would take up the work. If by any chance you are approaching retirement, consider the possibility. The labor need not be strenuous. Hours can be arranged to suit your convenience. Pay can be by the hour and adjusted so that you need not earn more than you are allowed by your retirement regulations. Your experience with children and with teaching will be invaluable. If you haven't the training to qualify for a certificate, you can easily secure it in extension courses and summer school, especially if you start a year or two before you are scheduled to retire. And you will find great satisfaction in continuing to serve children.

Teacher Assistants[5]

Back in 1898, in Batavia, New York, the superintendent of schools assigned two teachers to each room that had fifty or more pupils. One teacher was to handle group recitation, the other, individual instruction. In classes of less than fifty, a single teacher gave half time to each function. The individual instruction was designed to help all pupils, slow and bright, but the bright who advanced beyond the level at which the group was reciting were not expected to trouble the teachers with any difficulties encountered in their advanced work. Like so many other experiments in education, the Batavia plan was first widely adopted and then gradually abandoned.

Interest in "teacher's helpers" has been revived because of the shortage of qualified personnel. Some administrators have thought that if clerical, housekeeping, and out-of-class supervisory duties, for example in the cafeteria, could be delegated, the regular teachers could handle larger classes. Another possibility has been explored in the Yale-Fairfield Study, namely, that by delegating some duties to assistants without professional training but keeping classes at or near normal size (25 to 35 pupils), the regular teacher might pay more attention to individual differences. Part of the experiment involved a combination of three grades. The same subjects were scheduled at the same hour in each grade, and pupils attended the class which best suited their level of achievement. The assistant supervised the pupils as they changed rooms. The Fairfield schools called this a "multiple faculty" system. It is like the primary unit, plus certain features of the teacher exchanges described above. The twelve multiple-faculty classes averaged 30.42 pupils, as against 24.75 in control classes.

The Yale-Fairfield Study found that the teacher assistants saved the teachers substantial amounts of time in clerical work, routine classroom activities, and certain easy instructional tasks. Minor amounts of time were saved in out-of-class duties. Because of the time saved, teachers were able to make better provision for individual differences by preparing more special materials, carrying instruction further, and by organizing more-homogeneous groups. The results in terms of pupil achievement as measured by standardized tests were somewhat inconclusive, but pupils, parents, and teachers were almost unanimous in their approval of the plan.

Class Size

Class size is always a problem for administrators. As long as a regular system of grades prevails, some classes will have to be larger than others. The available evidence indicates that when achievement on standardized tests is used as a measure, pupils in classes of thirty or more do as well as pupils of similar ability in classes of twenty-six or less.[6] Our own experience suggests that both the teacher and the pupils in an extra-large class recognize an emergency and rise to the occasion. Class morale is consequently high. Moreover, the very best teachers are usually assigned to the large classes. Part of the explanation, however, may be that in the large class the teacher must shift to the pupils themselves much of the responsibility for what they learn. This automatically provides for individual differences and increases independence. In the small class, on the contrary, the teacher, as one pupil said, "always seems to know just what we are thinking and just what we're going to do." There is a natural tendency to supervise so closely that children become completely dependent and lose their desire to learn.

Regardless of achievement, there can be no doubt that the more pupils you have, the greater the drain on your time, strength, and emotional reserve. Moreover, you cannot know forty pupils as well as you can twenty-five, and adequate guidance becomes extremely difficult. If you have a large class, your first steps should be directed to establishing a good emotional tone in your room. Take the pupils into your confidence and plan with them how to make the best of the situation. Enlist them all as teacher's helpers, responsible not only for routine chores but also for their own progress. And if you have a small class, follow the same procedure!

Ability Grouping

The current emphasis on America's needs for fully trained specialists in many fields has revived ability grouping, but not without stirring old arguments against it. Strangely enough, there has never been much criticism of the standard practice of placing mentally retarded children together in a class under a teacher who has been trained to meet their needs. But putting gifted children together is called undemocratic. It is said to make the children conceited, not to mention turning them into bookworms. We have gone into the evidence for and against ability grouping more fully elsewhere.[7] In brief, we found that children in special classes for the bright and gifted continue to take full part in the general activities of their schools. They and their classmates in the slower sections all seem to recognize the advantages of grouping and to prefer it. The children learn more than children in ungrouped classes, and more of the bright and gifted go on to college and later into graduate work. If your school has a special class for the bright and gifted, we do not think you need hesitate to recommend a superior pupil for it.

When you are recommending placement in any group, consider all the evidence and interpret it with great care. It would be wise to review what was said in Chapter 2 about tests and other means of forming an accurate judgment of a child's abilities. Don't rely overly much on test results, but if they indicate a child is more able than you had thought, give him the benefit of the doubt. Be particularly on your guard against children's "halos" and your own prejudices. Talk with the class and ask them to nominate candidates for the top group. The children may be better aware than you are of who would work hard to meet an exacting challenge and who might rest on his laurels. Intelligence, achievement in the separate branches of the curriculum, work habits, interests, and goals are all important. In the doubtful, marginal case, consider also the personality and interests of the teachers a pupil might have. If it seems to you that one of the possible teachers is especially likely to get along well with him, that teacher may be the best for him.

If you yourself are teaching a class grouped by ability, be careful to avoid two surprisingly common mistakes. The first is to continue to follow the standard curriculum or basal texts at the same speed that you would with a heterogeneous group. If you do so, you will neither satisfy nor benefit anybody, least of all yourself. All the differences in learning that we discussed in the previous chapter under intraclass grouping apply here. Fit your materials, your methods, and the pace to the *range* of abilities in your class.

The second mistake is to assume that all the children in your group have about the same general level of ability and about the same achievement in each subject. Nothing could be further from the truth. No matter how carefully children are divided into groups, there will always be wide ranges in over-all ability and in achievement *in each subject,* and there will be great differences in interests, attitudes, and work habits. The 134 pupils in one sixth grade which is divided into five ability groups show some typical divergencies. The range for the total group on the battery median is 8 years 3 months. In some subtests there was an indicated range of 12 years between the poorest pupil and the best pupil in the whole class of 134. The ranges on the battery median in each of the five ability groups vary from 1.5 in the low-average to 3.8 in the high group. This indicates a considerable narrowing of the range. But when the results on the subtests are examined, differences as great as 8.6 are found in a single group. For practically every subtest in every group the range is at least 4.0. This is not an argument against ability grouping—cutting the range by two-thirds helps the teachers in every group organize the work and helps the pupils satisfy their particular needs. But in every group even the reduced ranges are still so great by subject that every teacher must use materials, books, and methods which provide for individual differences.

An examination of the test scores of pupils grouped by ability brings out two more important facts: there is sure to be some overlapping in the subtest scores of pupils in different groups; there are sure to be radical changes in the relative achievement of different pupils, especially during the summer vacation. The five groups described above had no overlap in battery-median scores in May, but there were 72 subtest average scores (for example, total Reading, total Arithmetic) above the median of the next higher group and 62 below that of the next lower group. In October, 4 pupils had scores on the battery median above the median of the next higher group, and 4 had scores below the median of the next lower group. Also in October, there were 79 subtest average scores above the median in the next higher group, and 84 below that of the next lower group.

Flexibility is the remedy in this situation. If in your judgment, based on all of your knowledge of a pupil and not merely on test scores, he belongs in a higher or lower group, his assignment should be changed. Of course you cannot keep shuffling the pupils' home rooms, but there ought to be regular opportunities for reassignment twice a year, say, in the middle of October and the middle of February. Not many pupils will be affected, but those who are will have a better chance to progress according to their abilities. If the interchange is a regular feature of grouping, pupils will accept it matter-of-factly. Very occasionally there will be a sudden shift in a pupil's attitudes or achievement or you will discover new evidence, for example a mistake in scoring or recording a test. In these cases changes in assignment might well be made at any time, especially if the pupil is consulted and agrees. One pupil writes:

> The nicest talk I ever had with a teacher was about Christmas time. He called me out of the room and said, "Jed, you don't belong in this group. You get too good marks. I have talked with the principal and it is okay if you go into a smarter group. It will mean losing some of your friends but I think it would be best. Is it okay with you?" I thought about it for a minute and said, "All right." This talk helped me to understand that it was worth while losing some friends during school hours to do the work I should be doing. Besides, I could make new friends.

Acceleration

If you teach a heterogeneous group, you may have one or several pupils each year who seem to you so far advanced academically in all subjects that they ought to be in a higher grade. Even if your system's official policy is against acceleration, you may want to suggest that an exception be made. If the policy permits acceleration, your recommendation is the most important factor in a sound decision.

The immediate advantages of acceleration are the challenge of work in line with the child's superior abilities and the association, competition if you will, with intellectual equals, who are more likely to share the bright child's interests than are slower children.

The remote advantages of some acceleration are so great that it should be considered in the case of the gifted child even when the teacher he would otherwise have is skillful in providing for individual differences or when he would be with a top-ability group in his normal grade. Today, when almost every professional career demands specialized education at the graduate level, a child who enters first grade at six will be from twenty-five to thirty years old before he can earn his living at a profession. In some much-needed specialties which, like psychiatry, require prolonged periods of training, a person may be thirty-five before he begins practice. A saving of a year or two produces disproportionately large savings in time, energy, and money because the individual gets a head start in his work and is engaged on it when his creative powers are at their peak. Moreover, all along the line the young student in a class is very likely to do superior work in order to live up to his reputation and his image of himself. All the members of Phi Beta Kappa in a recent Yale class were below the average age of the class as a whole, and their average was a year below the average of the class.

However, before you advise that a child be accelerated, you should investigate the probable make-up of the grade into which he is to move. His achievement in each subject ought to equal or exceed the medians of the new class. Otherwise he may be forced to work too hard to hold his own. Is the age distribution of the upper class such that he will fit in? If it contains an undue proportion of overage boys and girls and few near his age, he might be bullied, or left out of all nonacademic activities, or perhaps worse, made a pet. Are the children in the upper group good students, interested in their work—the type that will welcome and admire a superior pupil? Is the teacher of the upper grade skillful in providing for individuals, interested in gifted pupils, and ready to welcome this particular child? Is the child himself socially mature enough and physically tough and developed enough—quite different matters from mere size —to hold his own with the older group? Perhaps the best gauge of this is whether or not he now likes to play with older children and whether they accept him naturally as one of them.

A final consideration involves a look ahead. Under the present tradition it's practically impossible and probably not desirable to save more than two years of the normal sixteen between entering Grade I and graduating from college. Many colleges today accept pupils at the age of sixteen, but relatively few accept them at fifteen. A child in second or third grade has some years of school ahead of him, and if he is now in the least immature he might better wait, planning to skip an intermediate grade and perhaps secure early admission to college or finish college in three years.

While considering these points you should consult with the pupil and with his parents. The parents may hold very strong views one way or the other but be open to reason. If they are in doubt, they might be helped by reading the chapters on acceleration in *Bright Children, A Guide for Parents* and *Teaching the Bright and Gifted*.[8]

Summer Sessions

If your system conducts a summer session for elementary-school pupils or if there is one in a nearby community or at a neighboring teachers college, you will probably be asked to recommend pupils for attendance. Both slow and bright children are likely candidates.

The slow pupil sent to summer school to remedy a specific deficiency or as a condition for promotion may resent being forced to go. Because of poor motivation he may learn very little. One sixth-grader, who still needs to improve, writes: "Last year in school I didnit learn as much I would have like to learn more becouse I not do os good as I wont to and I had to go to summer school evry Momday tuseday and Wemdesday and I did't like because I cont do a lot of things I would have like to do." In a case like this you ought first to feel fairly certain that the child can, if he wishes, advance enough in the extra weeks of work to make the time and effort worth while. If you think he can, then you should try to make the pupil share your opinion. Talk with him and perhaps have him talk with the summer-session teacher. But you must be constructive. Making summer session a punishment for failure or holding it as a threat over a pupil's head is worse than useless.

Large numbers of children do want to go to summer school. New York City has for some years conducted a voluntary summer session. There are three eighty-minute periods five days a week for eight weeks. In 1956, a total of 28,630 boys and girls attended. Of these, 32 per cent went for advanced work, 55 per cent for make-up work, and 12 per cent for a mixture. Attendance was regularly higher than in the winter.[9] By 1958 the enrollment had grown to 35,000, and many more who begged for admission had to be refused for budgetary reasons. Summer school may be more attractive to city children than to suburban and rural children because the recreational facilities are in greater demand. But the experience in smaller communities shows that the well-run summer school is always popular. Perhaps the theoretically desirable twelve-month school is in the offing.

If you have an opportunity to teach in summer school you may well accept. The extra pay is usually welcome. The differences in the children who attend, some reluctant, many eager, challenge all your skill. But there is a relaxed and informal atmosphere—a good emotional tone—that helps you and your pupils do your best work. There are excellent openings for experimentation and research in how best to provide for individual differences.

NOTES

[1] Hedwig O. Pregler, "The Colfax Plan," *Exceptional Children,* XX, No. 5 (February 1954), 198-201, 222.

[2] Jack W. Birch, "Early School Admission for Mentally Advanced Children," *Exceptional Children,* XXI, No. 3 (December 1954), 84-87.

[3] J. Wayne Wrightstone, *Class Organization for Instruction,* What Research Says Series, No. 13 (Washington, D.C.: National Education Association, 1957), p. 5.

[4] E. R. Steadman, "Fifteen Who Were Not Promoted," *The Elementary School Journal,* LIX, No. 5 (February 1959), 271-76; L. A. Stringer, "Left-Back Child," *Child Study,* XXXVI, No. 2 (Spring 1959), 10-14.

[5] *Teacher Assistants, An Abridged Report,* The Yale-Fairfield Study of Elementary Teaching (New Haven, Conn.: February 1959).

[6] Herbert F. Spitzer, "Class Size and Pupil Achievement in Elementary Schools," *The Elementary School Journal,* LV, No. 2 (October 1954), 82-86.

[7] Norma E. Cutts and Nicholas Moseley, *Teaching the Bright and Gifted* (Englewood Cliffs, N.J.: Prentice-Hall, Inc., 1957), pp. 89-101.

[8] Norma E. Cutts and Nicholas Moseley, *Bright Children, A Guide for Parents*

(New York: G. P. Putnam's Sons, 1953), pp. 81-87; Cutts and Moseley, *Teaching the Bright and Gifted,* pp. 102-16.

[9] *Fifty-Ninth Annual Report of the Superintendent of Schools, City of New York, School Year 1956-1957, Statistical Section* (New York: Board of Education, 1958), pp. 204-5.

5

Art

EDWARD L. MATTIL

MAN IS DISTINGUISHED FROM ANIMAL BY HIS
ability to create, and children are born with this ability. The
most important resource of any society lies in the creativity of
its people, and the strength of a democratic society is based
upon the differences of people and the recognition and foster-
ing of these differences. Therefore it is imperative for schools
to provide not only for the intellectual, physical, and social
development of the child but also for his creative and aesthetic
development.

When the art program of the classroom is geared to the like-
nesses of children and tends to ignore the differences, there is
little possibility that it will rise above mediocrity or that it
will yield the rich results in child growth that should be the
outcome of any creative experience. Few, if any, teachers deny
the need for providing for individual differences, and yet all
too often we see as the products of the art work nothing more

79

than thirty identical "Pilgrims" or "Santas"—hectographs carefully filled in under the direction of the teacher. Such products are as unchildlike as they are uncreative. They do not represent true art experiences, and they do not provide opportunities for the recognition of differences in individual children.

How, then, do differences show themselves in the creative products of children? How can we as teachers provide for those differences and assure growth, and what are the basic areas in which differences assert themselves?

Levels of Development

It would be folly to assume that there are no standards in the arts. To be different just for the sake of being different is neither important nor justified. On the contrary, art educators have sought to find ways of recognizing the various stages through which children pass in their growth and development and have sought, through normative research, to establish certain broad areas in which characteristics of each level of development can be placed and ultimately evaluated. Numerous educators have done this effectively. Perhaps the most widely recognized and surely the most concise description of these levels of development has been provided by Lowenfeld.[1] These developmental levels are: Scribbling Stage (2-4 years), Pre-Schematic Stage (4-7 years), Schematic Stage (7-9 years), Gang Age (9-11 years), Stage of Reasoning (11-13 years), and Crises of Adolescence (13 years and older). In order to understand better how differences in children show themselves and how we can provide for the differences, let us consider some specific illustrations from the various age and grade levels.

Preschool

The very first stage of self-expression, which we might observe either in the home or in nursery school, is that of scribbling. Long before the child has any desire to use crayon or pencil to express an idea or thought, you may find him scribbling rather broadly in an uncontrolled fashion. Even in these very early scribbles, which are purely kinesthetic activities, or activities of movement, you can begin to distinguish differences in the works of children. One child may grasp a large crayon and scribble with careless abandon and tremendous vigor and vitality in a completely uncontrolled manner. A second child may grasp his crayon and make a series of very orderly, controlled strokes, perhaps all horizontal or all vertical or all circular. Still a third may reject the largeness of the paper and the crayon and may grasp a pencil and work in tight little areas almost duplicating or imitating writing. Another may scribble great varieties of circular, horizontal, and vertical movements, and at the end seek out the teacher and tell him, "This is my house," or, "This is my dog," or, "This is the swing in the yard." The teacher should listen when a child communicates ideas about what he has scribbled. He may not see any of the forms the child says are there, but he will realize that here is a child using his imagination, one who has begun to think of his scribbles in terms of images or pictures though he is not yet able to produce an image which is visually recognizable. Even within this very young preschool group, there may be one or two children whose scribbles are combined to form heads and legs and thus create a simple concept of man or animal.

At this level, the teacher's role is basically one of providing the class with proper materials with which to work and establishing a climate for work, giving encouragement to each child to seek out and develop his own potential. It would be wrong for the teacher to think that he should teach exercises in motor control and coordination at this early age or to withhold paper until the child has gained sufficient control to work neatly and "stay within the lines." If we think of the child when he is first learning to eat, smearing most of his cereal across his face and down his bib before he discovers how to guide his spoon to his mouth, we recognize that every child must have many misses before he has a hit. Only through constant trying can he develop the sureness and certainty necessary for proper eating—or for control of lines while drawing.

At the same time that the child is scribbling with crayons or with chalks on the blackboards, he is likely to be having very similar experiences with modeling clay. Careful observation will reveal that the child has experiences in three dimensions very like the ones he has in two dimensions. While he is scribbling broadly on his paper, repeating the same motion over and over again, we may find in his clay work that he is pulling off a little ball, rolling it, pulling off another ball, rolling it, pulling off a third, until he has used all his clay to repeat the same shape over and over. Or he may simply pound on his clay.

It is difficult to generalize about the meaning of each type of scribble which children may produce, and it may even be dangerous to try. Few people in teaching or in the arts are in a position to analyze the products of children. To do so may be to give them meaning they do not have. This does not mean that the teacher should fail to look for growth in the work of each child. It is more important to look for differences in the products of the same child than it is to seek out differences for purposes of comparison in the products of two children. At the kindergarten or nursery-school level, age alone could explain the differences which appear between members of a group.

Kindergarten—Grade I

As children enter kindergarten and first grade, we may see vast differences in their creative products. Let us take for example a first grade in which some of the children have attended nursery school and kindergarten and some have come directly from their homes and are having their first school experience. The teacher immediately recognizes many differences which are probably due to environmental conditions.

The children who have spent a year in a kindergarten or nursery school where suitable materials and good stimulation for creative work were provided may already have some type of form concept—that is, they may be making very simple figures based upon circles for heads and horizontal and perpendicular lines for bodies and arms. Perhaps they may be using some color here and there and on the whole working quite freely.

But children who have spent a year in a nursery school or kindergarten in which the entire art program was based upon stereotyped materials such as hectographs, mimeographs, or color books and in which the teacher was very severe in his demands for "keeping within the lines" and "using the proper colors" may show a tremendous dependency upon the teacher and upon hectograph or pattern materials. These children may have developed certain inhibitions and blocks and, when asked to work independently using their own ideas, may show the results of poor art experiences by saying, "I can't." Probably the first-grade teacher's most difficult job in encouraging creative work is the undoing of the stereotypes developed by earlier teachers who have shown the children "how" or have provided them with coloring books and patterns, thus imposing adult standards on them at a very early age.

The children who have come directly from homes where no materials have been provided for creative experiences probably have had no damage done to their confidence. They may begin finding themselves through large uncontrolled scribbles just like nursery-school- or kindergarten-age children, but they quickly pass through this stage, moving into controlled scribbles and soon catching up to the others' form concepts.

Some of the differences in the creative work of these first-grade children will be the result, not of environment, but of what we call "nature"; for some children are more gifted than others, some are more intelligent than others. There may also be differences resulting from nurture; some children may have a richness because of good personal experiences, some will have a richness because of their freedom and confidence in their own ability.

The range at the level of kindergarten and first grade is vast. Some children may still be at the very end of their scribbling experiences, and their form concepts will be extremely limited, perhaps only circles combined with horizontal scribbles, while other children may have even achieved what is commonly known as a "base line." That is, they may have discovered that all things appear upon a common line and may have already developed a very good spatial relationship and size relationship. Other children may be working in great detail.

It is important for the teacher to remember that children, like flowers, do not all bloom at the same time, but all need constant nourishment in order to come to bloom at all. Probably the single most important job of the teacher at this time is to see that each child develops confidence in his own means of expression. One of the most damaging or devastating things that teachers sometimes do with children of this age is to compare their works with those of other children or with those of adults. Teachers must look at differences not as the evils of the art program but as the strengths. We have become so accustomed to the use of standardized tests that we sometimes find ourselves trying to press our children into a standardized mold. Many times the teacher's strong drive to have all children achieve at the same level or at least at a certain minimum level is not based upon the needs of the children so much as it is upon the ego needs of the teacher.

Grade I

Most first-grade children develop the ability to think in terms of pictures or images, that is, they achieve some type of simple form concept. When the teacher realizes that most of his pupils have achieved this rather common ground, his role changes considerably. First, the teacher should provide art materials which conform to the child's desire for expression. (See "Suggested Art Materials for a Basic Program," page 101.) Generally, these are large colored wax crayons, thick easel paint and porous paper on which to paint, and modeling clay. Not every material should be introduced at this age. For example, transparent water color would not conform at all to the needs of the small child, who, when he puts a line on the paper, wishes it to stay where he puts it and not to flow all over the surface.

More important is the teacher's need to stimulate the child to want to express himself and to extend the child's frame of reference. The child's world at this age is limited and primarily focuses on himself. Many of his pictures will reveal this quite clearly. Since the child's first desire is to express his own experiences, the first motivations should be based upon an enrichment of his first concepts. These deal with the body parts. Topics can be derived from an immediate experience, or common topics typical of the activities of children can be used. "I am drinking my milk at breakfast," "I am running to catch the school bus," "I am walking with my mother and father," are examples.

A while ago one of my classes had a dental inspection by the school dentist just before I arrived. Some children were still excited and some still frightened, so the planned lesson was discarded and the topic "I am opening my mouth for the dentist to look at my teeth" was used. We quickly discussed what had been experienced, what was seen, and what was felt. Then I asked the children to draw their experience with the dentist. Most of the children placed a great deal of emphasis upon the mouth and upon the dentist's hands, and for the first time a large majority of the children drew teeth inside the open mouth and fingers on the dentist's hands. As one might expect from such an experience, the heads were all overemphasized and other body parts were somewhat neglected. Sometimes the eyes did not appear because they had been held so tightly shut, and sometimes the arms were absent. By comparing these drawings with ones the children had done earlier, it was possible to see that several new elements had been added to their drawings and thus the concepts were richer.

A very simple procedure for developing motivation at this level is described by Lowenfeld.[2] He recommends frequent discussions between the children and teacher based upon the words *what, how, where,* and *when. What* are you doing, or were you doing, or did you do? *How* did you do it? The children can either describe the situation verbally or act it out physically— "relive" it. *Where* and *when* are used to develop the general environment or atmosphere. Such stimulation will help children activate knowledge which was heretofore passive or unused.

You may now ask yourself, how then, if I desire to provide for individual differences in children, am I going to motivate each separately? Can differences be encouraged within the framework of one stimulus? In most instances this will be adequate to provide for all the differences which might occur within any single class, because the differences show themselves in the interpretation of the subject matter and not in the subject matter itself. To understand this more clearly, let us take an extreme example. Suppose we have a father and mother and three children, a boy age 12, a girl age 9, and a boy of 5. Then imagine that they all had an experience together. They visited the county fair and, following their visit, each desired to express his experience in painting. Most likely the 5-year-old would have been impressed by the ponies he rode or the merry-go-round or the ferris wheel. It would be activities of this sort which he would wish to express in his interpretation of the county fair. The 9-year-old may have been more impressed by the dancers at the square dance and the beautiful costumes they wore, and the 12-year-old may have been interested in the auto races or in the baseball game. The mother may have tried to paint a total visual impression of the scene of tents, gay colored banners, and crowds of people which she saw as she entered the fair grounds. The father may have been impressed by the faces he saw, the forms of clusters of people, or by the movement of crowds or the total spirit of the fair itself. While each has had a common experience and is trying to portray this experience the way he recalls and felt it, each places a completely different interpretation upon the subject matter, and each may be entirely right, according to what he saw and felt. If we were to examine six famous painters' renderings of one subject—a vase of flowers or a person—we would see precisely the same thing happening. One might concern himself with the interplay of planes, another might concern himself primarily with play of light and shadow, while a third might try to interpret the feeling or mood of the particular person being painted. A fourth might concern himself with the linear qualities which he see in the form. A fifth might concern himself primarily with color and mood, while a sixth may give a fairly literal interpretation, trying to come as close to visual reality as possible. Each of these paintings may be good, and none may be better than another, yet each is completely different.

At one time in art education, the highest achievement was considered to be the ability to draw or paint photographically, so that the picture looked lifelike. Because of this, much time was spent on technique and exercise, with great emphasis upon skill and practice. Sometimes people mastered all the skills only to find that they had nothing to say. The emphasis in recent years has been on the development of creativeness in our youth, not for use in the arts alone, but for use in any endeavor in which a child may ultimately engage. Art educators now seek to develop to the fullest potential the creativity of each child, and to do this means discarding any single standard. But we still find people in the arts who insist on generalizations such as, "All children must paint large"—as if largeness and creativeness were synonymous, which they certainly are not. The danger of such generalization will be evident as we consider the work of children in the second and third grade.

Grade II and Grade III

If you study a portfolio of a child's drawings during the first year or two of his work, you will note that his first concept of a figure may have been a circular scribble, which represented a head, and two verticals, which represented the legs. Then it began to change. Hardly a month would pass without the concept changing considerably. One week a circle would represent

the body, the next week a rectangle, and another week a tri-
angle. Generally, the body parts are represented by very simple
geometric shapes.

If you examine all of a child's drawings critically, you will
find that he seems to be searching for a personal and satisfying
concept of a person, animal, or tree. He finds one and soon discards it, discovers a new one, soon discards it, keeps some of
the old, adds something new, constantly changing and searching
until ultimately he comes up with a concept which seems to
appear over and over again. Many art educators call this the
child's search for a schema, the schema being the child's own
particular way of interpreting a person, tree, animal, flower, or
any other specific object. Some idea of the tremendous variety
of schemata which appear in the works of children can be gained
by looking at Florence Goodenough's article "Children's Drawings." [3]

It is generally in the second and third grade that the
child arrives at his schema and stays with it for a fairly extensive period of time. But during this period the children will
make many deviations from their schemata, sometimes by neg-
lecting parts, as was illustrated by the armless figures in the
drawings of the experience with the dentist, sometimes by the
overemphasis of certain parts or the exaggeration of parts, and
sometimes by a complete change in the geometric symbols for
various body parts.

I recall two drawings by a second-grade child which were
made several weeks apart. The first drawing appeared after there
had been a heavy snowfall and all the children had had a week
end of sledding, skiing, and so on. We had decided in our art
period that we would make pictures of the fun we had had over
the week end. Ken brought his first picture to me to examine.
Since it had an unusual number of arms protruding from the
shoulders of the one figure, I asked Ken to tell me about the
picture. I was eager to have him interpret the figure without
my asking about the multiple arms. When he reached the part
of the picture in which the arms appeared, he said, "Say, do

you know what was happening here?" and I replied I didn't.
He said, "It was so cold, I was flopping my arms up and down."
In order to get his feeling of flailing arms into the picture,
he simply put on four additional arms. Several weeks later,
during the art period, he made a picture of himself walking to church with his family. Because the motivation of the
particular lesson had been, "How do you dress?" "Who is in
the family?" and, "How do you walk?" attention had been
focused away from the arms—not intentionally—and his completed picture failed to have arms on any of the figures. When
we talked about our pictures, Ken seemed entirely unaware of
their absence and not at all concerned about it.

It is during second or third grade that children generally discover the meaning of the base line, that is, they begin to use
the bottom edge of the paper as a common base on which to
place all the objects in the picture, or they draw a horizontal
line across the page and place all the figures upon that line.
This is a definite sign of growth, for now the child has begun
to depart from his self-centeredness and begins to see himself
more in relationship to the world. He begins to see the relationship of one thing to another. It is generally during this time
that reading greatly improves, as does the child's ability to work
in group or cooperative activities.

Probably the greatest number of differences in ways of ex-
pressing ideas or thoughts occur at this age. This is, in fact, a
period in which children are able to express more in a single
picture than at any other time in their development. They may
make X-ray pictures, that is, they draw the inside and the outside of the same thing at the same time. For example, you may
find a picture of a dog that has eaten a bone: the dog is drawn
with all sorts of views into his body so you can see where the
bone has gone down his throat and is resting in his stomach. Or
the picture may be of a cat that has eaten a mouse, or of a house,
where you see the inside and outside simultaneously. A child
will make pictures in which time is represented in many sequences; that is, he may show you his whole trip to his grand-

father's farm and back, and he may appear in the picture six or eight times. In a single picture a child may mix up different views; that is, in making a picture of himself playing checkers at the table with his friend, he may first draw a side view of the table and of himself and his friend and the chairs on which they sit. But when he wants to show the checkerboard on the table, he simply gives a top, or bird's-eye, view of the table so that you can see all the squares on the checkerboard and all the checkers in place.

Probably the best evidence of a teacher's success at this level is a great variety of differences in the works of his pupils. And the greatest danger is a propensity to concern oneself with teaching proportion, perspective, proper color, and other matters which are inconsequential to the ideas that the child is trying to express and which actually interfere with his ability to express much about himself.

At this level certain definite characteristics begin to show themselves which will probably be retained in much of the future work of each child. Earlier in this chapter there was a mention of bigness. Some children at this age level do love to "work big," and get on the floor and express themselves freely in large paintings. Certainly, every classroom ought to have materials for large work and should try to provide the space for children to have such an experience. But at the time when some children are enjoying this freedom from restricted size and space, other children are concerning themselves with minute details. It is important for the teacher not to become bound by single ideas lest he prevent the child who is interested in detail from having the opportunity to work in his own way.

I remember a young man who was in my classes many years ago. When he was in second grade he made a picture of the kitchen where he was helping his mother wash the dishes. Every mechanical device in the kitchen was shown. After he had completed the picture, he picked it up, took it to the window, and carefully traced the outline of the stove, the refrigerator, and the clock on the reverse side. Then, within the tracings, he proceeded to draw all the mechanical parts in the clock, the stove, and refrigerator. This young man kept his interest in details and mechanical things. He continued to show the same characteristics all the way through high school. Today he is an engineer, still working with his small details and interested in parts.

During the second and third grades it is necessary to introduce a larger variety of materials with which children may work. In addition to the tempera paints and bristle brushes, crayons, and modeling clay, the teacher may begin to supply a variety of scrap materials such as paper bags, boxes, fabrics and buttons, colored papers, scissors, and paste, and thus introduce a simple crafts program to parallel the arts program.[4] However, it is important in the crafts as in the arts for the teacher not to start by some standardized method or procedure and have all the children make "something for a Christmas gift." Children need to develop their own techniques in the crafts as well as in drawing and painting.

Since children at this age level have come to recognize themselves in relation to their environment and are showing themselves capable of cooperative activities, the kinds of topics or the subjects of the topics which are now presented can include "we" instead of "I." Because the child's world is growing and his variety of experiences has enlarged, the topics are almost endless. In fact, any experience with which the child can closely identify becomes a good experience for personal expression. For example, there are many wonderful films which can provide an intense experience—one even more intense than a firsthand experience in some cases. And many a story which teachers read aloud or children read to themselves can be the basis of good creative experiences.

Grades IV and V

As we look at the children in the fourth and fifth grades, we observe a completely new set of characteristics creeping into their work. Generally, up until this period most of the children have used symbols, that is, geometric forms, for the parts of all the things they have drawn. While these symbols have been used in highly individual ways in their schematic drawings, there has been little relationship with visual reality. As a rule of thumb, one might say that younger children are inclined to draw what they know about things rather than things as they appear. A simple test of this is to take the first or second grade out into the schoolyard and tell them to draw the school building. By the time they have seated themselves and gotten into a position to draw, a large proportion of them are facing away from the school and they proceed to draw the school as they know it to be rather than as it appears visually.

In the fourth and fifth grades, children begin to draw by using characteristics which are no longer geometric but cannot yet be considered completely visual concepts. They have changed considerably in their interests and in their activities. This is the time in which they are inclined to group together in boy gangs or girl gangs. It is the period of the Brownies and the Cubs and secret societies. The boys want to be boys, and girls want to be girls. The girls now develop their early strong drives to be like certain feminine movie stars, and boys want to be identified with very masculine types. Although the child has probably by now developed a highly personal way of working or a highly personal technique, there is a tendency for the child to focus upon characteristics of the different sexes. Here, boys will place a good deal of emphasis upon the drawing of trousers or of costumes or uniforms representative of masculine types, while girls tend often toward careful, precise drawing of dresses or costumes that are specifically feminine, such as those of nurses, WAC's, airline hostesses.

At the stage when the focus is upon a specific costume, there is a tendency toward a much greater stiffness in the work of both boys and girls. Frequently much ground is lost during this phase of development because the children pick up certain easy stereotypes from the comic strips which portray either the masculine or feminine types. For example, many boys around this age are drawing Tarzan types or Flash Gordon types, while the girls are doing Blondie or Penny types or Dixie Dugans. To overcome or to avoid such stereotypes, the teacher can plan drawing or painting activities which are related to the use of the human figure and with which each child can identify. "Rescuing the child who has fallen from the boat" could be a topic. The teacher might ask who has seen a child who couldn't swim, flailing about in the water. Are his movements full of action and excitement, does he stir up the water as he flails about? How would you rescue him? Would you kneel and stretch out your arms, would you throw him a rope, or would you dive or jump from the boat? How would the other occupants of the boat behave? Such a motivation can help the child re-engage in the emotional qualities so evident in his earlier drawings and may cause him to deviate from the rigidity of stereotypes. On occasion during this stage, the teacher may also suggest the use of a posed model, but a model should be given meaning. Pose a child swinging a stick toward the floor. "Have you seen anyone do this?" "Surely, this could be a woodsman killing a rattlesnake, or a railroad-track man driving in a stake, or a miner picking coal or gold, or a soldier preparing his foxhole." "Have you ever swung like this? What were you doing?" Such a motivation will start much thinking and bring about a keener awareness of oneself and will call for many different interpretations.

It is during the fourth and fifth grades that the child is apt to discover the meaning of the plane. He leaves the simple concept of a line for a base line, and the space between two base lines becomes meaningful, or a plane. It is at this time, too, that you begin to see the child pull the sky down to make the horizon. This is a perfectly natural phenomenon. Teachers should respect it and have sufficient patience to wait until it occurs spontaneously. Of course, a first-grade child can be made to paint the sky down to meet the ground, but if he is forced to do this he is usually confused.

During this period, children show great differences in progress. Certain children with visual tendencies will progress very rapidly in their ability to portray things visually and may soon be showing depth by means of diminishing size or a change in color. Other children may retain the simple geometric approach of the schematic period. The large majority of the children will be in the gang age, in which the tendency is more to characterize, rather than generalize as they did in earlier years or to visualize as they may do as they become older. The inclination, natural at this age, to group in gangs or clubs can be put to constructive use in many creative activities, such as the making of murals, dioramas, and wall hangings and block-printed drapes for the use of the group. The kinds of things the children are able to do are limitless.

If the child has been encouraged in each of his creative endeavors so far, we should find him working freely and flexibly, that is, able to attack every new problem without fear of failure. We should see him grow in physical coordination through the many experiences he has had with the use of his hands and materials. We should see growth in aesthetic judgment through the numerous choices he has made in the selection of his colors, in the placement of his figures, and the constant decisions he has made for himself in choosing and selecting. We should see creative growth in his ability to think originally and emotional growth in his ability to work independently and to be free of stereotypes or clichés.

As the teacher works with the children of this age, he might focus his attention upon a number of topics which are of special interest and significance to them. It is desirable to choose topics which bring a greater consciousness of space, thus allowing the child to make the discovery of the plane for himself. For example, interest in uniforms might lead to drawings of a policeman directing traffic or of a nurse wheeling a patient down a hospital corridor. Interest in athletics is capitalized by topics like, "We are playing hockey on the ice rink," or, "We are watching the football game from high in the stands."

Craft projects such as block printing or clay modeling or

sculpturing, weaving, stitchery, papier-mâché and mask making, making puppets and putting on a puppet production would all be effective additions to the arts-and-crafts program. The great differences which show themselves in drawing and painting will be evidenced in very similar ways in such craft activities as mask making or puppetry. In puppetry some very slow children may never get much beyond the simplest form, while bright children have a very intense creative experience, making many new discoveries and explorations in materials, solving many problems of construction and function, and finally identifying strongly with the puppets they make.

Recently I observed one of my classes for children of this age level, who chose to draw on the blackboard during some of their free time. Each child was self-motivated, that is, no one suggested that he go to the blackboard or suggested what he might do. One of the children immediately began to draw a very romantic version of a wild horse. The next child concentrated all her attention upon her idea of a beautiful and seductive mermaid sitting among the rocks. The third child made a very mechanical drawing of the United States and placed most of the states in their proper locations and began to mark in the names of the states and their capitals. The fourth was a boy who has a most intense interest in fire fighting and fire engines. This child drew a very careful, very accurate, perspective drawing of a fire engine, with fire fighters, ladders, and all the speed and activity one might expect from a fire engine in motion. It is impossible for me as a teacher to know what makes each of these children different, beyond knowing that the existence of individual differences is a normal condition of nature which is present in all characteristics and abilities.

The Preadolescent—Grade VI and Grade VII

In order to complete our picture of the elementary-school child as he passes through the many stages, it is necessary to look at the preadolescent child. A goodly number of our sixth-

and seventh-grade children have arrived at this stage. In the arts this is most frequently seen in the ability to observe visually. We recall that the children's drawings during the first years were merely generalizations, and that during the middle and upper elementary grades they became characterizations. Now the drawings often become visualizations. With many children this is seen in a very sketchy quality in their drawings; with others it may be seen in the inclusion of joints such as knees and wrists and elbows; with others, in an eagerness to make "correct proportions"; and with still others, in the use of light and shadow or diminishing size. With some children it may be a combination of any or all of these factors.

As we observe our groups of children, we may note that there are two basic ways of working. One group of children may tend toward sketchy free drawings, while a second group may tend to concentrate a good deal on details. Lowenfeld [5] describes the two basic types emerging in this period as the visual and the haptic, or nonvisual, child. The child with the visual propensity tends to concentrate upon the total picture and plays the role of the observer or spectator, while the nonvisual child tends to focus his attention on important details and concentrates more on self than on environment. In fact, environment may appear only when it is absolutely essential.

A very interesting manifestation of these two main types of expression occurs in the use of modeling materials. The so-called visual child has a tendency to take his entire lump of clay and see in it the image which he wishes to have emerge, and begin to pinch or pull it out of the whole lump. The nonvisual child has a tendency to take his clay and pull it apart bit by bit, building first a foot and a leg, then a second foot and a second leg, a body, arms, hands, and fingers, working from parts toward the whole concept.

Many years ago the art schools taught that the "right method of modeling" was that of beginning with the lump of clay as a whole and squeezing all the parts out of the whole. But it would be wrong to insist that there is a right and a wrong method of modeling or painting at any level. Most children will use a combination of the basic methods. Careful observation of a whole class of sixth-graders will reveal that there are probably no two children who work in precisely the same manner in their clay or in their paints. By now each child has probably developed his own personal style or technique, which is highly individualized, in fact as individualized as his handwriting or his speech or his manner of walking.

The preadolescent child is probably at the most critical point in his creative development. It is now that his thinking becomes more adult, and he becomes highly critical of his own production. He begins to look at his work with the eyes of an adult but may yet be working with the hands of a child. This discrepancy between what he wishes to do and what he can do sometimes causes him to stop working creatively.

There is no easy solution to the problem of how to prepare children for this period of self-criticism. Perhaps the best approach is through discussion of their creative products. Following a lesson in which the children may have gone outdoors and painted landscapes from nature, the teacher might ask, "Betty, how did you get this cluster of trees to look so far away?" "Larry, you have the door on the house standing open. How did you get the effect of having it open?" "Clara, you have created an unusual color. How did you make this color?" Such questions and the children's answers help guide children to a greater awareness of what they have achieved. With the child who has nonvisual tendencies the question may be: "Mat, your picture has such fine feeling of balance. What did you do to achieve this fine feeling?" or, "Ned, you have selected a most unusual and interesting variety of colors to portray your ideas. How did you go about selecting colors to arrive at such an interesting arrangement?" or, "Dorothy, your picture seems to be very strongly designed. Do you have a special way you go about simplifying the content of your picture to arrive at this beautiful design quality?" Each of these questions, in pointing out the most positive qualities of the individual, is also pointing out the differences which exist within the group. In essence, the teacher is an adult placing his stamp of approval on the differences. Such experiences strengthen children's confidence in their own creative work and also teach them to respect the works of others regardless of how different one may be from another.

Self-confidence and respect for others also come from familiarity with the works of our great painters. If the children are constantly exposed to books of drawings and of paintings of the artists of all times, they will realize that no two great painters have ever worked identically. Excellent reproductions that can be exhibited in the classroom are available in all kinds of periodicals. *Life,* for example, has featured in color the works of literally hundreds of artists. Moreover, daily contact with these works will not only raise the level of awareness and the sensitivity of the children, but it can have a like effect on the teacher. Too often the only "art" on classroom walls is in the form of sweet calendars which have absolutely no claim to quality. We cannot raise our cultural level if we do not seriously try to provide our children with a means of raising theirs.

The Gifted Child

The gifted pupil is not always easily identified. This is especially true in the arts, where individual differences are commonplace and are to be expected. Frequently, technical facility (such as the ability to draw slick horses or cartoons) is the main criterion for identification. Far more important than mere facility are enthusiasm, originality of ideas, the ability to express ideas with feeling, and a relatively advanced level of development.

Most schools have as yet no workable way of providing for the child who is gifted in art. In many the only resource is a part-time or out-of-school class in which adult art-school methods are applied, with great emphasis on the product and little on the child. Unless classes for the gifted are directed by persons specifically trained to meet the particular challenge, it is altogether possible for them to do more harm than good.

The classroom teacher who feels that he has a gifted child in need of special attention will, of course, ask the assistance of the art supervisor if one is available. The principals and guidance counselors of both the elementary and secondary schools should also be consulted. If all work together as a team, it is conceivable that some effective plan can be drawn up to assist the continued growth of the child. In the meantime it is up to the classroom teacher to supply the greatest possible challenge to each pupil.

In Conclusion

What, then, are some of the main points which the classroom teacher might keep in mind for developing an art program and providing art experiences to take care of individual differences in children?

1. At each grade level the program must have a very broad base in order to take care of those children who may be working at levels below and levels above what may be the norm for the class.

2. The best motivations are based upon intense experiences, whether real or vicarious.

3. No single material or medium can satisfy the needs of all children. Therefore it is imperative that every program be broad enough in kinds of activities to take care of the special interests and special needs of all children. For example, some children who are unable to express themselves adequately or well in the painting of a landscape may find that they excel in a problem of designing a piece of stitchery or a block print based upon abstract forms.

4. Every teacher should seek an outlet for his own creative abilities. Each one of us has some creative ability, though often it has lain dormant for many years. To know the thrill that comes from writing one's own poem, decorating one's own home, creating one's own clothing, painting a landscape, building a fireplace or a work table, or teaching creatively is important. To exercise our full powers as creative individuals is an obligation to our pupils and to ourselves. Only through the awakening of the teacher's own potential of creativity can he fully comprehend its importance to the child. We would not excuse the child who has two good hands and uses only one. We cannot excuse ourselves as teachers when we fail to exercise our full abilities.

5. There should be some record of each child's development. Try to keep a portfolio of samples of the works of each child spaced over intervals of several weeks. If possible, ask the child to make a brief statement about each of the samples kept, and attach this to the picture. A simple check sheet can be clipped to the folder of each child. The check sheet might include items which relate specifically to the philosophy of art teaching; for example, originality, flexibility (the ability to attack new ideas and new processes without fear of failure), motor control, work habits, and attitudes. Such a check sheet helps the teacher recall a better total image of the child and evaluate his progress. Samples, statements, and check list used together provide tangible evidence of growth or lack of growth, as the case may be.

6. We must respect differences as a normal condition in the arts at any level, childhood or adult. It is fair to assume that a good program tends to increase rather than decrease differences in creative work. Differences are a positive factor in much of the richness of living and in some of the most important achievements of man. They are evident in the paintings of famous artists of all times. And in those societies in which civilization has reached its highest peaks, there have always been the widest ranges of differences among individuals.

SUGGESTED ART MATERIALS FOR A BASIC PROGRAM

		Grades				
Materials	*K-1*	*2*	*3*	*4*	*5*	*6*
Newsprint	x	x	x			
Manila drawing paper	x	x	x	x	x	x
White drawing paper				x	x	x
Colored construction paper	x	x	x	x	x	x
Colored poster paper	x	x	x	x	x	x
Kraft wrapping paper	x	x	x	x	x	x
Finger-paint paper	x	x	x			
Kindergarten crayons	x	x				
Standard crayons			x	x	x	x
Paste	x	x	x	x	x	x
Water colors				x	x	x
Powder paints	x	x	x	x	x	x
Easel brushes	x	x	x	x	x	x
Plastic modeling material	x	x	x			
Clay		x	x	x	x	x
Scissors	x	x	x	x	x	x
Chalks	x	x	x	x	x	x

SUGGESTED MATERIALS FOR AN IDEA BOX

Metal foils
Beads
Buttons
Burlap
Boxes
Cans
Cellophane
Cloth remnants
Costume jewelry
Felt scraps
Feathers
Paper bags
Paper plates
Newspaper
Wallpaper books

Nature materials
Pine cones
Burs
Seeds
Twigs
Shells
Reeds
Bushes
Pods
Ribbon
Screening
Spools
String
Wire
Wood scraps
Yarn

GENERAL REFERENCES

Cole, Natalie R., *The Arts in the Classroom*. New York: The John Day Company, Inc., 1940.

D'Amico, Victor, *Creative Teaching in Art*. Scranton, Pa.: International Textbook Company, 1953.

de Francesco, Italo L., *Art Education: Its Means and Ends.* New York: Harper & Brothers, 1958.

Erdt, Margaret H., *Teaching Art in the Elementary School.* New York: Rinehart & Company, Inc., 1954.

Lindstrom, Miriam, *Children's Art.* Berkeley, Calif.: University of California Press, 1957.

Lowenfeld, Viktor, *Creative and Mental Growth* (3rd ed.). New York: The Macmillan Company, 1957.

————, *Your Child and His Art.* New York: The Macmillan Company, 1954.

Mattil, Edward L., *Meaning in Crafts.* Englewood Cliffs, N.J.: Prentice-Hall, Inc., 1959.

Wickiser, Ralph L., *An Introduction to Art Education.* Yonkers, N.Y.: World Book Company, 1957.

ART EDUCATION MAGAZINES

Arts and Activities. The Jones Publishing Company, Skokie, Ill.

Craft Horizons. Craft Horizon, Inc., 601 Fifth Ave., New York, N.Y.

Design. Design Publishing Company, Columbus, Ohio.

School Arts. The Davis Press, Worcester, Mass.

FILMS ON CHILD ART

(Most of these films can be obtained from university film libraries or from the film libraries of state departments of education.)

Children Are Creative. 11 min., color. Bailey Films, Inc.

Children Who Draw. 38 min., black and white. Brandon Films.

Meaning in Child Art. 10 min., color. The Pennsylvania State University.

Report in Primary Colors. 33 min., color. Virginia State Board of Education.

Understanding Children's Drawings. 10 min., black and white. A. F. Films.

NOTES

[1] Viktor Lowenfeld, *Creative and Mental Growth*, 3rd ed. (New York: The Macmillan Company, 1957). By permission of The Macmillan Company.

[2] *Ibid.*

[3] Florence Goodenough, "Children's Drawings," in *Handbook of Child Psychology* (Worcester, Mass.: Clark University Press, 1931).

[4] Edward L. Mattil, *Meaning in Crafts* (Englewood Cliffs, N.J.: Prentice-Hall, Inc., 1959).

[5] Lowenfeld, *Creative and Mental Growth*, p. 262.

6

Music

ROBERT E. NYE *and*
VERNICE TROUSDALE NYE

ALMOST FROM THE HOUR OF THEIR BIRTH, AMERI-
can children live in an environment overflowing with music.
Beginning with mothers' lullabies and continuing from radios,
television sets, and high-fidelity record players, come patterns
of melody, rhythm, and harmony. Moreover, the vast body of
music, from nursery songs to symphonic and operatic music,
forms a part of man's cultural heritage.

The elementary school has a duty to see that *every* child finds
meaning in music and shares the rich musical experiences so
readily available. When music is well taught, the rewards extend far beyond the bounds of the subject. Children, through
individual and group musical experiences, learn to comprehend
concepts of beauty. They can become increasingly creative.
They have the opportunity to express themselves emotionally
and so are helped to develop wholesome personalities. The
teacher, through the medium of music, speaks to children in a

104

language that carries no personal threat or fear. Adequate musical experiences can provide an avenue by which children may attain a feeling of acceptance, success, and importance as contributing members of a group.

A generation of music teachers has proved that there is no such thing as a "nonmusical" child. To be sure, there are wide differences in musical ability, but *every* child can learn to share in the recreational, cultural, and emotional wealth which music affords. This chapter is planned to help teachers help all children progress in knowledge and enjoyment of music.

The Good Teacher of Music

The teacher is the most important factor in providing for the growth of the individual in music. The good teacher of music is able to analyze and understand the musical needs and abilities of each child. He is professionally qualified to teach music in the classroom. He plans for and with the children the musical activities necessary to build success and confidence in each child in terms of the child's potentialities and limitations. He selects and organizes objectives, activities, and materials in order to meet the specific needs of individuals and of groups. Therefore, he knows the precise reasons for his choice of any particular song, activity, or material of instruction. Needless to say, he enjoys music, and his enthusiasm is contagious.

It is folly to assume that every classroom teacher in the United States has these qualities, that every teacher can teach music successfully. Unfortunately, many boards of education and school administrators too frequently act on this assumption. Others rationalize a failure to provide good instruction in music in every grade by claiming that the deficiencies of one teacher will be balanced by the excellences of the next. The results of these assumptions are deplorable, as anyone who visits classrooms with an open mind—and ears!—will agree.

You may, then, ask what you can do if you yourself are not a good teacher of music. Obviously, you should have help. Ideally this will be provided by having a teacher who is a specialist in music work with you in your classroom. The amount of teaching he does will depend on your knowledge and skill at the time. There should never be an instance in which you as the classroom teacher are divorced from the music program. Your counsel concerning each child is essential, as is your part in planning with the child and the specialist. But the specialist, with a sympathetic understanding of your limitations, will show you what you can do to guide the children's activities along the right lines when he is absent and will help you improve your music-teaching skill. He will provide a good deal of direct instruction. And he will help you evaluate the musical progress of each child.

As a classroom teacher you can't insist that your school system employ a music specialist, but you can agitate for one. In the meantime, if you feel you are weak in music, you can ask your principal to work out some method by which you can get help, perhaps a limited exchange with a teacher in another classroom. (See Chapter 4, page 63.) And consider taking private music lessons or enrolling in summer-session or extension classes in music education.

The Classroom and the Program

Each classroom should have a *center of interest* for music. There should be shelves for books, wall space for pictures about music, a bulletin board for current news items, cartoons, and educational information concerning music, and easily accessible storage space for instruments and for materials for experiments with sound. There should also be basal and supplementary music books, chalkboards, flannel boards, staff liner, and a record player with recordings of quality.

The program should include opportunities to experiment with aspects of music that interest the individual and musical experiences undertaken as an outgrowth of other areas of the curriculum or as a contribution to them. In every case there should be provision for participation by the children in planning, directing, and evaluating music activities. Such participation can encourage the development of creative ability and help build wholesome pupil relationships.[1] There should be a regular allotment of time each day to be devoted to music. And there should be an agreement with the children that those who wish can spend any free time they may have in music activities when these will not disturb the other children.

Participation in planning and carrying out specific music activities, and in their evaluation, helps a child establish goals which he understands and can realize. This is very important, because learning music is essentially an individual matter. For example, take a child who cannot sing well at a certain phase of his musical development. Among his immediate, and attainable, goals may be rhythmic responses, playing the bells, experimenting with percussion instruments, or learning about certain recorded music. His interest and success in these activities can be utilized to stimulate interest and effort to achieve future goals in singing and other aspects of music.

Identifying Individual Differences

Individual differences in standards and in achievement are to be expected. *Realization of this is the beginning of an effective music program.*

Wide variations in general musical background are always present. Some children come from homes where the parents sing and play and where they hear good music from a large collection of recordings beautifully reproduced by a modern record player. Other children come from homes where uncontrolled broadcasts constantly bombard them with confusing sound. Still others come from meager surroundings in which music plays slight part.

Besides these differences in background, each child brings

with him all the other influences, musical, mental, emotional, and physical, which affect his relationship with music. All types of differences are intensified where the music program is under-developed and inconsistent from year to year, and where the student population is unstable.

To assemble the information necessary to identify individual differences in music and the different degrees of musical apti-tudes, you need to employ most of the techniques available for studying the individual. (See Chapter 2.) If your program is such that it stirs the child's interest in music and encourages him to express himself, alert observation helps you identify his strengths and weaknesses. *Cumulative records* of each child should contain anecdotes and specific information which reveal individual attitudes, appreciation, special interests, and talent. (Too often, the only mentions of music in the records of a class describe the extremes.) *Conferences with a child's prior teachers, including private teachers of music,* are an important supple-ment to the records. *The health records* should describe defects and their origin, so that the teacher can provide for musical activities which are logical in view of a hearing loss or other handicap. *Conferences with parents and visits to homes* should include a deliberate effort to find the family's musical in-terests and activities and the part the child takes in these; points to be noticed are the instruments available, the presence of a record player, the type of records, and the types of broadcast to which the parents and the child listen. An estimate of cul-tural and economic levels will help if the family needs guidance in promoting the child's musical development. *Classroom ac-tivities, including discussion about music and dramatizations concerning music,* give opportunity for direct observation of attitudes, appreciations, special interests, ability to interpret the content of songs, and creative tendencies. *Personal talks* with a child give him opportunity to discuss, identify, plan, and evaluate his musical interests, skills, and problems, and to decide with the teacher the types of activity in which he is to partici-pate.

Differences in Intelligence, Physique, and Aptitude

Mental differences. Above-average musical abilities may be found in children of below-average intelligence—musical talent is not confined to the intellectually gifted. Moreover, superior intelligence is no guarantor of musical ability. But a child of normal musical abilities and high intelligence, though he has a poor musical background and is at first below average in musical accomplishment, may make rapid progress when he and his teachers establish suitable goals for him.

Physical differences. These include response to rhythm, coordination (see pages 120-22), physical size and structure, and impaired hearing.

Physical size often governs a child's choice of musical instrument. Tiny hands may make fingering on some instruments extremely difficult. The stringed instruments, such as violin, viola, and cello, can be obtained in three-quarter and half sizes to accommodate small hands and arms. However, the playing of many instruments cannot begin until the body has grown to a size which makes playing physically possible. Mouth and teeth formations also dictate whether or not certain wind instruments can be easily played. A specialist in musical instruments should be consulted before an instrument is purchased for any child. Parents should be made aware of this and be helped in finding expert advice.

Some children seem unable to hear certain pitches, but other hard-of-hearing children seem able to hear music better than other sounds. Remember that vibrations from a piano or record player are more readily felt in some parts of the room than in others. A seat in the front row may not be as good as a seat near the wall. Enlist the child's help in finding the seat that is best for him.

Differences in ability. These appear to be most crucial in singing, because they are audible. Some children may not be able to sing alone, others only a phrase with the group, and still others two phrases of a simple song. Teachers are commonly confronted with differences in pitch comprehension and in the range of voice. A superior ear can be a problem when its possessor finds it easier to "do what comes naturally" than to think about what he is doing in terms of the specifics of music instruction. An example of this is the child whose superior musical ability becomes a puzzling barrier to his learning to use notation either vocally or instrumentally; the tonal memory of such a child is so keen that he comprehends and reproduces melodies after one hearing. Because of this he sees no logical use for notation simply because he does not need it in this particular situation, and the teacher will have to contrive activities for him in which music notation has a needed and understood use, for example, playing an added part on the bells which requires use of notes.

Children vary greatly in their capacities to comprehend harmony. A few six- and seven-year-old children may be able to identify simple chord changes readily. Many children do not make marked progress in this kind of musical skill until they are ten years old or older, when they become capable of being helped to do part-singing activities successfully. Other children may not have this ability until they are in their early secondary-school years.

Singing

The child who cannot sing. While attempting to discover the reasons for this condition, it is exceedingly important to keep the child trying: *keep him trying; he may never sing if he is not encouraged to try.* The number of adults who cannot sing today is traceable to teachers of past years who said, "Billy, you can't sing like the others, so I want you to stop singing from now on." If a child cannot read, teachers do not tell him to stop trying to read for the rest of his life; it is the teacher's responsibility to help him to read. The same responsibility exists in music. The child is to be helped by beginning on his level, whatever it is, and working technically and systematically on his individual problems. Specific suggestions for this follow.

The child who tries to sing with his speaking voice. There are many ways to aid this child. Have him try to imitate how his mother or his friend calls him when he is far, far away.

This is sustaining vowels, which is a simple definition of singing. Other ways of doing this include sustaining the final vowel of spoken words such as "hello" or "grandma." When the pitch has been found by the child, have him try singing short sentences on this pitch. Next, sing an easy, familiar song to him which begins on this pitch and ask him to sing with you. Another often-used aid in helping the child find his singing voice is having him imitate the sound of a siren. Sometimes if the child plays easy parts of familiar songs on an instrument such as the bells or the piano, he finds it easier to match these pitches with his voice.

The child who fails to identify high and low pitches with his voice. The concept of high and low in pitch is one which must be taught. In teaching it, the teacher should use as examples pitches which are far apart, not adjacent. Since high and low are understood by the child as descriptive terms explaining the position of objects, the teacher usually begins with these understandings, then attaches pitch concepts to them. Some little songs explain high and low by suggesting high and low bodily movements which coincide with high and low pitch. One such song tells of a jack-in-the-box. The children crouch low; the pitch of the melody remains low. At the end of the song the lid of the box is opened, and Jack leaps high—as does the pitch of the final note. This is essentially a listening experience through which a concept is learned aurally, then applied vocally. The use of hand motions for high and low pitches often helps. Other aids in teaching high and low pitch will be found under "Listening," pages 117-18.

The child who can match only one or two tones. The teacher should discern the singing range which is normal for the child at the time; this is often a small range which is low in pitch. Ask him to try to match tones in this range, or, sometimes better still, ask him to sing a pitch which the teacher or the class will match. Lead him to create little chantlike sentence songs on scale tones 5 and 3, using the descending minor third as follows:

```
5      5              5  5
          3  3              3 -
    sol   sol  mi mi  sol sol  mi -
    "Rain  is  fal-ling, fal-ling down."
```

The child should do this in his own easiest-to-sing range. When he has done this many times and has attained competence, scale tone 6 can be added very easily to the two pitches already learned, and he can proceed to create songs using three pitches:

```
                    6
    5 -              5 -
          3              3 -
    sol   mi   la   sol   mi
    "We   won  the  ball-game."
```

When this has been accomplished, add scale tones 2 and 1 to those learned, and guide him to create his own songs on the five tones of the pentatonic scale:

```
              6
    5    5          5  5
          3              3 -  3 -
                             2 -
                                  1 -
    sol  sol  mi la  sol  sol  mi - mi - re -  do -
    "What  is  al-ways good  to  eat? Pump-kin  pie!"
```

(The pentatonic scale is a five-tone scale. If this scale were superimposed upon a major scale, it would consist of major-scale tones 1, 2, 3, 5, and 6—do, re, mi, sol, la.) Next, inventing similar melodies in adjacent higher keys will help extend his singing range. Some children are helped by playing the bells along with their singing, and like to use them when they make up their tunes. Bells that can be separated are particularly useful because the teacher can let the child have only those tones he is to use when creating his songs. However, the goal is to be able eventually to sing without their support. This type of creative approach can be useful in helping people of any age group. Note that scale tones 4 and 7 are avoided. They can be added later when the other tones have been mastered.

The child who lacks sufficient tonal memory to enable him to sing satisfactorily. The use of songs which have short repeated sections can be valuable in developing tonal memory in both individual and group work with children. These repeated sections can be used in the spirit of a game, the teacher calling upon children to be "echoers." One such song which has been used for this purpose for many years is "The Echo."

THE ECHO

KATE FORMAN   *Old Children's Air*

1. Ech-o I can hear you, hear you, hear you,
2. Now the rain is fall - ing, fall - ing, fall - ing,

Though I can't get near you, near you, near you,
So I'll stop my call - ing, call - ing, call - ing,

You're so far a - way, a - way, a - way.
Won't you say good-day? good - day? good-day?

Another way to help develop tonal memory is to hum familiar songs and ask the child to identify them. An often-used aid is the teacher's calling the class roll in song and having the child "play the game" by trying to answer in the same pitches sung to him. Since tonal memory is related to other problems in listening, the above are only a few of the many ways a teacher will take to help the child to hear and remember musical sounds. More suggestions will be found under other headings in this discussion.

The child who fails to try. Sometimes this is a health, emotional, or social problem, not really a musical one. Nonmusical means which give the child status may solve this. Dramatizations in which the child forgets himself often help. In the primary grades, when the child takes part in a dramatization in which he is a cuckoo clock that sings "cuc-koo" (5-3), or where he is a rooster and sings "cock-a-doodle-doo" (55553——), he may forget himself and sing. In the intermediate grades a child may be so carried away by the pleasure of, for example, a nonsense song that he will forget his hesitancy to sing and join with the others.

Some children fail to try because they are bored; the music is too simple.

The child who wants to imitate his father's voice and who doesn't want to sound like his female teacher or like girls when he sings. This is a psychological problem. The teacher's task is to explain the changing voice, that it is seldom before the seventh grade and sometimes not until the ninth grade that boys' voices change. Most important of all is the information that immediately before the change begins, some boys can sing with better high-pitch tone quality than girls, and this is an indication the change is about to begin. The teacher can hope the boy will act on the idea that singing with an excellent high voice may mean that his voice will change before long! (Some fathers have made singing difficult for their sons by holding up an erroneous ideal of manliness which excludes singing.)

The child who sings satisfactorily some of the time, but who often fails to start a song on pitch, and thus sings off pitch part of the time. This frequently results from the failure of the teacher to take the time to make reasonably certain that every child has had ample opportunity to hear the pitch of the first note of the song. Many children sing off pitch because they have been asked to begin singing before they have located the beginning pitch. In the lower grades everyone can "tune in" (as a radio is tuned in) to this pitch as sounded by the teacher's voice, bells, piano, or pitch pipe. In the upper grades the playing of the tonic chord (I-chord) or the I-V-I chord sequence on the piano, Autoharp, or bells is a good additional help since it aids the children in establishing the beginning pitch of the song in its harmonic setting.

The child who has not yet learned to sing correctly, and whose singing sometimes detracts from the efforts of the class to sound well. In the lower grades try to seat him (without his knowledge) where he can hear the example of good singers. In intermediate grades he can be assigned a friend who sings well as a seating partner and helper. Since children in this age group usually realize fully that they cannot sing well, they welcome and appreciate any efforts to aid them which do not embarrass them. Plan things for the child to do, such as obtaining and distributing materials, playing on the bells or piano, and keeping time with percussion instruments, when the class is learning a new song. After the class has learned the song, his out-of-tune efforts should not handicap the group. Continue working with the child as an individual and in small-group situations.

The child whose inability to sing well interferes with his enjoyment of music. The teacher should recognize that a child who does not sing well may not enjoy a classroom program which consists entirely of singing. But this does not mean that such a child cannot enjoy music if the program is properly varied. He needs help in his voice problem, but he needs other music activities, too. A child who cannot sing in tune may *hear* music very well. He may be able to tell when he himself or his teacher is singing incorrectly. Lack of singing ability does not necessarily prevent a child from appreciating music or even from becoming a good instrumental musician.

The child who stammers. A stammerer is freed from his speech difficulties when he sings. Sometimes he can gain confidence through successful communication by singing which can aid in reducing his speaking problem.

The child who cannot yet sing harmony parts. Children in the intermediate grades who have not yet developed a harmonic sense should continue singing the melody; they should not be asked to sing parts they cannot sing. However, they profit from practice in singing or playing chord roots. (When the "Autoharp chords" are marked in a song, singing the notes by which the chords are named constitutes singing chord roots. For example, if the G and D7 chords are called for, the children will play or sing the pitches G and D, which are the *roots* of these chords.) Playing chord roots on the bells, piano, or cello can help develop the harmonic sense; some children can do this well in third grade. Others need this experience in Grades IV through VIII. When this basic harmonic concept is learned, singing songs written in parallel thirds or sixths is a logical next step.

The child who has superior harmonic sense. As early as the third grade this child can utilize the chord roots mentioned in the preceding paragraph. He will be interested in playing the Autoharp and playing simple types of chording on the piano. He can sing simple chants and descants (counter melodies), and can add harmonic endings to songs. In fourth grade and above he will be able to sing the parts of true part songs and thus enrich the musical experience of the class. His activities may attract the interest of others, and the growth of other children in part singing and instrumental chording should occur. All of this implies that the teacher should be prepared to provide for this type of musically advanced child.[2] Opportunities for membership in a fifth- and sixth-grade chorus should be offered.

The musically advanced child who possesses a high vocal range. In the intermediate grades this implies that this child and others like him should continue to develop their ability to sing high pitches with ease and enjoyment. It is recommended that he be guided to work on selected high descants outside of class for the purpose of adding this part above the melody at an appropriate time in class. Certain collections of songs with descants are mentioned in the references at the end of this chapter; some of these descants are to be found in basal texts. Incidentally, many songs of this type are excellent program material. Such a child may be a good vocal soloist in the classroom or on special programs. Teachers should be prepared to transpose songs into higher keys at times for such voices, as they are prepared to transpose songs into lower keys for voices which have natural lower ranges. It should be remembered, however, that while differences in range should be recognized, and at times accommodated, one of the goals of classroom singing is to extend these ranges until everyone in the class can sing comfortably in a normal, average range. Membership in a special choral group should be provided for any child who has the ability and interest. Most children will not be ready for such membership until they are in the fifth or sixth grade.

Listening

The child who seems to fail to comprehend pitch differences. Under "Singing" on pages 111-13 some aids to pitch were given. Mechanical means such as the song bells can also be used to explain "up and down" in pitch by turning them on end, with the large bars down. When they are played in this position, the child can both see and hear what we mean by high and low pitches.

The child who does not associate the notes on the staff with high and low in pitch. If the song bells can be suspended by the small end upon a chalkboard or light cardboard, the lines of the staff can be drawn to extend from the proper bar of the bells, and notes drawn on this staff. When these notes are played, the child can see the connection between the sounded (played) notes and their position on the staff. To go on from this, have the notation of very simple songs—perhaps one each week—in the music center ready to be played on the bells. Children can teach themselves a great deal about music notation if such provision is made. A further step might be the placing of melodies of recorded instrumental music on the chalkboard to continue relating what is heard to man's ingenious picture of musical sound—notation.

The child who doesn't seem to "hear" music. He may not know what to listen for. The teacher should provide (and also be alert to seize upon) objectives in listening which encourage interest and concentration. The child needs to be helped to discover and to listen for the elements of music in every possible way. Since these same musical elements and concepts should continue to expand in every grade, these ways are innumerable. For example, a boy in fourth grade suddenly "heard" what part singing was for the first time when the teacher had the class sustain scale tones 1 and 3 to produce a simple harmonic ending to a song. He was enormously thrilled by his personal discovery, and the teacher yielded to his requests for singing this over and over again, first each pitch alone, then the combination of them sung by different groups of children. The teacher wrote the notes on the chalkboard so all could *see* what they *heard.* When a fifth-grade clarinet trio performed for a first grade, one child said, "They aren't playing the same song; they are playing *different* songs together." At this, the teacher had each of the clarinetists play his part alone, then had them play their parts together again, so the first grade might begin to understand that the parts can be different, yet sound well together. The concept of ensemble playing was expanded for that child and his classmates because the teacher made an effort to explain it to them. At all age levels the teacher makes plans to help the child enlarge his understanding of the many concepts involved in hearing and listening to music. This is a never-ending task because listening is a part of every music activity.

The child who does not want to listen to recordings. This could be a reflection of lack of motivation or of an unbalanced music program. Just as there are teachers who concentrate upon singing to the exclusion of other music activities, there are teachers who concentrate upon listening to recordings to the exclusion of singing and other activities. Since children want to sing (as well as to listen, to play instruments, and to move to music), they quite rightly resent a music program which lacks variety and as a consequence fails to provide for individual differences. This child is probably tired of a music program which is not meeting his needs.

The child who needs experience in listening and practice in repeating vocally what he hears. Some suggestions that would help such a child have already been given on pages 113-14 in the discussion of tonal memory. An interesting listening experience is provided by placing a child in each far corner of a room and having one make up and sing simple tone groups to another. Some supposed out-of-tuners have made remarkable progress through having to listen carefully to relatively far-away voices in this manner. (Some simple tone groups are scale tones 53, 53653, 321, 531, 58, 8765, 5678, 54321.) Usually, neutral syllables such as "loo" are used.

The child who has special listening interests. These interests sometimes need both to be encouraged and to be kept within bounds. For example, the child who has more enthusiasm than judgment about wanting to bring recordings from home to play for the class should be held accountable for explaining specifically to the class why he believes the recording is superior and worth the time of the class. Encourage special listening interests of individuals and small groups in the classroom by employing the type of record player which has earphone attachments. These children can then listen without disturbing their classmates.

Reading about music and musicians is a naturally related activity for children who have developed special listening interests. Appropriate books should be available in the classroom or in the school library for both the music listening program and the special-interest reading program. A superior list of books for this purpose is in *Recommended Records and Books for the School Curriculum*; this list is useful to both the teacher and the school librarian.[3] Collections of recordings for school use obtainable from Sound Book Press Society, Inc., are accompanied by books designed for both the child and the teacher.[4]

Rhythmic Responses

The child who lacks average skill in coordination. What may be a normal, natural rhythm to one child may be neither normal nor natural to another; children vary in their responses to rhythm as they do in other respects. The teacher should find the natural response of the child who seems to lack rhythmic feeling; that is, the teacher should watch the child and select a rhythm to which he can respond. After this has been done successfully and continued for a time, the child should be able gradually to synchronize his movements with slower or faster tempos. When a six-year-old cannot march to music, it is probable that he does not yet realize that there is a relation between what he hears and what his feet are supposed to do. It often helps to have the child march with children who "show him how to do it" by their example. Sometimes a paper streamer or scarf helps a child feel a motion he cannot yet feel with the unaided arm at his stage of physical development. Responses which use the large muscles should be emphasized at first, then responses calling for increasing use of smaller muscles should be introduced. Since clapping in time to music requires more coordination than striking both hands on the thighs, the latter motion will be easier for some children.

The child who needs a rhythmic approach to note values. Musical understandings are believed to come initially from bodily movements. Later on they become more intellectualized. Quarter notes and eighth notes as marks on a staff mean exceedingly little to children unless they can identify them in terms of bodily movement. The feeling of walking is basic to eventual comprehension of the quarter note, and the same is true of running and the eighth note. It is an easy matter for the teacher to make this concept clear to the child, and it is not difficult to invent bodily movements which will make clear other note values and combinations of note values.

The child who needs bodily movement to aid his understanding of musical concepts. With any age group, rhythmic dramatizations of songs and of recordings of instrumental music often make more clear to individual children both the message of the music and aspects of the music itself, such as its form. Understanding of the musical phrase is commonly enhanced by such means, as are some musical terms. For example, accelerando (gradually faster) and ritardando (gradually slower) can be explained to children through the use of song material which employs these devices. Despite this, some children will still have only a tenuous understanding of the terms. To make the meanings clearer, bodily movement can be utilized. This can be done on the playground, using large bouncing balls and a drum, or in a gymnasium. A piano can be substituted for the drum, if the teacher prefers. If the children face each other and bounce (or bounce and catch) the balls in time to the teacher-sounded accelerando and ritardando, they will feel physically what these terms mean in relation to throwing and catching the balls faster and slower, and in having to move closer together and farther apart in order to accommodate the gradually changing tempo.

Another example of bodily movement serving to enlarge intellectual concepts is that of taking part in and observing the rhythmic dramatization of a round. First, children learn the song and make up their dramatization of the words. Then they divide into two to four groups, according to how many parts they will sing, and dramatize the song. As they sing their different parts, they act out the dramatization of the words in turn, as the parts enter, each group doing the same thing but at different times—exactly as the melody does in a round. Doing this rhythmically, and at the same time seeing how the other groups (parts) are doing the same thing—but not at the same time—helps to expand the concept of a round, something which the notation of a round seldom does.

The child who has above-average coordination. Encourage creative responses by means of which the child can employ his superior coordination and can continue to advance at his own rate. More-advanced dance steps may be introduced.

Playing Instruments

The child who lacks knowledge of the keyboard. Introduce the keyboard to him by means of simple playing on the song bells; later expand this knowledge to include the piano keyboard. Have a cardboard keyboard suspended from a chart holder so you can quickly refer to it as a visual aid to explain many things about music. The child may have his own keyboard on his desk after he understands (through his introduction to the song bells and piano) what it represents.

The child who has above-average facility at the keyboard, probably due to private piano lessons. Make it possible for him to perform for the class at suitable times; help him to utilize simple chords[5] in improvising accompaniments to classroom songs; have him help other children who are interested in learning how to chord accompaniments.

The children who reveal varying degrees of interest and adeptness in playing simple wind instruments. There are many different recorder-type instruments, such as the Tonette, Song Flute, and Flutophone. Children who find playing them quite easy should be guided to the more challenging and rewarding ones such as the true recorder and the Melody Flute. Children who find the most simple of these instruments difficult should be encouraged to play the Autoharp, song bells, and percussion instruments instead.[6]

The child who plays a band or orchestra instrument, or a "social" instrument, such as the ukulele, guitar, or accordion.

Certain instruments, such as the violin, viola, cello, string bass, and flute, blend with children's voices and can enrich the experience of the class by being used to play the melodies of songs or to play chant, descant, chord root, or other parts, as in two- and three-part singing. Other band and orchestra instruments generally have too heavy a quality to blend with the light voices of children. However, all of these instruments can be played in solo and ensemble performances. Sometimes they can be used to accompany large groups of children in special events when the instrumental score is available.

If a child plays the trumpet or the clarinet, he can probably play the melody of many of the songs a class sings, and he may have a special interest in doing this at home or for some special situation in the school. Since these instruments are built in the key of B-flat, whatever note is played from the song book will *sound* one whole step lower than written. Therefore, for the trumpet and the clarinet to play correctly with a piano accompaniment, the child will have to play each melody one whole step higher than written. Or, if he cannot do this and must play the notes as written, the piano accompaniment will have to be transposed into a key which is one whole step lower than the key of the written accompaniment.

The history of this development in instrument manufacture and a study of the complete band and orchestra score may be worthwhile special-interest projects for individuals or small groups of instrumentalists. An E-flat alto saxophone sounds a major sixth lower than the written note; when the C written on the fourth space is played, the result is the pitch of E-flat on the first line. When an F horn plays this same C, the sound is that of F on the first space.

Players of guitar, ukulele, and accordion can contribute to chording and accompanying activities with appropriate songs.

The child with special interests in instrumental music. An intermediate-grades classroom presents a large variety of talents in instrumental music, which should be employed at times in connection with singing. Besides some of the experiences mentioned above, the "singing classroom orchestra" [7] is an activity which can accommodate many individual differences and interests in the classroom. Many instruments can be used in conjunction with singing: the strings and flute mentioned above, the recorder and recorder-type instruments, flute-type instruments, the psaltery, bells, Autoharp, Harmolin, piano, percussion instruments, ukulele, guitar, and accordion. In addition, appropriate opportunities for solo performance should be planned; special-interest reading and listening activities should be suggested to further a child's interest; he may participate in the band and orchestra program, which generally begins in the fourth or fifth grade.

Music—A Dynamic Force in Personality Development

Creative musical activities. These offer one of the most effective ways to build or reconstruct an individual's self-concept and his feeling of self-adequacy, and thus can greatly aid the shy, submissive, or overly aggressive child. As a child participates in creating songs and instrumental pieces, creating words for known melodies, and creating rhythmic responses and dramatizations, he develops skills, knowledges, understandings, attitudes, and appreciations that affect his entire outlook on the world. He sees himself as one who can contribute to and understand the beauty of sound, movement, color, and form. He sees the beauty in other personalities; he learns to appreciate the contributions of others. As his feelings and acceptance of self improve, he generalizes these attitudes and feelings; thus he becomes more appreciative and understanding of other people and the world around him.

Two examples will show how opportunity to create, to build self-confidence, and to perform on one's own level can aid a child in finding himself. Owen, a daydreamer and a very disinterested student, was asked by his teacher, "Owen, what are you thinking about?" He answered, "Oh, I was just thinking of some day when I will become a big band director." When the children and teacher planned a Christmas program, Owen was chosen to create the part of John Wesley as a choir director who conducted the group in "Away in a Manger." Through participating in this and in many similar roles, Owen's interest and skill in music grew, and because of his successes he became happier and better accepted by his peers and every aspect of his work improved.

Paul, when given the opportunity to create words to a song while studying a unit in social studies, wrote words which he and the class put to music. Paul's song was reproduced in the school paper. The recognition he received from members of the community, his peers, and teachers was a significant force in helping him develop the feeling of success and importance which is essential in the building of wholesome personalities.

GENERAL REFERENCES

Andrews, Frances M., and Clara E. Cockerille, *Your School Music Program.* Englewood Cliffs, N.J.: Prentice-Hall, Inc., 1958.

Britten, Benjamin, and Imogene Holst, *Wonderful World of Music.* New York: Garden City Books, 1958.

Davis, Marilyn K., and Arnold Broido, *Music Dictionary.* New York: Doubleday & Company, Inc., 1956.

Huntington, Harriett E., *Tune Up: Instruments of the Orchestra and Their Players.* New York: Doubleday & Company, Inc., 1942.

Keyboard Junior, a magazine for Grade VII and up, and *Young Keyboard Junior,* for Grades IV-VI, 1346 Chapel St., New Haven 11, Conn.

Krone, Beatrice, and Max Krone, *Our First Songs to Sing with Descants; Very Easy Descants; Songs to Sing with Descants; Descants for Christmas; Great Songs of Faith; From Descants to Trios.* Park Ridge, Ill.: Neil A. Kjos Music Co.

Lacey, Marion, *Picture Book of Musical Instruments.* New York: Lothrop, Lee & Shepard Co., 1942.

Landeck, Beatrice, *Children and Music.* New York: William Sloane Associates, 1952.

McMillan, L. Eileen, *Guiding Children's Growth through Music.* Boston: Ginn & Company, 1959.

Murray, Ruth L., *Dance in Elementary Education*. New York: Harper & Brothers, 1953.

Nye, Robert E., and Bjornar Bergethon, *Basic Music for Classroom Teachers*. Englewood Cliffs, N.J.: Prentice-Hall, Inc., 1954.

Tooze, Ruth, and Beatrice Perham Krone, *Literature and Music as Resources for Social Studies*. Englewood Cliffs, N.J.: Prentice-Hall, Inc., 1955.

FILMS

Jam Handy Organization, 2821 East Grand Blvd., Detroit 11, Mich. *Music Stories; Stories of Music Classics; Opera and Ballet Stories.* Filmstrips in color with recordings.

Pitts, Lilla Belle, ed., *Handbook on 16 mm. Films for Music Education*. Music Educators National Conference, 1201 Sixteenth St., N.W., Washington, D.C., 1952. Contains annotated listings of films for correlated units of study, for music, and for the sciences.

INSTRUMENTS

Autoharp. National Autoharp Sales Company, 560 31st St., Des Moines 12, Iowa. Also obtainable from mail-order houses.

Harmolin. The Harmolin Company, Box 6157, San Diego, Calif.

Organ. "Little Estey Reed Organ." Estey Organ Corporation, Brattleboro, Vt. A three-octave, 45-pound organ with an electrically driven pump.

Percussion instruments. Peripole Products, Inc., 2917 Avenue R, Brooklyn 29, N.Y.

Song bells. Walberg and Auge, 31 Mercantile St., Worcester 8, Mass.

RECORDINGS

Bowmar Records, 4921 Santa Monica Blvd., Los Angeles 29, Calif. Catalogues:
> *Annotated List of Phonograph Records.* Children's Reading Service, 1078 St. John's Place, Brooklyn 13, N.Y.
> *Catalog of Outstanding Records for Education and Entertainment.* Children's Record Guild and Young People's Records. The Greystone Corporation, 100 Sixth Ave., New York 13, N.Y.

RCA Victor Educational Record Catalog. Radio Corporation of America, Educational Services, Camden, N.J.

Recommended Records and Books for the School Curriculum. Issued annually by Children's Music Center, 2858 West Pico Blvd., Los Angeles 6, Calif. Fifty cents.

Sound Book Press Society, Inc., Box 222, Scarsdale, N.Y. Companion recordings for the music-appreciation books of Lillian Baldwin.

Vox Productions. Obtainable from local dealers and large distributors. *Master Series of Composers* albums. Example: *Mozart: His Story and His Music.*

NOTES

[1] Robert E. Nye and Vernice T. Nye, *Music in the Elementary School* (Englewood Cliffs, N.J.: Prentice-Hall, Inc., 1957), chap. i.

[2] *Ibid.*, chap. viii, "Teaching Part Singing."

[3] *Recommended Records and Books for the School Curriculum.* Issued annually by Children's Music Center, 2858 West Pico Blvd., Los Angeles 6, Calif. Fifty cents.

[4] Lillian Baldwin, *Tiny Masterpieces for Very Young Listeners* (Bryn Mawr, Pa.: Theodore Presser Company, 1958), for Grades I-III; Lillian Baldwin, *Music for Young Listeners, The Green Book,* for Grade IV and up, *The Crimson Book,* for Grade V and up, *The Blue Book,* for Grade VI and up (New York: Silver Burdett Co., 1951); Lillian Baldwin, *Music to Remember* (New York: Silver Burdett Co., 1951), for Grades VII-VIII. Companion recordings are obtainable from Sound Book Press Society, Inc., Box 222, Scarsdale, N.Y.

[5] Marion Egbert, *Piano Handbook for Classroom Teachers* (New York: Bourne, Inc., 1959); Marion Egbert, *Suggested Keyboard Experience Lesson Plan* (obtainable from American Music Conference, 332 South Michigan Ave., Chicago, Ill.); Nye and Nye, *Music in the Elementary School,* chap. iv, "Teaching Melody and Harmony Instruments"; Hallie Webber, *The Piano Hour: Favorite Melodies Using the I, IV, and V Chords* (New York: Carl Fischer, Inc., 1949).

[6] Nye and Nye, *Music in the Elementary School,* chap. iv, "Teaching Melody and Harmony Instruments."

[7] *Ibid.,* pp. 82-84, 195.

7

The language arts

VIRGIL E. HERRICK

THE LANGUAGE ARTS ARE COMMONLY DIVIDED
into reading, handwriting, spelling, oral and written composition, grammar, and literature. A simpler division is into the
four related functions of language: writing and reading; speaking and listening. In many schools reading is considered separately. But any division magnifies the teacher's task of adapting
instruction to deal with children who vary widely in the nature
and degree of their learning.

Another way of considering the language arts is to see three
related and necessary parts in all language instruction. The
first part is the *social situation* which gives rise to the need for
language, furnishes its content, and provides its controls. The
second consists of the *media of language,* the talks, letters,
stories, notes, poems, signs which are the vehicles of verbal expression. The third is the *mechanics of language,* namely the
grammar and usage, the conventions, which are the specifics of

128

language itself. All instruction of all children in language involves all three of these parts.

This chapter is written with the conviction that individual differences are best provided for when the teacher starts with the social situation, which gives purpose and meaning to learning, and then relates the appropriate media and mechanics to the situation, rather than reversing this process. For example, it is easier and better to begin with a conversation or story and show the need for punctuation and grammar and spelling than it is to begin with rules.

Quality in language teaching depends on solving the problem of putting the three necessary aspects of language together in a fashion and in proportions which will best promote each child's growth in language skill. The nature of children and the nature of the language-arts program determine what arrangements are meaningful for grouping children, for varying instructional procedures, for modifying the allotment of time, and for diversifying materials.

The Subject Matter of the Language Arts

The nature of the language arts separates them from other subjects in several ways which affect a teacher's methods of providing for individual differences in this area of the curriculum. First is the fact that language has no content or subject matter of its own. Language is merely a convenient way of conveying ideas. It does not generate them. Most other subjects, for example history or biology, are organized around germane topics, major generalizations, and factual detail. But all that a study of the language arts as such offers is a knowledge of their structure and processes. Structure and process are important, but the teacher, in making adaptations in his instruction, must always realize that the child is reading, writing, and speaking about, or listening to, people's experiences, feelings, and ideas. This means that one of the best ways to start helping a child to learn to read, speak, listen, and write is to make sure he has some knowledge of the things, activities, and people forming the subject matter of his language activities. This knowledge is the basis on which rests the choice of the form or structure in which a writer or speaker expresses himself.

In one sense, the total language curriculum confronts the child as soon as he comes to school. His oral expression already involves most, if not all, of the forms of speech and of sentence structure. Long before he leaves the sixth grade, he will be using all the forms of sentences and of grammatical structure in reading and writing as well as in speaking. The language-arts teacher who is trying to adapt his instruction to the wide variation in children must feel free to help each child use the forms necessary to express himself adequately at any given time. This means that the teacher must not be limited (as is frequently the practice in elementary schools) to the simple sentence and to "name" and "action" words. He must also be released from the common curricular sequence which follows an artificial division and laying out of the matter to be learned.

Language as a tool is an essential part of all learning experiences. Unfortunately, all the resources of the school, the home, and the community are rarely marshaled to promote the fullest possible development of each child's language skill, although competent over-all instructional planning could make important contributions to the education of all children and especially to that of gifted children.

In the last analysis, growth in the use of language is always a highly individual process. Granted that it is only the individual who can learn any subject, there is an especially personal quality in speaking and writing and, to a lesser degree, in reading and listening. This quality, which the language arts share with the other arts, gives to any use of language a personal and creative character. It is just this individuality and creativity that call for wise and constructive provisions for individual differences in the field of language arts.

The foregoing discussion shows how important it is for a teacher to see the relationships among the various phases of language and to be able to relate his teaching of the mechanics of form and structure to the growing language skills of individual children. The quality of a teacher at any level is evident both in his knowledge and in his willingness and ability to impart this knowledge as soon as a pupil can use it.

The Problem of Standards

Every person is judged by his use of language. The hard facts are, however, that adequate standards are only very slowly incorporated into the language behavior of a child and that individual children vary widely in their rate of learning and in the degree to which standards of form and usage are attained. Therefore the teacher, while helping each child grasp a conception of correctness which will direct the child's language growth, must be willing to allow different children to be at different points in their development. It is also obvious that to drill a class on the spelling of words which many of the children already know, or to teach them about parts of speech or punctuation which they already use correctly, does not meet the individual language needs of these children. The teacher should remember too that, while grammar helps in writing and sentence structure, it is not very valuable for dealing with matters of language usage. Here the development of a good "ear" is more important. This ear depends more on extensive reading and listening than it does on drill.

Some Matters of Time

Studies of the oral language of normal children show how prevalent—some adults say continuous—is their use of language for all kinds of purposes. Some surveys of instructional practices in the primary grades have shown that around 90 per cent of the school day is spent on activities directly related to the language arts. Moreover, at every age level and both in and out of school there are endless opportunities for a broad range of language experiences: conversations, conferences, "doing and telling times," reading periods, library hours, writing of planning charts, TV and radio programs, books, magazines, and newspapers.

Quality in language development is enhanced when the teacher makes sure that proper attention is paid to the need for balance and for emphasis on all necessary aspects—writing and reading as well as speaking and listening, acting as well as thinking, enjoyment and enrichment as well as study and drill, individual creative expression as well as discussion. Unfortunately, adequate attention to each aspect is not assured by anything as simple as planning a period a day for the language arts, or making sure of two reading periods a day. The teacher will want to examine the language opportunities that occur during the entire day and week. Attention to a child's language needs in the arithmetic period is just as important as attention to these needs in reading and spelling classes. Discussion in the language-arts class becomes more meaningful when it is related to experiences in the science class or to rules needed for playground games.

Quality is also a product of the significance of what is read, spoken, or written. Essential here is an educational setting where each child is cherished for himself and where he can distinguish his concept of self-worth from his attempts to read, speak, or write. What the child says and the form he uses must be accepted as the basis for building more significant thought and more appropriate form. Harsh criticism and the imposition of adult standards or the impatient refusal to listen to an idea that is sincerely but incorrectly expressed destroy the child's interest in working at his language development.

Materials

Complete dependence on basal readers, other texts, workbooks, and the official curriculum decidedly limits the teacher in his attempts to provide for individual differences. About all he can do is to vary the amount of time devoted to the books by different children or have different groups of children working at different levels. Important as good materials are, they are most effective when a topic or area of activity gives purpose and control to their use.

Texts, workbooks, and supplementary text materials. Most school systems have basal texts in reading, handwriting, spelling, and the language arts. The language-arts text is usually introduced at about the third grade. Many kindergarten children are given reading-readiness materials to prepare for "real" reading in the first grade.

Most reading series have materials on two or three different levels of difficulty. At least one basal text deals with the same topic at three levels, thus permitting different children in the same class to read about the same center of interest but on levels appropriate to their reading development. Many teachers employ workbooks, designed to accompany the basal text, as a means of promoting reading for thought, vocabulary development, skills of vocabulary attack, and so forth. Tied to each basal series are teacher's handbooks with plans for all lessons and keying the available supplementary materials to each lesson. As many as twenty-six kinds of supplementary materials may be offered—phrase materials, vocabulary cards, picture books, check lists and tests, and the like—to aid the teacher in dealing with the reading needs of all of his children.

Children's books. There are many materials which help the teacher go beyond the traditional three groups in reading in each grade. Wonderful riches are available in children's literature, periodicals, and pamphlets which can be easily linked to the interests and educational needs of individuals and small groups.[1] Perhaps children's books afford the most effective way to deal with individual reading interests and abilities.[2]

Some suitable books and periodicals may be available in the children's homes, but the resources of the home are usually meager. Therefore the teacher should set up a reading corner where the children will find books that cater to different interests and abilities. Color and variation in format increase appeal. The volumes in the book corner may be on loan from the school, community, or state libraries. The corner should also display children's newspapers and magazines and appropriate adult magazines, particularly if they are illustrated. The up-to-dateness of these materials in the eyes of the children makes them especially valuable.

Bulletins and pamphlets may be written for use on an individual basis. The staff at Fond du Lac, Wisconsin, has attempted to provide for individual needs by writing a number of booklets on such topics as "So You Want To Be an Author," "Outlining," "Writing Friendly Letters," "Preparing a Talk," "Making Introductions," and "Writing Poetry." The flexibility of using these pamphlets with children on many different grade levels is obvious.

The library. A school is unusually fortunate if it has a good library under the charge of a competent librarian or even has easy access to a good public library. The library can have many more materials of all kinds, including records and pictures, than can a classroom. The librarian gives the teacher skilled advice in his selection of them and arranges for their distribution on loan to the classroom or directly to the children. Frequently the library has a large collection of teaching materials and of professional books for teachers.

Audio-visual materials. Many teachers have the advantage of radio and TV programs on such topics as "Creative Writing," "Story Telling," and "An Hour with Books," which are beamed at children and teachers in school. The State Radio Program, WHA, University of Wisconsin, is a good example. The programs in the public schools of Chicago, Milwaukee, and Cleveland have dealt with reading. Many other school systems are developing similar programs. Records and tape recordings are excellent means of presenting stories, poems, and dramas. Recordings can also capture the language and speech of any group of children and be used for their study and enjoyment. Such materials offer boundless possibilities for enrichment and flexibility.

Materials developed with children. The stories, poems, dramatic episodes, and letters of children are valuable for enrichment and for evaluation. A file of a child's writings helps the child study the nature of his development and determine areas that need special attention, and it lets him enjoy again some of his previous efforts.

Experience stories and charts developed by the teacher and the group are among the best vehicles for writing, reading, and listening. Children can use their art skills to illustrate these charts or to make picture notes for oral compositions. In these ways children of widely varying abilities can make important contributions to the group task. Difference, in this context, is enriching and productive.

Children's drama scripts are especially valuable when they are used with puppets to stage a dramatic story for other children. This is also true of make-believe radio presentations. The many parts and other activities necessary to the success of the play give the children opportunities to contribute in line with their abilities and skills.

Reference materials. Frequently the teacher is the sole provider of the "word not known" in spelling or reading and the "social convention not known" in a social application of language. The time spent in imparting this knowledge would be much better spent in helping the child to assume this responsibility for himself. Mere correction leads to physical and emotional exhaustion on the part of the teacher without improving the competence and resourcefulness of the pupil.

The child needs training in the use of reference materials to learn to help himself. The dictionary, style book, thesaurus, handbook of grammar, and books on the history of language should be introduced in the program of instruction as the child develops the ability to use them. Even in the primary grades, children can use their own vocabulary lists, children's dictionaries, card files, handwriting scales, and appropriate hand-books. Research has shown that first-grade children can evaluate and diagnose their own writing, speaking, and reading difficulties, frequently as well as adults can. The "editorial" sense so important in future language use can start its development in many ways at this age. Self-evaluation and self-help must be emphasized, and the tools and resources for such help must be provided at every grade level.

Every elementary classroom should have at least an unabridged dictionary, a style book, a handbook of grammar and usage, a thesaurus, a good children's encyclopedia, and a file catalogue of books and materials used for learning. Scales for handwriting diagnosis and a recorder and tapes for speech and oral reading are highly valuable. Not all children in the primary grades can use these tools, but from the beginning some children, with the teacher's example and help, will make increasing use of them.

Professional references. Many books present material on the developmental sequences in language and help the teacher to adapt procedures and materials to the instruction of individuals. The notes at the end of this chapter include titles of standard works on vocabulary development,[3] indexes of stories in various reading series,[4] specialized indexes of poetry and children's books,[5] recent materials on readability and difficulty,[6] some books on the structure and nature of language,[7] and recent books on the teaching of the language arts.[8] The teacher should obtain from the publishers of the basal reading series which he uses any available studies of the vocabulary.

The Limitations of Materials

No matter how superior the available materials are, their wise use depends on the teacher and the learner. Here are some points to be considered.

Generalization. Generalizations are made by the writers of the textbooks and even put into lists for the reader to learn. But the process of generalization takes place when a child abstracts the essence of a number of experiences. It is very difficult for a textbook to marshal all the related specifics which facilitate generalization. Every teacher will want to go beyond the text and make sure that every child is given additional help and time for thinking through what he has read and seeing its general meaning for future behavior. Only the teacher and the learner can make the adaptations and reinterpretations so necessary to this kind of learning. Filling out blanks in workbooks and drawing connecting lines on work sheets are not the same as applying knowledge of language and its uses in a personal and therefore unique situation. This kind of application—call it transfer or training or what you will—is the reason and justification for all teaching. It is in this context, too, that many of the provisions for individual differences are made.

Practice. Children are constantly using language. Their language skills are improved as materials and aids are applied to this use. Reading about how to read, write, or speak makes no change in these skills by itself.

Putting together the parts of a language experience. As has been pointed out, there are three related components in any adequate language experience: a social situation, a medium, and form, structure, or convention. Language maturity grows out of the increasing skill with which the learner selects and uses the best medium and form to serve the needs of a given situation. The learner must do this for himself, though the teacher can help him achieve both understanding and skill.

Sequence. It is relatively easy for the teacher and learner to know what should be done next. Their planning meets the needs of the individual better than does some fixed order in the text or workbook.

Creativity. Creativity does not exist apart from the individual. It must come from within himself and from his perception of his world and be experienced in a way that is right for him.

Evaluation. Personal evaluation of one's own use of language is the major tool of improvement. The teacher must help each child become more effective in this evaluation and in putting the results into practice.

This review of the role of materials suggests the following conclusions: 1. Different types of instructional material should be used in different ways. A story is a language experience with its own validity. The textbook on grammar can only be a resource, not an end in itself. 2. The teacher and the child have the responsibility of determining how instructional materials are to be used. They can exhaust the potential of a book or use it poorly. 3. Instructional materials have a place in an educational program but cannot be the complete program. This is especially true of any program concerned with individual differences.

Minimum Essentials

The opinion persists that if the learning task could only be reduced to its minimum essentials, then the problem of providing for individual differences could be solved by grouping children and by modifying the amount of time allotted for study. Able children could go through the essential experiences as fast as possible, while slower children took more time. Although this neat logical teaching scheme comes apart when arbitrarily applied—children just do not learn in this simple, economical manner—there are enough values in this approach to justify a consideration of some of its contributions.

The child's oral vocabulary is the basis upon which his reading and later his writing vocabularies are built. Because of this, the basic words used in most reading series are presented in the readiness materials and carefully developed in the initial reading experiences.[9] Edward William Dolch's basic word list,[10] used by many teachers as part of the children's self-help work in vocabulary, consists of the essential words found in the most frequently used reading series. A teacher in the primary grades can easily examine the series which he uses and get some feeling for the words introduced and their sequence of development.

In spelling, much good work has been done by W. Franklin Jones ("one hundred demons"),[11] Ernest Horn,[12] Henry D. Rinsland,[13] and James A. Fitzgerald.[14] Fitzgerald's list of 2,650 words supposedly represents the words which children use in 95 per cent of their writings. Of these words, 222 account for 55 per cent of the spelling errors made by children.

In handwriting, although logically the alphabet defines the range of letters to be learned, the words most needed in writing show which letters and combinations are most frequently used. In the transition from manuscript writing—which is composed of two basic formations, the circle and the straight line—to cursive writing, every child needs help in forming the slant, making the connections, and learning some new letter forms. Some children may now have to learn to read cursive writing. Studies by S. L. and L. C. Pressey,[15] and Donald H. Rolliston[16] show that *a, e, r, t, v, u, o,* and *s* provide more than 45 per cent of the illegibilities in the handwriting of children and adults. Ernest Newland [17] has found that the numerals 5, 0, and 2 are those more frequently written illegibly.

In the area of oral and written expression, Robert C. Pooley[18] points out that a small number of errors repeated many times constitutes over 90 per cent of the usage problem in the elementary grades. T. Keith Goltry[19] reports that 40 per cent of all usage errors come from confusion of the past and past-participle forms of fourteen common verbs: *see, come, run, write, begin, break, drink, lie, do, give, take, ring, sing,* and *sit.* Another difficulty for both teachers and children is that a large number of the "errors" listed in textbooks and workbooks are commonly accepted forms of colloquial English.

Enough has been said to justify the following generalizations, which may help the teacher deal with problems of individual differences in the language arts:

1. Relatively few words, letter forms, and matters of usage account for a large proportion of the errors which children

make. In a positive sense, attention to the language problems underlying these errors will pay big dividends; in a negative sense, these errors are keys to remedial instruction.

2. A child's ability to use language develops *very slowly*. Instruction of the kind considered here cannot be given at one time by one teacher, once and for all. Individual children will need help and encouragement from all their teachers.

3. Direct help on specific forms needed by a child in a situation requiring the use of language is always more effective and efficient than specific help on forms occurring in lists or in teacher-made exercises.

4. Instruction given to the whole class at the same time will soon fail to meet the needs of many children—especially the bright ones. The teacher will have to add instruction of individuals and small groups on specific needs.

Common Situations

A child's writing and speaking occur in a few common and persistent situations. If special attention is paid to these, many developmental needs will be taken care of.

The social situations in which people write and speak have been analyzed in studies by Paul McKee and others,[20] and the following have been identified:

SPECIAL SITUATIONS IN ORAL LANGUAGE	SPECIAL SITUATIONS IN WRITTEN LANGUAGE
Conversations	Letter writing
Discussion	Outlining
Telephoning	Filling in forms
Storytelling	Notices and announcements
Dramatization	Labels, signs
Reporting, reviews	Memoranda, rules
Participating in meetings	Receipts
Announcements	Minutes
Using social amenities with people	Written reports
Creative expression	Creative writing

An examination of these two lists indicates that the usual individual spends much more time speaking than he does writing. Moreover, most writing is brief; relatively little need be extensive or carefully organized. It is obvious, too, that both types of activity involve the same skills and demand the related functions of listening and reading.

Because the activities listed above are so common, children at every grade level can engage in them. At first, writing will be done through dictation, but soon each child can participate at his own level in both speaking and writing. Reading and listening afford other ways in which children can make individual contributions and learn. This is particularly true if in each situation each child thinks, acts, and evaluates.

The wise teacher will take advantage of the fact that the same usage, grammar, and rhetoric are employed in speaking and writing. This permits many and highly varied illustrations of their use and development. Time and effort usually spent on drill and workbook exercises can be much better spent in learning to deal effectively with situations as they commonly arise in speaking and writing.

Centers of Interest

One of the most effective ways to further the language development of children is to organize one's teaching around topics or centers of interest that are important both to the area being studied and to children. A good center of interest has a comprehensiveness which opens up many avenues of learning: looking, feeling, hearing, smelling, reading, discussing, and so forth. It supplies subtopics and activities which lend themselves to many forms of grouping and to individualization, all within a meaningful, manageable context. A good center has a subject matter of its own for study and understanding. It stimulates talking, reading, listening, and writing. A good center has continuity in space and time and thus permits checking, tying back, and future study in a way that more-limited learning activities never do. Teachers and children can keep track of where they are in relation to a common problem.

The social experiences of children form the basis of many important centers of interest. Topics from the social-studies and science programs, current events, and special events in the classroom, all involve language. There is no difficulty in finding many and continuous opportunities for using all forms of language in planning, discussing, reporting, research, creative activities, and in the evaluating and culminating phases of a unit. There are also ample opportunities for direct attention to language difficulties in a context important to the children.

Group and Individual Experiences

Two procedures commonly used by primary teachers have possibilities at higher levels. These are the experience chart and the "doing and telling time," also called the "sharing time" or "planning period."

The experience chart reflects a significant group experience. The oral vocabulary is meaningful to the children and capable of many extensions. Planning the chart, exploring the many possible forms of expression, evaluating these and selecting and arranging the most appropriate, writing, punctuating, titling, illustrating, and creating the final punch line, all provide invaluable language instruction which can be readily adapted to individuals. After the chart is completed and hung up, it can be used for many purposes by the group as a whole and by individuals. It will be admired, talked about, discussed, and read again and again. It will become a basis for new experience charts.

The experience chart soon evolves into other types: the planning chart, flow chart, and log of writing. At the upper grade levels it expands into individual creative writing.

The sharing and telling times capture the individual experiences of children and provide training in how to communicate through language. Oral language and related listenings are usually emphasized, but frequently the oral reading of a poem, story, or article serves as the initial stimulus. Most teachers find it advisable to discuss with their children points to watch for or consider in telling times. The suggestions are recorded on the planning chart or chalkboard and referred to for guidance.

Sometimes experiences tend to be considered private tales and so are not shared extensively by the rest of the group. Lack of real participation hinders the tryout of new language patterns and evaluation. Another danger is that a few highly articulate children will monopolize the period. The teacher should plan deliberately for general participation. He should encourage shy children so that they will gain confidence in their ability to talk to the group. Frequently it is necessary to plan for the next day with some children so that they can prepare what they are going to say and get the help and encouragement that they need. Some children find it helpful to make picture notes of what they are going to say.

Choral Speaking

Choral speaking is a good way to support individual children in a group situation. There are many degrees of responsibility, but each person's contribution is necessary. Able children have ample opportunity to make the project a better one.

Choral speaking also permits the discussion and tryout of different ways of interpreting the meaning of a word or passage. It is valuable in dealing with some speech problems. It is naturally related to the reading of poetry and prose by the teacher and the class. The dramatic character of choral speaking adds incentive to each child's participation. A tape recorder helps children enjoy and evaluate their speech productions.

Children do not move into choral speaking easily. The interested teacher should seek help from one of the many good books on speech.[21] In general, a slow simple start is best. Many groups find fun in beginning the day with a choral selection, especially one that combines speaking in unison with a repetitive refrain or two-part question and answer.

Dramatic Episodes

The writing and production of short dramatic episodes by a class group provide many worthwhile experiences in language and many activities and responsibilities suited to the varying capacities of children. One advantage is that much help can be given to individuals and small groups in a context where the content of language is at once important and open to constant evaluation and improvement. Intensive polishing of the written and spoken line is necessary and frequently leads to improved language power. What is said, written, and done makes a lot of difference to the success of the production, and therefore language power suddenly becomes important to the children.

Radio plays, puppet productions, finger games, and shadow plays, as well as brief dramas and skits, are also excellent means of encouraging language development. Short pieces which grow out of the children's interest and activities are much more profitable than one ambitious overpracticed production for parents.

As in choral speaking, dramatic episodes can include many children and utilize their various abilities in a way that supports and makes significant each child's contribution.

Reading and Language Classes

Many teachers have examined the traditional pattern of the reading class and have found how to broaden the possibilities for more effective learning by making broader use of the individual interests and abilities of each child.

Scrutiny of methods used by outstandingly successful teachers reveals that they have emphasized certain aspects of the reading lesson, modified the order of steps, and used the story as a springboard for a number of individual reading and language activities. These teachers do much more than their less successful colleagues in introducing a story, in tying it into the experiences of their groups, in establishing purposes and setting up questions to direct the reading, and in skimming, overviewing, or "reading the pictures" as a means of pretesting.

A feature in the practice of these teachers is the place of vocabulary and phrase study in the lesson. These do not come before the child takes up the story, and they are not based merely on someone's guess as to which new words will prove difficult. Instead, they grow out of a prereading or skimming phase which lets individual children identify the words they need to work upon. Thus the teacher has the context of the story to help in vocabulary attack and in improving reading.

Another feature is the effort these teachers make to associate the story with the children's individual experiences by rereading pertinent phrases or sentences in order to verify, extend, and enrich the thought. The children are also led to move from this story to others, which they may read to the group or by themselves for their personal pleasure. Some teachers help the children locate in the story things which the children like and might wish to incorporate into their own story writing.

All teachers can help individual children in their regular language classes if they will follow three precepts: prepare for the story by stimulating the children's interest in it and giving them a purpose in reading it; tie reading skills and vocabulary attack to actual reading situations; extend the use of the story to verify and broaden understandings and to reach out to new language and reading experiences.

Recent professional books on the teaching of reading will be helpful to the teacher. Some contain materials valuable for improving instruction.[22]

Creativity

Perhaps the most effective way to build language power is to encourage each child to extend his participation in creative reading, writing, and speaking. Here each child goes on his own. His language experience reflects all that he is, all that he understands, and all that he can express. Where better to provide for individual differences in the language arts?

The room's reading corner, the school library, and home and community libraries offer the children the resources they need to extend their reading. As a child reads more, he increases his reading power, broadens and deepens his interests, and acquires assets which he can share with others.

Many teachers have found it desirable to discard the old "reading report" and the large charts showing thirty-one books read by Ellen and only one by Quentin. Instead, each child writes on a three-by-five card his reaction to each book he reads. The cards are placed in a file. From time to time the teacher goes over a child's cards with him and discusses other books he might like to read. Some teachers ask the children to make duplicate cards which can be kept with the books. Then another child has the benefit of his classmates' opinions when he examines a book with a view to reading it. When a child has liked a book especially he is given an opportunity to report to the group on it.

Discussions with children lead them to identify the things they should keep in mind as they explore the world of reading. Each child develops these criteria as he reads, and carries them with him into his next reading experience.

In the minds of many teachers of the language arts, creative writing affords the most fertile place for distinctive language growth for all children, and particularly for the gifted child. Creative writing first forces the child to become more aware of himself and of his world. Then language becomes the medium for saying what he wants to say. He is no longer satisfied with sloppy, careless expression but works to find the exact word or phrase which will convey the precise feeling, tone, or meaning that he wants to communicate.

In encouraging creative writing, the teacher should remember that writing skill develops very slowly. The children in any group will write at many different levels, and the same child in the same poem will have verses of widely differing quality.

I sensed this one autumn in an after-school visit to a one-room rural school in Michigan. The teacher had encouraged her children to write about what they felt and understood as they walked home in the bright, late-afternoon sunshine, when the wooded hilltops were casting long shadows across the paths. She showed me some of their writing. The selections ranged from, "I walked home," through, "My shoes kicked puffs of dust in the air," to, "The long black shadows extended like fingers to grasp at the coming night," and, "The crows shouted their anger at the end of day." I was quite sure that the teacher herself would have written, "I went home in my car at 4:00," but I could see that she was encouraging her children to write what they saw and felt. She could accept, too, the fact that some of the children were writing better than she was.

Creative writing[23] takes many forms on many levels. It gains in power slowly, primarily because the child has to grow and develop before his writing can grow and develop. Varied and extensive reading helps writing a great deal. Extensive and deepened experiences are the sources of enriched language expression.

Creative storytelling[24] is a handmaiden to creative writing, and each gains from the other. The skillful teacher will encourage both as a means of endowing each child with the gift of individual language power. Naturally, the role of the teacher is to encourage and help children to write and speak creatively. One hopes that children will have teachers who will encourage writing like the following:[25]

On the way to school this morning I keep poking down my shirt. I pulled the front and the back would come out and I pulled the back and the front would come out. I kep on doing it. I was mad.

Huhwayun music is hundred times pertier than other music. I think of one night My Grandma took a sick spell. Now the room was shut up tight as a jar with a lid on it. She gave a scream. When she gave a scream it was high. But it got lower lower lower and lower till you could hardly hear her. Huhwayun music is something like when she was getting lower. I can play Huhwayun music on my gettar.

Yesterday some smoke was coming out of a chimmney. And what made it queer the smoke mached the house because the paint was woren off the house. And the smoke got lost in the sky.

Some Characteristics of Instructional Method

There are several principles of instructional method which seem to recur in successful attempts to deal with the individual differences of children. Every teacher can adopt these principles as directives for his own instructional procedures.

1. The importance of every child's seeing some purpose in what he is learning has been demonstrated again and again for children at all levels of intelligence. Many instances have been given in this chapter of how the teacher can assure this for all levels of purpose and in all areas of the language arts. It is especially important that purpose in learning extend beyond the specific step of learning the letter "r," spelling the word "receive," or writing a simple sentence.

2. The center used for organizing learning must provide for children on many levels of understanding and ability and carry children naturally from one phase or aspect of language to another. Unless the teacher understands what is essential in a center to enable it to provide for differences among children, no fundamental adaptation can be made in the instructional method to deal with such differences adequately.

3. The learning activities must have their own valid meanings. Language alone can have little significance. The meaning of the reading story is paramount over the sounds of the letters or the names of the words. Form, usage, and grammar can only clarify and support what the story is saying to the reader. What the boy says to the class is more important than how he stands or where he looks. These latter aspects are valuable only as they contribute to meaning. Many of the procedures advocated in this chapter are worth while because the activities themselves have importance.

4. The long-time hope for providing for individual differences among children lies with the child himself and his increas-

ing ability to improve and give direction to his language development. If a child can be helped to help himself, then, because he has better access to the necessary data, he can do far more than any teacher can to maintain the continuity of his effort and learning. Essential in self-evaluation are a sense of purpose, some skill in using the tools of learning, and a willingness to improve one's own language behavior. Only by these means can the dignity of the individual and the resources and gifts of his own intelligence come to their fullest fruition.

GENERAL REFERENCES

Chappel, Bert, and Others, *The Gifted Child in the Elementary School,* Twenty-Sixth Yearbook of the California Elementary School Administrators Association. Sacramento, Calif.: The Association, 1954.

Cincinnati Public Schools, *Challenging the Able Learner: Intermediate Grades,* Curriculum Bulletin 401. Cincinnati, Ohio: 1957.

Dawson, Mildred A., and Marian Zollinger, *Guiding Language Learning.* Yonkers, N.Y.: World Book Company, 1957.

DeHaan, Robert F., and Jack Kough, *Teacher's Guidance Handbook,* elementary ed., Vol. II, *Helping Children with Special Needs.* Chicago: Science Research Associates, Inc., © 1955-56.

Greene, Harry A., and Walter T. Petty, *Developing Language Skills in the Elementary School.* New York: Allyn and Bacon, Inc., 1959.

Herrick, Virgil E., and Leland B. Jacobs, eds., *Children and the Language Arts.* Englewood Cliffs, N.J.: Prentice-Hall, Inc., 1955.

Klausmeir, Herbert J., *Improving Learning through Grouping of Pupils in the West Bend Public Schools.* Mimeographed. Madison, Wis.: Cooperative Educational Research and Services, School of Education, University of Wisconsin, 1959.

Miel, Alice, ed., *Individualizing Reading Practices,* Practical Suggestions for Teaching Series, No. 14. New York: Bureau of Publications, Teachers College, Columbia University, 1958.

Strickland, Ruth G., *Language Arts in the Elementary School* (2nd ed.). Boston: D. C. Heath and Company, 1957.

Witty, Paul, *Helping the Gifted Child.* Chicago: Science Research Associates, Inc., 1952.

————, ed., *The Gifted Child*. Boston: D. C. Heath and Company, 1951.

NOTES

[1] *Recommended Children's Books*, compiled by E. Louise Davis, yearly reviews reprinted from the *Junior Libraries* section of *Library Journal* (obtainable from Junior Libraries, 62 West 45th St., New York 36, N.Y.); *Magazines for Elementary Grades* (Madison, Wis.: Curriculum Division, Madison Public Schools, 1949), bulletin.

[2] *More About Reading* (Washington, D.C.: 1959). Obtainable from Association for Childhood Education International, 1200 Fifteenth St., N.W., Washington 5, D.C.

[3] Henry D. Rinsland, *A Basic Vocabulary of Elementary School Children* (New York: The Macmillan Company, 1945); Edward L. Thorndike and Irving Lorge, *The Teacher's Word Book of 30,000 Words* (New York: Bureau of Publications, Teachers College, Columbia University, 1944).

[4] Eloise Rue, *Subject Index to Books for Primary Grades* (Chicago: American Library Association, 1946); Eloise Rue, *Subject Index to Books for Intermediate Grades*, 2nd ed. (Chicago: American Library Association, 1950).

[5] John E. Brewton and Sara W. Brewton, *Index to Children's Poetry* (New York: H. W. Wilson Company, 1942, First Supplement, 1954); Elvajean Hall, *Books to Build On*, 2nd ed. (New York: R. R. Bowker Company, 1957); *Children's Catalogue*, 9th ed. (1956), with supplements (New York: H. W. Wilson Company).

[6] Rudolf Flesch, *The Art of Readable Writing* (New York: Harper & Brothers, 1949); Glenn Leggett, C. David Mead, and William Charvat, *Prentice-Hall Handbook for Writers*, 3rd ed. (Englewood Cliffs, N.J.: Prentice-Hall, Inc., 1960).

[7] S. I. Hayakawa, *Language in Action* (New York: Harcourt, Brace and Company, Inc., 1941); Otto Jespersen, *Growth and Structure of the English Language*, 9th ed. (New York: Doubleday & Company, Inc., Doubleday Anchor Books, 1956).

[8] Mildred A. Dawson and Marian Zollinger, *Guiding Language Learning* (Yonkers, N.Y.: World Book Company, 1957); Harry A. Greene and Walter T. Petty, *Developing Language Skills in the Elementary School* (New York: Allyn and Bacon, Inc., 1959); Virgil E. Herrick and Leland B. Jacobs, eds., *Children and the Language Arts* (Englewood Cliffs, N.J.: Prentice-Hall, Inc., 1955); Robert C. Pooley, *Teaching English Grammar* (New York: Appleton-Century-Crofts, Inc., 1957); Ruth G. Strickland, *Language Arts in the Elementary School*, 2nd ed. (Boston: D. C. Heath and Company, 1957).

[9] Donald D. Durrell, *Improving Reading Instruction* (Yonkers, N.Y.: World Book Company, 1956), pp. 359-94.

[10] Edward William Dolch, *Teaching Primary Reading*, 2nd ed. (Champaign, Ill.: The Garrard Press, 1950).

[11] W. Franklin Jones, *Concrete Investigation of the Material of English Spelling* (Vermillion, S.D.; University of South Dakota, 1913).

[12] Ernest Horn, *A Basic Writing Vocabulary*, University of Iowa Monographs in Education, First Series, No. 4 (Iowa City, Iowa: College of Education, State University of Iowa, 1926).

[13] Rinsland, *A Basic Vocabulary of Elementary School Children.*

[14] James A. Fitzgerald, *A Basic Life Spelling Vocabulary* (Milwaukee: The

Bruce Publishing Company, 1951); James A. Fitzgerald, "Spelling Words Difficult for Children in Grades II-VI," *The Elementary School Journal,* LIII, No. 4 (1952), 221-28.

[15] S. L. Pressey and L. C. Pressey, "Analysis of 300 Illegibilities in the Handwriting of Children and Adults," *Educational Research Bulletin,* VI (1927), 270-73.

[16] Donald H. Rolliston, "A Study of the Handwriting of College Freshmen" (Unpublished master's thesis, University of Iowa, 1949).

[17] T. Ernest Newland, "A Study of the Specific Illegibilities Found in the Writing of Arabic Numerals," *Journal of Educational Research,* XXI (March 1930), 177-85.

[18] Robert C. Pooley, *Teaching English Usage,* National Council of Teachers of English, English Monograph No. 16 (New York: Appleton-Century-Crofts, Inc., 1946).

[19] T. Keith Goltry, "Analysis of Sentence Structure in Oral Composition" (Unpublished doctoral dissertation, University of Iowa, July 1935).

[20] Paul McKee in *Teaching Language in the Elementary School,* The Forty-Third Yearbook, Part II, of the National Society for the Study of Education (Chicago: University of Chicago Press, 1944), chap. ii.

[21] Mardel Ogilvie, *Speech in the Elementary School* (New York: McGraw-Hill Book Company, Inc., 1954); Carrie Rasmussen, *Speech Methods in the Elementary School* (New York: The Ronald Press Company, 1949).

[22] Leland B. Jacobs, Irene Vite, Robert Sperber, Jeanette Veatch, Mary A. McCune, and Ann Ragland Noel, *Individualizing Reading Practices,* Practical Suggestions for Teaching Series, No. 14, ed. Alice Miel (New York: Bureau of Publications, Teachers College, Columbia University, 1958); Robert F. DeHaan and Jack Kough, *Teacher's Guidance Handbook,* elementary ed., Vol. II, *Helping Children with Special Needs* (Chicago: Science Research Associates, Inc., © 1955-56).

[23] Mauree Applegate, *Helping Children Write* (Evanston, Ill.: Row, Peterson & Company, 1954); Alvina Treut Burrows, June D. Ferebee, Doris C. Jackson, and Dorothy Olton Saunders, *They All Want to Write* (Englewood Cliffs, N.J.: Prentice-Hall, Inc., 1952).

[24] Ruth Sawyer, *The Way of the Storyteller* (New York: The Viking Press, Inc., 1947); Marie L. Shedlock, *The Art of the Story-Teller* (New York: Dover Publications, 1951).

[25] Hannah Trimble, "They Call It Creative Writing," *Progressive Education,* XX, No. 2 (February 1943), 69-70.

8

The social studies

J. RICHARD CHAMBERS

IN TEACHING THE SOCIAL STUDIES, MORE THAN IN
any other field, the teacher becomes responsible for helping each
child develop lifelong habits of good citizenship, realize the tremendous past with its vital effects on the present and future, and
know a multitude of facts necessary for successful living in the
modern world. No teacher can accomplish this great task if he
relies on uniform assignments in a basal text. The pupils differ
so decidedly in reading and language ability, not to mention intelligence and interests, that no one text can serve them all satisfactorily. Here as elsewhere the good teacher must adapt materials to levels of ability, note individual rates of progress in
the learning of skills, give special help at points of weakness,
enrich learning and make it significant, build on interests and
experiences, and encourage self-direction and initiative.

Unfortunately, many teachers who would never dream of asking all their pupils to read from the same page of the same

152

reader at the same time give them all the same social-studies text and expect them to study it in accord with a predetermined schedule. Instead of carefully introducing new words and slowly building the basic understandings needed for comprehending the abstract generalizations of the text, they order a blind attack. Regimentation of this sort is futile as a means of promoting knowledge of facts. Moreover, it is an example of the worst kind of leadership and imposes on the pupils an experience diametrically contrary to the ideals of democracy.

Pertinent Differences

Earlier chapters of this book discussed the differences to be expected in children and the ways in which a teacher might study a child. Here it is only necessary to point out the particular effect which some differences have upon a child's ability to achieve the commonly accepted objectives of the social studies, and consider some relevant ways of discovering a given child's status.

Differences in intelligence. Children of low ability have difficulty in understanding and personalizing vicarious experiences, especially those remote in time. For example, children of low ability cannot be expected to have a vivid comprehension of the colonial period in the United States because that era cannot be directly experienced. They may have trouble grasping abstract theories of government. They prefer short-time units and specific tasks rather than work which requires sustained independent effort.

Differences in reading and language abilities. Much of the work in social studies depends upon learning from books and involves written and oral expression—reports, panel discussions, dramatizations. The special vocabulary of the social studies, because it is rich in concepts, may be extremely hard for the poor reader, especially if he is also low in intelligence. The pupil who has not learned how to use the dictionary and encyclopedia is at loss in reference work.

The wise teacher will pay close attention to the ways in which different pupils tackle any research. In one fourth grade which was starting a unit on "Florida Today," members of the class were to report on the Seminole Indians, tourists, and birds and plants. One child turned immediately to the index in the textbook, another selected a volume of the encyclopedia, and others went to the shelves to find what other books were available. But one boy just sat still, looking rather bewildered. The teacher recognized that this last child needed special help in techniques of research and proceeded to teach him how to find available materials, how to use them, and how to organize a report on what he found. Because the child realized that he needed these skills to accomplish his job, he had a true purpose in learning.

Most standardized tests of study skills include questions on the principal techniques which a pupil must use for independent work in the social studies. By examining the children's responses, the teacher can quickly discover what kinds of mistakes each pupil makes and which pupils have superior skills.

Differences in home environment. The socioeconomic status of a child's family may be reflected in many ways in his work in the social studies. His knowledge of current affairs is affected by the kinds of programs his family watches on TV, their conversation about world affairs, and the books, magazines, news magazines, and daily papers available in the house. Home influences may also be felt in his ability to communicate, in his observational powers, in his intellectual curiosity. His reaction to political and social questions probably resembles his parents' reactions. Any travel that he has done himself, and to a less extent any that he has heard his family talk about, increases his understanding of terms and of concepts which are outside the experience of most children.

Florence, a ten-year-old friend of the writer, has motored across the United States and back, spent two years in Germany and two in Jordan (during the political upheavals there), and visited Egypt, Syria, and Saudi Arabia. She has traveled by automobile, ship, plane, and train in four continents in the last four years. She attaches real meaning to such terms as "ocean," "river," "desert," and "mountain." She is a veritable resource person when the class is studying transportation, time belts, climate, and international trade. In current events, when there is a revolution in the Near East, she can tell what it feels like to be evacuated from an unfriendly territory. When the class was studying the deserts, Florence's father showed them his colored pictures of the Sahara. In contrast, many of Florence's classmates have never been out of the state in which they live or ridden on a train. None of the other children has ever seen a ship hull down on the horizon. They have read that the world is a sphere but have never had an experience that makes the idea real to them.

A simple questionnaire about states and countries visited can be filled out by each pupil at the beginning of the year. This will disclose which pupils have had experiences that implement their work in the social studies and which pupils will probably need help in comprehending geographical terms and concepts. Questions about what magazines the family takes might well be included. *Holiday* and the *National Geographic,* for example, broaden a child's knowledge. Old copies can be shared with other members of the class. If a pupil mentions any unusual travel by a parent, ask if pictures are available.

Social adjustment. If a child is to become a good citizen when he grows up, he must learn to be a good classmate while he is in school. He must see the need of cooperation, fair play, and tolerance. He must have the security of being accepted by the group and the recognition that comes from making contributions to the group. Exploring a child's status in these respects is not easy. Systematic observation, friendly talks, and an ear open to the comments of other children are all necessary.

Differences in subject preferences. When a pupil thinks he doesn't like a subject, he has a mental set against it, and vice versa. One study of 13,483 fifth-grade pupils in 65 New England towns and cities showed that only 9.4 per cent of the pupils preferred social studies over all the other subjects of the curriculum. This put social studies in a tie with spelling for fourth place. A similar study, made ten years later in 78 communities with 19,135 fifth-grade pupils, found the social studies ranking fifth.[1]

In contrast, when children were asked to indicate the type of questions to which they would like answers, nearly 50 per cent listed questions dealing with social-studies topics.[2] It is interesting to note that slow and bright children and good and poor readers seemed much alike in wanting answers to questions about social-studies topics.[3] Furthermore, many pupils complain that a topic of special interest to them has not been taken up in social-studies class.

If all the pupils in a class are asked to indicate on a check list which subjects they like best, next best, and least, and which they find hardest and easiest, the teacher will have a guide to the subject-matter strengths and weaknesses of individuals. He will be able to capitalize on the former and to give special help where it is most needed. If the check list is used at the beginning of the year and again, say, early in December, the teacher may find a clue to what, if any, subject he is slighting.

At the beginning of any unit or when a new topic is scheduled by the course of study, the teacher can present an overview of the content to be studied and ask the children to list pertinent topics that they would particularly like to learn about. This helps the teacher be sure that he is not ignoring a strong interest. It gives him an opportunity to increase the pupils' purpose in learning. And it may indicate a basis for setting up small groups of children who have common interests which they can pursue together. When this technique is used in the social studies, the children give the social studies a high rating and learn well.

Grouping

An outstanding feature of the social studies is that their very nature facilitates cross-ability grouping. Groups of children of the same intelligence or reading ability are not ruled out. They are useful when a particularly difficult book must be consulted, a rather abstract theory is to be considered in connection with a unit, or a small number of children are having trouble learning a new concept. But, because the social studies are forcibly charged with the responsibility for developing desirable social skills and habits in children, the teacher must seize every opportunity to have children with different abilities and backgrounds work together.

Actually, the social studies involve many activities which a whole class can share. These include making plans, viewing films, listening to recordings, talks, and reports, observing the culminating activities of a unit, and taking field trips. Moreover, there are frequent occasions when the subject matter to be introduced next is strange to all the members of the class so all can profit from the same explanation. For example, when a class is beginning to use maps, all of the children will probably need help in understanding and using a scale of miles. Of course, children vary in both the amount they learn and in what they learn when the whole class works together. But this is also true of small groups or even of a team of two pupils.

Groups formed on the basis of a common interest are often very satisfactory. One class was studying the western states. Four children, Ralph, Grace, Harriet, and Sam, all indicated an interest in mining. They discussed together what they ought to find out; for example, what minerals are, where they are found, and how they are mined. Then they pooled their ideas on where information could be secured, and planned how they would report their findings to the class. Ralph and Grace did the hardest part of the book work and shared their findings with the other two. Harriet gathered illustrations from the classroom file and from magazines. Sam planned the display of the pictures and set it up.

In this kind of situation the children realize very quickly the necessity of working together courteously, sharing, taking initiative, assuming responsibility, and meeting a deadline. Each learns as much about the basic content as he would working alone, and separate work would have contributed little or nothing to the goals of social learning.

Children's existing friendships and a particular child's need for new friends affect grouping.[4] Both are revealed by the sociometric technique of asking each pupil to list in order of preference the three other pupils with whom he would like to work.

A group made up of children who like to work together can be very efficient in work-type activities—preparing exhibits, handling service projects such as a lost-and-found department, and working in the school store. The individuals have a better knowledge than the teacher can ever expect to have of what each child does best and of how the members can help each other.

The child who needs friends, the unchosen pupil, can be greatly helped by the experience of working in a small group with a child whom he admires. Care must be taken not to assign the unpopular child to a group whose members are already closely knit and likely to exclude him from their common task. Equally, it is unfair to ask a particularly popular, kindly boy or girl always to work with unpopular, slow, or disorderly children.

A child should have frequent experiences not only of working independently but also as one of a pair or of a small team. Recitation teams of two or three pupils eliminate the lonesomeness of silent study, provide extra practice, and make knowledge more lasting. This type of grouping frees the teacher and the class from many regimented activities and leaves the teacher more time to work with groups of children who are experiencing the same difficulty or following a common interest. Several examples of team learning activities are included in this chapter.

Flexibility is essential in all grouping in the social studies. Each pupil should have the opportunity to work at one time or another with each of the other children in the room. He may belong to two or three groups simultaneously; for example, to a group that is painting a mural and to one that is studying mining. In the meantime he may be carrying on independent work connected with a special interest of his own.

Texts and Supplementary Books

When a teacher discovers that a basal social-studies book in use in his room is too difficult for some children and too easy for others, he must work out expedients to help all of the children acquire the understandings and facts covered by the book and to challenge each child to do his best. Because a series of social-studies texts may take up the same topic in more than one grade, it is often possible to provide harder and easier books which present very similar information. In any case, the teacher should be familiar with all the books in the series he is using. Another possibility is to find a different series that takes up the topic in a different grade. Best of all is to have on hand or secure from the library children's books that are related to the topic under study. Practically every subject that is taken up in the usual elementary-school social-studies curriculum has been dealt with in many books of different degrees of difficulty. The school or public librarian will be glad to help locate books, or the teacher can select them from one of the graded book lists. (See page 176.)

One teacher has described a situation where, because of a lack of library facilities and an insufficient number of books at different levels, he could not provide any books suitable for the poorest readers. He solved the problem by having some of the better readers read aloud to them. Actually, poor readers may have an astonishing untapped facility for learning by listening. One study[5] disclosed that mentally retarded children in the primary grades had a listening comprehension 14 months higher than their mental age and 16 months higher than their reading achievement. In the intermediate grades listening was 8 months ahead of mental age and 23 months ahead of reading achievement. It has been suggested that children could acquire much social-studies information from a nonreading curriculum.[6]

Vocabulary

In the writer's experience as an elementary-school teacher, he has found that difficulties with vocabulary are a major source of trouble in the social studies. Texts and reference materials contain a multitude of words not in the ordinary vocabulary of the pupils or even their parents. Many of these words are difficult to understand unless the child attaches a correct image to the word. A child who has never seen an ocean or a desert is in far different case from Florence; he may use the words without any mental picture of what they represent or any understanding of how an ocean or desert might affect a way of life. Moreover, abstract words like "democracy" are hard for slow children to understand.

In addition to the differences in background which affect pupils' social-studies vocabulary, there are differences in the ability to learn new words. Some children are more able than others to grasp the meaning of a new word from the context. These are usually the good readers with a good ability to analyze and pronounce words. They have no difficulty in understanding "desert" when they read the sentences, "The camel is an animal which can go many days without water. It is used for transporting goods on the desert." Other children, though slower to pick up meanings from the context, are adept at using a dictionary. Still others cannot understand a strange word without the help of many illustrations or even a filmstrip. Many children make mistakes due to errors in perception ("surf"—"serf"), in connotation ("coppersmith" taken for an article), and wrong associations ("fleet"—a fleet of ships; fleet animals).[7] Oftentimes the locality in which children live affects the meaning of a word, as when plains dwellers think of a mountain as the small hill which they call a "mountain."

The teacher may predict and determine the vocabulary needs

of children in several ways. He may pick some of his average readers and have them read the text while he notes the words they do not seem to know and questions them to check up on their understanding. The same procedure can be followed by a small group, with a "secretary" to list the doubtful words and give the list to the teacher. The latter system does not work well with poor readers because they do not know which words they do not understand. But the chances are that words which average readers do not understand will not be understood by poor readers.

A pretest has the advantage of showing the teacher immediately which words which children need help on. It can be either of the multiple-choice type ("Gorge means: cave; narrow passage between hills; a waterfall") or of the word-association type ("The word that best describes a gorge is: deep; swift; hollow"). The words may be selected by the teacher as those likely to occur in work on a unit or text, or they may be taken from the glossary in the text. One rather serious disadvantage of pretesting is that when a child picks a wrong meaning he automatically tends to fix that misconception in his mind. This is probably outweighed by the fact that the teacher can immediately correct the mistake and provide practice.

Another method of determining vocabulary needs is to prepare flash cards of words that may be unknown. The teacher holds up the card, for example, "COFFEE," and asks a question about the word—"Do people drink this?" If each child has "yes" and "no" cards, all can flash their answers, and the teacher can quickly see who is mistaken. Much humor can be added by the types of questions the teacher asks. The children enjoy the game, and it makes a good way to practice on words as well as to test knowledge.

Learning of new words is speeded up if each chapter or unit has a special glossary.[8] The glossary calls the children's attention to words they need to know. Because only one meaning is given and that is to be used immediately, the glossary is less confusing than a dictionary. If an appropriate one is not available

in a text, the teacher should prepare his own. The pronuncia-
tion and definition should both be given. For example, in connection with work on Egypt: "fellahin (fĕl-á-hēn'), Egyptian
farmers; papyrus (pá-pī'-rŭs), the plant from which Egyptians
made paper; shadoof (shä-doof'), an ancient Egyptian water lift
of a type still in use." If glossaries are written on durable paper,
they can be used again in later years.

A knowledge of the vocabulary used in the social studies is so
important in later life that the teacher is justified in spending
a great deal of time and effort to be sure that it is learned. Even
the slow child, to whom a word remains just a word all through
school, may eventually find himself in a situation which suddenly gives it meaning and usefulness. Pictures, filmstrips,
movies, word games, flash cards, verbal descriptions, review, and
reteaching—all the techniques employed in teaching vocabulary
in reading and other subjects—should be called upon. A chart
of geographical terms which provides pictures to help establish
concepts is well worth the purchase price.[9]

Because of the importance of vocabulary, teachers serving on
committees for the selection of social-studies books should give
careful consideration to the way vocabulary is handled in them
and may well spend the time necessary to apply a readability
formula.[10] Teacher's manuals should be examined to see
whether they give helpful suggestions for handling the problem.
In at least one series, the *Living Together* books, new words
are listed at the beginning of each chapter, the words are itali-
cized in the text, and wherever possible they are illustrated by
pictures which use the word in the captions.[11]

Graded Study Guides

Graded study guides, used by pairs or teams of children, have
been found an aid in overcoming children's difficulties in comprehension and recall.[12] Three types of guide can be constructed. The first, for use with poor readers, consists of detailed
questions and answers on each paragraph of the text. The ques-

tions are listed on the left-hand side of the paper and the answers on the right so that the answer column may be folded back until it is needed to check the pupils' responses. An example of a detailed guide written for use with *Beyond Our Borders*[13] follows:

Page 364—"Guayaquil to Quito" from "Around Guayaquil" to page 366, "To the Plateau from Lima"

Paragraph 3—Beginning with "Sugar cane and other tropical farm crops"

Where do sugar cane and other tropical farm crops grow? .... On the lowland.

What do farmers raise on the wetter part of the lowland? .... Rice.

What is grown on the higher land elevations? .... Cacao.

What product is still a leading export of Ecuador? ...... Cacao.

What is raised on the slopes at the edges of the lowland? .... Coffee.

What is another important food crop? .... Bananas.

This type of guide is best used with pairs of pupils or teams of three under the direction of the teacher or of a pupil who is a good reader. Each child has a copy of the guide, with the answer column folded back. The leader reads the first question orally *before* the pupils read the text. The pupils then read to find the answer to the question. One pupil answers the question, and the others check his answer against that in the answer column. The same procedure is followed for each question listed. The easiest type of question to answer is one phrased like the text. The oral reading of the question reduces the vocabulary difficulties of the pupil who is reading the text to find the answer.

A more advanced type of guide is suitable for use by pairs of better readers. These guides consist of general questions on each paragraph followed by a listing of the related facts. The pupils read the paragraph *first,* then look at the question, attempt to answer it, and check their answers against the list. The procedure can be made more difficult by having the children read several paragraphs before looking at the questions. The answers may be written down and then compared with the answer sheet. Superior readers may read an entire section and try to recall the contents orally while another pupil uses the guide to check them. A sample based on the same section of *Beyond Our Borders* follows:

Page 364—"Guayaquil to Quito" from "Around Guayaquil" to page 366, "To the Plateau from Lima"

Paragraph 3—Beginning with "Sugar cane and other tropical farm crops"

What is said about crops:

Grown on lowland:	Sugar cane _____ other tropical farm crops _____.
On wetter part of lowland:	Farmers raise rice _____ used for food _____.
On higher land:	Cacao _____ has been grown for a long time _____. Cacao is still leading export of Ecuador _____.
On edge of lowland:	Coffee is grown _____.
Important food crop:	Bananas _____.
Other crops:	Oranges _____ other warm-climate fruits _____.

A third type of guide uses an outline which calls attention to the major ideas of the paragraph. The outline lists three titles for each paragraph. The children first read the paragraph in the text, and then try to agree on the best title. After they have agreed, they unfold the answer column and check their accuracy. For example:

Page 364—"Guayaquil to Quito" from "Around Guayaquil" to page 366, "To the Plateau from Lima"

Choose the best title among the three suggested below for each paragraph.

Paragraph 3—Beginning with "Sugar cane and other tropical farm crops"

(A) Products of Ecuador's Lowlands
(B) Growing Coffee in Ecuador   (A)
(C) The Lowlands of Ecuador

The built-in organization of these study guides aids in eliminating difficulties in comprehension and recall, which are often complicated by lack of organizational ability. The technique also gives each child an opportunity to respond rather than "waiting his turn." Oral recall is generally preferred by children over written recall, yet it results in an increase in written-recall ability. Any technique overused is apt to be abused, and use of study guides more than two or three times a week or for extended periods is likely to bore the children. But used with discretion, they are worth the trouble it takes to prepare them, especially as the same sheets can be used over and over again.

Reference Work

There should be readily available to the children, preferably in each classroom but surely in the school building, the major types of reference material used in the social studies. Each type should include books written for children on different levels. There should be a junior dictionary, a collegiate, and an unabridged; a children's encyclopedia and an adult encyclopedia; touring maps and a big atlas. There should also be a *World Almanac.*

Many pupils in any grade may still need training in the skills necessary for efficient use of reference materials. They should know the alphabet perfectly, how to use an index, how to interpret symbols and legends and where to look for the key when they meet a new set of symbols, how to read maps, how to read graphs and charts, and so forth. They may need training in how to skim.

One teacher, whose class was studying its own community, found that six of the children could not read a map. He took the six as a group and instructed them in the cardinal points of the compass. On the playground at noon, he had them stand with their backs to the sun so that their shadows pointed north. He explained that south was behind them, east to the right, and west to the left. Then he asked questions like, "Is your house north or south, Ted?" "In which direction is Mr. Wilson's house?" Back in the classroom, he had the six children draw a chalk compass rose on the floor and label each wall of the room to indicate its direction. Next they made a simple map of the neighborhood and located the school on it and noted the directions in which the streets ran. The rest of the class used the map, and each child wrote his name on a piece of paper which he pinned to the map to show where his home was. As the study progressed, several field trips were taken. The six children were responsible for drawing symbols on the map to show where the places they had visited were located—the first fort, the oldest meetinghouse, and the city hall. By aiding these six children who lacked some of the map-reading skills, the teacher was able to improve their skills and to give them an opportunity to contribute to the general activity of the class.

Two, three, or four children of different ability can work together to secure information on a topic and each learn more about how to use reference materials than he would working alone. They pool their ideas about what topics they should study, what books they should use, and where they can find the books. Each child assumes responsibility for part of the work, but they all help each other and exchange experiences. When the teacher sees that the group or any child needs help with a specific method, he comes to the rescue. Because the children are already trying to learn and have had some experience, the teacher's help is welcome and meaningful.

Thinking

One of the commonly accepted objectives of social-studies teaching is to enable children to use the knowledge they gain. Essentially, this means that children should become skilled in critical and elaborative thinking and learn to organize their knowledge so that it is effective in any given situation. All human beings, regardless of their general intelligence, do think. The more intelligent can deal more effectively with complicated lines of thought and with abstruse generalizations. However, there are wide differences in the ability to think in different ways, and these differences do not necessarily depend on intelligence, nor do they bear much relationship to each other.[14] A very bright child may score lower on a test of elaborative thinking than an average child does. A child may do well on a test of critical thinking and poorly on a test of organizational thinking. But luckily all children can be taught to think better and be given useful experience in applying knowledge.

Elaborative thinking. This involves the ability to associate many related topics. It is stimulated by people's working together. It is particularly useful in school and in life in the initial planning stage of any project. Children can be given experience and practice in elaborative thinking if they are encouraged to contribute their ideas in class and group discussions. For example, the teacher may say, "More children have been hurt by automobiles this year than last. I think it may be because traffic is heavier. Who can think of something else?" The ideas will probably come in a flood and include specific reasons based on what different children have seen, read, or heard. If the teacher is alert, he will notice which children are slow to advance ideas and opinions. He can direct leading questions at these children and praise their answers. He should be careful to comment favorably when a diffident child volunteers a suggestion. If possible, some general principle should evolve: "Most children are hurt because they step from behind parked cars. We should teach children never to do this."

Groups of not more than five children, chosen on the basis of friendship or a common interest rather than intelligence or reading ability, gain experience in elaborative thinking whenever they work together to achieve an end. Activities which stimulate elaborative thinking by the whole class or by small groups include listing questions not answered in the reading, seeking for inferences and generalizations, planning activities, dramatizing episodes from books, and writing different endings to stories.

Critical thinking. This involves the ability to distinguish between relevant and irrelevant information and between fact and fiction—a valuable attribute in these days when we are bombarded by misleading propaganda. Pupil study teams gain experience in critical thinking when they try to answer such questions as, "Which of the things this author states appear to be based on facts and which on opinion?" Or they may be asked to tell sense from nonsense ("Pick out the parts of this story that probably could never happen") or to find differences in points of view ("Why do more city dwellers than farmers want daylight saving?") or to select information pertinent to a topic ("As you read this section about communication systems, think about the ways in which they make our lives more enjoyable").

Organizational thinking. This includes the ability to classify major and minor ideas that are met in reading. Teaching of organizational thinking begins in first grade when the teacher, after reading a story, asks, "What did Dick do first?" or "What was this story about?" Activities which aid its development include finding the topic of a paragraph, locating topic sentences, building headlines, writing topic sentences from headlines, writing telegrams, and, ultimately, building outlines.

Pupil Specialties

The use of pupil specialties may be salvation for the busy teacher.[15] They are particularly suited to the needs of the gifted child because they depend primarily on self-direction and self-discipline. They combine many of the favorable aspects of unit teaching and individual instruction and allow pupils to work at their own ability levels and rates. Capitalizing upon worthwhile interests in the social studies not only serves to encourage the child who has a specialty but also stimulates the curiosity of the other pupils and enables them to share the specialist's knowledge. For the gifted child this technique adds purpose to practice in locating, selecting, and evaluating materials, in making reports and setting up displays, and in using higher mental processes. It allows him to use multiple texts and reference books, which he prefers to a single text.

The technique for carrying out this type of work is relatively easy in any classroom. The teacher first attempts to discover the range of interests already present in the classroom by simply asking all the children to list the things that interest them most. Then the list is compared with the topics the teacher expects the class to be working on a month hence. Children with pertinent interests are given assignments to report on them at that time. Each report is scheduled for a definite day. The teacher makes sure that the pupil understands the standards which his report is expected to meet. A ten-minute time limit for the report is usual.

The *Pupil Specialties Guidebook,* by Walter J. McHugh, gives both teachers and pupils help in the technique.[16] It suggests sources of materials, methods for organizing and presenting information, criteria for a good oral report, criteria for a good display, and ways to evaluate a report.

Units

A good unit offers endless opportunities for providing for individual differences. Every step—outlining the content, setting up objectives, planning activities, and evaluating outcomes —entails responsible independent work, either alone or in close cooperation with the members of small groups. Unit teaching requires a great deal of effort on the part of both teacher and pupils. Allocating tasks in line with abilities, needs, and interests, securing the necessary books, supplementary materials, and audio-visual aids, and checking on the pupils' learning are all time-consuming processes. But when learning experiences are organized around a unit, the pupils' increase in knowledge —and in their liking for the social studies—leaves little doubt that unit teaching is necessary and desirable.

Introducing the units—the approach. Rarely will there be a time when a teacher can cause thirty children to be equally interested in the same topic. But the advantages of a unit are lost to any pupil who does not at least accept it willingly. Some sort of mass motivation is essential.

The children in one third grade entered their classroom on Monday morning and found themselves literally surrounded by elements of transportation. Everywhere there were pictures of trains and planes, ships and autos. A model helicopter hung from the ceiling. The bulletin boards were covered with clippings: "Airline Strike Cripples Miami," "New Cars Widest Ever," "Boy Injured in Bicycle Mishap." The library table displayed books ranging from *The Little Train* to Lucius Beebe's latest, many open to show attractive illustrations. A poster showing a Swiss train snaking through the Alps was pinned to the front of the teacher's desk. A filmstrip viewer was set up with a strip about transportation in the city. Printed on the board in large letters were the words, "I KNOW. . . ."

The children scattered excitedly about the room. Some gathered in small groups about pictures. Others turned the leaves of books. One boy climbed on a chair to get a closer look at the helicopter. The teacher called for attention and told the class they were going to study transportation. Then he pointed to the words on the board and said, "I know something about trains because I took the train to Washington last summer. Who else has had a trip lately?" The accounts of experiences came in an eager flood. To be sure that all were noted, the class divided into small groups, and a secretary for each group took notes about where the children had been and how they had traveled.

The next day, when the children arrived they found on the board, "I WANT TO KNOW. . . ." The same groups set to work to list all the children's questions about transportation. The first lists showed the teacher what experiences different children had had that might contribute to the unit and, perhaps more important, showed him which children had had so little experience that they might need extra attention, either to stir their interest or to increase their understanding. The second list was used as a guide in planning and for setting up individual group activities.

Developing the unit—the core. One sixth-grade teacher uses a combination of units and basal text. His class was studying our Latin neighbors when the revolution in Cuba suddenly gained momentum. He decided to alter the schedule. He and the class collected all the clippings they could on Cuba. Three bright students who showed real interest read through the chapter on Cuba in the text quickly and then took on the job of organizing the clippings. They summarized their classification under appropriate headlines in a paper called *Cuban Capers.* The other children in the class were allowed to select the topics which appealed to them and, working in groups, began to collect clippings and information from other sources about their special topics. One child from each group reported to the class each week on what his group was finding out. A few pupils with special interests were scheduled for specialty reports on topics featured in the classification of the clippings or in the text.

Once the main headings were agreed upon, the groups set up, and the reports scheduled, the whole class moved back to the text and completed reading the chapter on Cuba. Teacher-made study guides were used by teams of pupils, and the text was read aloud to three very slow readers. Travel films and slides were shown to the whole class. Sugar cane, raw sugar, and molasses were brought to class and sampled, and in general everything was done that could help make the accounts in the clippings, books, and text real to all the children.

This teacher felt that the use of a current event gave the children a real interest and purpose in studying Cuba. The combination of the topics selected by the pupils and those covered in the text resulted in a much more complete study than either method would have by itself. Individual differences were carefully considered. Children with special abilities, special sources of information, and keen interests had an opportunity to contribute. Slow pupils made their own contributions and at the same time were given individual help to compensate for their handicaps.

Concluding the unit. Just as it is very difficult to assure that each pupil is well motivated for the study of a unit, so also is it difficult to arrange a culminating activity which at one and the same time gives each child a real part and helps fix in his mind the knowledge, skills, and attitudes which the unit was planned to promote. One emphatic warning is in order. The differences in interests and abilities are so great that the teacher cannot count on all pupils' learning equally when they hear reports or observe the demonstrations of others. On the surface of the matter, it is absurd to expect one child to learn from the ten-minute report of another everything that the reporter has spent weeks in studying. All these difficulties are compounded when the children are young. Therefore, the best type of culminating activity is one which excites the children. The general effect is not to impart new knowledge but to help fix in each child's mind what he has learned in the course of the unit.

A second-grade class decided to have a farm breakfast at the conclusion of their unit on farm life. The room was decorated with a mural of cows in a pasture near a red barn. There was a morning paper at each place, featuring an account of the class's visit to the farm. Instead of the speeches which adults endure at club breakfasts, there were brief reports on books as varied as *Animal Stories in Basic Vocabulary* and *In the Forest*. The big thrill, of course, was eating the breakfast. Juice squeezed from real oranges (no frozen concentrate would do!), milk from the dairy they had visited, muffins baked by the children in the school's kitchen (after a very practical and wholly successful use of arithmetic in measuring and multiplying the recipe), and butter churned by vigorously shaking a jar of heavy cream. Each child had contributed to the project, but the great value lay in the vivid evidence of the importance of the farm in their daily lives.

Evaluation

The threefold nature of social-studies objectives—facts, attitudes, and behavior—complicates the problem of evaluation. This is further complicated when the work, whether in a text or unit or combination of text and unit, is adapted to the individual interests and abilities of the pupils. Moreover, the measure of progress is change, and changes in behavior and attitudes are difficult to discover and to gauge.

The bulk of the evidence for progress in factual knowledge will come from teacher-made tests. To be fair to children who have not been required or perhaps even had the opportunity to learn as much as others, the teacher will be wise to copy the test expert and arrange questions in ascending order of difficulty. This prevents the slow children from being discouraged and perhaps giving up at the beginning. Because the slow child has neither the knowledge nor the speed to answer all the questions, the teacher may well divide the class according to ability and instruct the slower half to do only the first so many questions on the test, and the brighter half to do them all. If a child in the slow group finishes his section of the test and wants to continue with the harder questions, he should certainly be allowed to do so. It is interesting to note that when tests are given in this way and each group is scored on the basis of the questions which were to be answered (a given number for the slow group, all for the bright group), the distributions of score in the two groups resemble each other in terms of range and scatter.

Teachers who stress the acquisition of understandings may be dissatisfied with the strictly factual nature of most standardized tests. A new series of achievement tests, the STEP tests, is designed to overcome this difficulty.[17] They are good measures of understandings and of the ability to apply knowledge.

No test can replace the teacher's own efforts to discover each child's needs and attitudes as a basis of helping him learn to behave better and better now and eventually become a good citizen. The teacher's knowledge comes principally from observing children at work and play, in a classroom discussion or a playground game, when they are listening to a talk by a visitor, on a field trip, asking questions, and receiving criticism. Anecdotal records of behavior, both for this year and prior years, alert the teacher to changes. They can be made the basis of the best means of evaluation, a friendly talk with the pupil about what he thinks, feels, and hopes.

An Organizational Pattern[18]

This chapter has stressed examples of social-studies programs which recognize individual learning needs of children. It has considered:

Whole-class activities. There are times when the children in a class must come together as a group. These occasions include the introduction of a new unit, the showing of a motion picture or filmstrip, the presentation of a pupil specialty report, dramatizations, exhibits and displays, field trips, and visits by resource persons.

Group activities. Much work will be done in small groups or teams of two to five pupils. In general these will be formed on the basis of friendship or needs or interests rather than ability. But pupils of different ability may differ in the level on which they engage in an activity, the depth they reach, and the distance they go. Some types of activity are better adapted to bright pupils than to slow, and vice versa.

High achievers. Bright pupils profit from the use of advanced study guides, experience and training in making specialty reports and other reports, and instruction in advanced skills in using reference materials. They need systematic reviews of facts and concepts to be sure they are not losing sight of the initial goals.

Average achievers. These pupils profit from the multiple-response techniques described in the section on vocabulary. A study guide used by a team of two or three will generally help them make rapid progress in factual and conceptual learning. Team specialty reports may be assigned on the basis of common interests. These children will need special individual and group instruction to overcome weaknesses and for the teaching of skills.

Low achievers. Children of low ability who are poor readers may need an oral presentation of text material. Others may be able to work under the direction of a pupil teacher, using detailed questions in a study guide. The classroom teacher should give them practice in the use of the guides and in vocabulary attack, including the use of glossaries. Slow pupils need much individual instruction and work in small groups.

The programs that have been described have proved that they increase the amount of material learned, provide opportunities for real social learnings, and create a sense of accomplishment on the part of the teacher. They involve much work, but the results are truly gratifying.

GENERAL REFERENCES

Beatty, H., "Social Studies and the Slow Learner," *High Points,* XXXI (September 1949), 13-26.

Chase, W. Linwood, "Individual Differences in Classroom Learning," in *Social Studies in the Elementary School,* ed. Nelson B. Henry, Fifty-Sixth Yearbook of the National Society for the Study of Education, Part II, pp. 163-86. Chicago: University of Chicago Press, 1957.

D'Ambiosio, L. M., "Adjusting Social Studies to the Nonacademically Inclined Child," *High Points,* XXXIV (January 1952), 13-18.

Gavian, Ruth Wood, ed., *The Social Education of the Academically Talented,* National Council for the Social Studies, Curriculum Series, No. 10. Washington, D.C.: The Council, 1958.

Hanna, Lavone A., Gladys L. Potter, and Neva Hagaman, *Unit*

Teaching in the Elementary School. New York: Rinehart & Company, Inc., 1955.

Jarolimek, John, *Social Studies in Elementary Education,* chap. vi. New York: The Macmillan Company, 1959.

Kenworthy, Leonard S., *Introducing Children to the World.* New York: Harper & Brothers, 1956.

Krug, Edward, and G. Lester Anderson, eds., *Adapting Instruction in the Social Studies to Individual Differences,* Fifteenth Yearbook of the National Council for the Social Studies. Washington, D.C.: The Council, 1944.

Michaelis, John U., *Social Studies for Children in a Democracy.* Englewood Cliffs, N.J.: Prentice-Hall, Inc., 1956.

Miel, Alice, and Peggy Broggan, *More Than Social Studies.* Englewood Cliffs, N.J.: Prentice-Hall, Inc., 1957.

Otto, Henry J., *Social Education in the Elementary School.* New York: Rinehart & Company, Inc., 1956.

Preston, Ralph C., *Teaching Social Studies in the Elementary School* (2nd ed.). New York: Rinehart & Company, Inc., 1958.

——, ed., *Teaching World Understanding.* Englewood Cliffs, N.J.: Prentice-Hall, Inc., 1955.

Sullivan, Helen B., "Skills Instruction for the Slow Learning Child in the Regular Classroom," *National Elementary Principal,* XXIX (December 1949), 41-46.

BOOK LISTS

A Graded List of Books for School Libraries. New York: Harcourt, Brace and Company, Inc., 1959.

Harrington, Mildred P., *The Southwest in Children's Books.* Baton Rouge, La.: Louisiana State University Press, 1952.

Literature for Human Understanding. Washington, D.C.: American Council on Education, 1948.

Reading Ladders for Human Relations. Washington, D.C.: American Council on Education, 1955.

Sattley, Helen R., *et al., Children's Books About Foreign Countries.* Chicago: National Council of Teachers of English, 1951.

Strang, Ruth, *Gateways to Readable Books.* New York: H. W. Wilson Company, 1952.

Sullivan, Helen B., and Lorraine E. Tolman, "High Interest-Low Vocabulary Reading Materials," *Journal of Education*, CXXXIX, No. 2 (December 1956).

Tooze, Ruth, and Beatrice Perham Krone, *Literature and Music as Resources for Social Studies*. Englewood Cliffs, N.J.: Prentice-Hall, Inc., 1955.

NOTES

[1] W. Linwood Chase and Gilbert M. Wilson, "Preference Studies in Elementary School Social Studies," *Journal of Education*, CXL, No. 4 (April 1958).

[2] Emily V. Baker, *Children's Questions and Their Implications for Planning the Curriculum* (New York: Bureau of Publications, Teachers College, Columbia University, 1945); Edythe T. Clark *et al.*, "What Children Want to Know About Their World" (Master's thesis, Boston University, 1952).

[3] Chase and Wilson, "Preference Studies in Elementary School Social Studies."

[4] J. Murray Lee, "Grouping in Social Studies," *The Grade Teacher Reprint*, XLII (April 1958), 103-4.

[5] Elizabeth B. Speidel, "Language Achievements of Mentally Retarded Children" (Doctor's thesis, Boston University, 1958).

[6] W. Linwood Chase, "Individual Differences in Classroom Learning," in *Social Studies in the Elementary School*, ed. Nelson B. Henry, Fifty-Sixth Yearbook of the National Society for the Study of Education, Part II (Chicago: University of Chicago Press, 1957), pp. 163-86.

[7] J. Richard Chambers *et al.*, "Studies Based on the Earley and Wolffer Social Studies Vocabulary Tests for Grades IV, V, and VI" (Master's thesis, Boston University, 1953).

[8] Donald D. Durrell, *Improving Reading Instruction* (Yonkers, N.Y.: World Book Company, 1956), pp. 257-58.

[9] Good charts are *Chart S100x—Geographical Terms*, obtainable from Denoyer-Geppert Company, 5235-59 Ravenswood Ave., Chicago, Ill., and *BG 051—Map Symbols Chart*, obtainable from Rand McNally & Company, 405 Park Ave., New York, 22, N.Y.

[10] Edgar Dale and Jeanne S. Chall, "A Formula for Predicting Readability," *Educational Research Bulletin*, XXI (January 21, 1948), 11-20, 28.

[11] *Living Together Social Studies Series* (New York: The Macmillan Company, 1958).

[12] Durrell, *Improving Reading Instruction*, pp. 290-97.

[13] J. Warren Nystrom, Emlyn D. Jones, and Helen Harter, *Beyond Our Borders* (Chicago: Rand McNally & Company, 1957).

[14] J. Richard Chambers, "The Relationships Among Measurable Mental Tasks Related to Reading" (Doctor's thesis, Boston University, 1956); Donald D. Durrell and J. Richard Chambers, "Research in Thinking Abilities," *The Reading Teacher*, XII, No. 2 (December 1958), 89-91.

[15] Donald D. Durrell and Leonard J. Savignano, "Classroom Enrichment Through Pupil Specialties," *Journal of Education*, CXXXVIII, No. 3 (February 1956); Joseph A. Gattuso *et al.*, "An Evaluation of Curriculum-Related Specialties in Grades Five and Six" (Master's thesis, Boston University, 1957).

[16] Walter J. McHugh, *Pupil Specialties Guidebook* (n.d.). Obtainable from Reading Aids Press, 198 Mt. Vernon St., Dedham, Mass.

[17] *Sequential Tests of Educational Progress* (Princeton, N.J.: Educational Testing Service).

[18] Much of this material has been suggested by unpublished mimeographed materials from the School of Education, Boston University. These are part of a research project being sponsored by the United States Office of Education.

9

Science

MARY E. SHECKLES

CHILDREN ARE CURIOUS ABOUT THE WORLD IN which they live. If there is any doubt of this in your mind, just listen to a child who is in a free, informal setting. The following are the kinds of questions you might collect in a short time. What is air? Why do we breathe it? Why can't I see it? What are those bubbles that come out of the ground when I water Mommie's flowers? Where is space? Does the goldfish breathe? Why do jet pilots wear such funny-looking suits? Why will my magnet pick up my penny but not Billy's? Where do babies come from? What is a satellite? Yes, children are curious about many things. But they are not all curious about or interested in the same things at the same time. Neither are children able to learn the same things just because they are all the same age or all have the same intelligence quotient. Too often we have tried to fit children into the same mold with little regard for the obvious differences. Through experimentation some teachers have found that it is more rewarding for them and their children if they use some individualized instruction during the day.

Science for All

Science should be an important part of each day's program for each child throughout the elementary-school years. This is extremely important in a democracy such as ours, where the individual through his vote helps to determine the governmental policies concerning our scientific and technological programs. We need to have a voting public in which the individuals know some of the fundamentals of science, are interested in the welfare of all men, are aware of the interdependence of life and the interaction between living things and their total environment, are able to see the relationships between behavior and the resulting conditions, and are capable of independent thought.

Science experiences should be provided for *all* children—our future day laborers, merchants, scientists, mechanics, lawyers, farmers, physicians, and the host of others needed to satisfy our needs in the world of today as well as tomorrow. Whatever their future role in society, children will profit by learning to work and to play together. They will learn through experiences that each has strengths and that each has weaknesses. Through the guidance of skilled teachers each child will learn that ability in reading, in playing baseball, or in manipulating scientific equipment does not make one a better person than one's classmates. But such ability may be very important in helping a child to decide on the kind of adult role for which he is best suited and in which he will be happiest. In our present society it is important that each child, regardless of his future vocation, know some of the fundamentals of science and have some degree of understanding concerning his environment.

Science experiences need not be identical for all children in the same grade or in the same age group. Studies in child growth and development have shown us that children have an individual growth rate and that growth is not uniform on all fronts. Some children who mature slowly have great potential, but they are likely to be lost in a program where children are grouped according to ability. This is especially true if it means denying some children an opportunity to study a particular subject. To tell a child that he has little or no chance of learning science or to deny him entrance into the science group are both more than likely to inhibit his growth in this area. There is some evidence that these or similar procedures do great damage to his concept of self, for as the child perceives himself so does he act. A few children have enough inner stability or support from sources outside the school to succeed in keeping an interest in science alive until they get into a more favorable school setting. But most of the children who are slow to mature give up and accept the label placed on them. Children who mature at the usual rate or faster can profit by being in classrooms where they are guided and stimulated to work at their own speed and to pursue in depth that which is challenging to them. Many classroom teachers who are working in science with all their boys and girls find that each can learn some things. They do not all learn the same things, but each profits in his own way.

In addition to the variation in growth rate, there is wide variation in the background experiences of children in any classroom. The variation in background may be used to broaden the experiences of all. The child who has grown up on a farm may know much about animals, plants, and farm machinery but may be quite limited in his formal experiences with aquaria, chemistry sets, the study of the universe, prehistoric animals, and the like. Each child, regardless of his background or level of maturity, should be helped to feel that he can contribute to others as well as learn from them. In addition to this learning, it is vitally important that each of these children have experiences in many areas of science and that each be helped and encouraged to take from these experiences what is meaningful.

Girls and boys are equally interested in the biological and the physical parts of the world about them unless they have been conditioned otherwise. In the past many people have felt that children of elementary-school age could not deal adequately with physical phenomena. Others have felt that it was natural for boys to be interested in machines, magnets, and electricity but that girls would have no interest in these areas. Anyone who has worked with youngsters who have not been conditioned by thoughtless adults has found that there are no sex differences in scientific aptitude. Some girls can wire doll houses and make electric motors just as efficiently and enthusiastically as some boys. And some boys can become excited about planting seeds or bulbs and watching them grow. Children should be given an opportunity to explore as widely as possible and to develop their interest in all parts of their environment.

Objectives and Purposes

As you begin to plan your program in science, you will need to be clear on the objectives toward which you wish to work. What are the purposes of including science in your program? The purposes and objectives must be ones you can accept and feel are worth working toward. Although you will have to decide on these for yourself, you may get help from reading about some of the things that others consider important. The following or similarly stated objectives are held by some classroom teachers who are teaching science in the elementary schools of our nation today. The objectives listed are ones to which not only science experiences but also other parts of the curriculum can make a significant contribution. You may wish to modify some of these and add others so that your objectives are truly yours.

The study of science should contribute toward each child's growth in his ability:

to observe and to record accurately the happenings in a planned science experience be it classroom experimentation or a field trip;

to use resource people and resource materials to gain information from a variety of sources;

to examine evidence and not accept as fact everything he hears or reads;

to manipulate with skill materials used in testing out hypotheses or checking the results of experiments reported by others;

to consider all information available before formulating generalizations or conclusions and to change these generalizations or conclusions if change is justified by new evidence or a reevaluation of earlier information;

to communicate his thoughts, ideas, and reactions to others and to listen with an open mind to the contributions of others.

Objectives such as these cannot be achieved without the learning of content, but there is no specific body of content that is needed to reach any one of the objectives. For example, children may grow in manipulative skill through experiences in learning about the nature of air, setting up a system of pulleys to move a heavy object, or making an electric motor. Similarly, children may learn to communicate thoughts and ideas growing out of a study of seed germination, of propagation of plants from cuttings, of the effect of different soil mixtures on plants, or of the effect of sunlight on green and nongreen plants. Since learning the same facts is not needed to achieve our objectives, it is no longer necessary to provide the same experiences for all children of a given age or in any given classroom.

Working to achieve these objectives, you can explore and learn with children. You can become an active participant in the search for scientific information. You can begin to allow for more individual selection of content at the time when it has the greatest appeal. And as you work with your children, you will be able to stimulate, to challenge, to encourage, and to open up new sources of information. Because you will be working for the greatest development of each individual, you will not set predetermined upper limits. When you first begin working in this way, you are likely to be pleasantly surprised at the progress some children make when they are free to use their own initiative and to work at their own individual rate.

A Framework[1]

Many classroom teachers feel insecure and inadequately prepared to deal with science in their classrooms. When they look through some of the books on methods and the wide range of subject matter in books for children, many become even more insecure. They realize that all areas of science are dealt with to some degree in the elementary school. If you have some of these feelings, you may be interested in exploring briefly a framework with which you can begin to bring some order out of confusion.

This framework is made up of seven basic science patterns of the universe: time, space, change, adaptation, interrelationships, variety, and energy. The concepts you have associated with these patterns will depend upon your experiences. You have been building concepts related to these patterns of the universe since early childhood and will continue to do so as long as you remain mentally alert. And as you have more and more experiences, you will add new concepts and reorganize some of your old ones.

All the traditional units of science can be fitted on this framework, which also provides for the development of new materials. For example: 1. *Time*. Minute, hour, day, night, month, year, season, decade, century, tomorrow, today, yesterday, all deal with concepts related to time. Another group of time concepts has to do with the age of things such as rocks, soil, the earth, living things, and historical monuments. 2. *Space*. Concepts related to distances, such as inch, foot, yard, mile, meter, rod, and light years, play a part in the meaning space has for you. Chances are that your concepts related to space beyond the earth and to distances in outer space have increased in number rather rapidly since the launching of the first successful satellite. 3. *Change.* Everything is changing. One might think of changes as they occur in nature and as men make them. Some natural forces bring about weathering, erosion, volcanic action, earthquakes, and changes in the weather. Men make changes as they clear land, build cities, build roads, dam rivers, drain swamps, and cut waterways. 4. *Adaptation.* Living things on the earth today are here because of successful adaptation of the species and of the individual to their environment. Those species of living things that did not make a successful adaptation to their environment, such as the dinosaurs, passenger pigeons, and dodo, are now extinct. 5. *Interrelationships.* There is an interrelationship between members of our solar system. On the earth there are interrelationships between different parts of the environment: between the physical and physical (as the forces that cause weather), between physical and living (as human beings in a crowded auditorium where humidity is greatly increased), and between living and living (as dependence of animals on plants for food). 6. *Variety.* There is great variation in the living and nonliving things on the earth. Variation among human beings is great. Notice the great variation in the breeds of dogs and the differences among individuals of one breed, such as cocker spaniels. Variation in the rocks along a stream bank is usually great. 7. *Energy.* Energy may be in the form of something in motion or something that has the potential ability to produce motion. The study of energy includes studies of heat, sound, light, magnetism, current electricity, static electricity, machines, chemistry, nuclear energy, and weather.

It is not likely that each year you will be able to provide an equal number of experiences in each of these basic science patterns for each child. For example, some years you may do a great deal of work that helps to develop concepts of space, change, variety, and energy, but you would also be careful to provide some opportunity for growth of concepts of time, adaptation, and interrelationships. Such planning will enable you to make use of subject matter from both physical and biological science. If you have made the seven large patterns of the universe a part of your thinking, you will have a framework for your planning and will be able to see many opportunities to help children gain real understanding when they are asking and are ready to be helped.

Programs That Provide for Individual Differences

Your planned work in science may follow one, or a combination of all three, of the following ways of providing for individual differences. 1. You may be working with an entire class in a given content area. In addition to the planned work in which all participate, you allow each child to study in depth some part of the work that is of special interest to him. 2. You may be working with an entire class in a given content area. In addition to this classwork in science, each child is encouraged to study in depth an area of science that has no direct relation to the classwork. 3. You may be working with no organized classwork in science. Each member of the class is doing individual work. At any given time all individual work may be within one large content area, or there may be no restriction placed on the area to be studied. Now let us explore some of the ways of working and some of the possible outcomes from each of these general plans of work.

Entire Class with Provision
for Directly Related Special Interest

You may wish to provide common science experiences for your group early in the school year while you are beginning to learn some of the background, interests, and abilities of individual members. Common experiences may also be provided as you begin a study which is new and different to almost all your children. It will be helpful to introduce the material to all and to discuss their present information on the topic. Such discussions will guide you as you plan experiences that will help to broaden present concepts and to change behavior where this seems desirable. If in your school system there are certain units or bodies of content that all children are required to study, you may wish to work with the total group as you introduce such material.

Suppose that you discover from the questions that many of your children ask and the comments they make on news items related to trips to the moon that they lack basic information not only about the moon but also about the other members of our solar system. Together you decide to study the solar system. Some of the basic information all members of the class study and discuss may be: the names and approximate sizes of the planets, the order in which they occur as you move from the sun outward, what other heavenly bodies are a part of the solar system, some of the reasons why it is believed that people similar to ourselves cannot be living on any of the other planets.

You will need to provide as wide a range of resource materials dealing with our solar system as can be assembled. Then, using these materials, you may wish your children to read independently on each of the topics to be studied and afterwards come together for a discussion of what they have read. Or you may wish to give them some small-group experience. You might form groups to study about the four smallest planets, the five larger planets, the sun, satellites, meteors and comets, or perhaps you will want to use some other organization of materials to be studied by the groups. On completion of their group study each group will share information and ideas with the entire class.

During the study suppose you discover that some are reading the more difficult and fundamental materials. The contributions and questions of these students go beyond those of most of the group. You realize that about six of your boys and girls are interested in some of the fundamental problems of space, space travel, and astronomy. One child in this group is interested in jets, missiles, and a proposed trip to the moon as are the others, but his interest goes much deeper in astronomy. He is concerned with such problems as how astronomers calculate the distances between the members of our solar system, how they can estimate the heat on the surface of the sun, how they build and use telescopes, and how they study the speed and direction of travel of our solar system.

These children with special interests continue to participate in classwork in science, but you make it possible for them to spend some time in the school day in pursuit of individual interests. You also find time to listen to new learnings and to offer suggestions for additional sources of information. Children who are interested in what they are doing and who have usable resources available can develop much independence in their work. They need guidance, but much of this can be given in brief interviews, with only an occasional longer conference.

A study of the solar system and related topics may provide opportunities for helping your children to expand their concepts of the seven basic science patterns. 1. *Time* can be dealt with in connection with the study of rotation and revolution of the members of the solar system and the time required for light to travel from some of the stars to the earth. 2. *Space* can be dealt with in relation to distances between members of the solar system and between the solar system and the other members of the universe. 3. *Change* may be dealt with in relation to the changes observed on Mars and the difficulties of observing changes on some of the distant members of the solar system. 4. *Adaptation* might be included in the discussion of possible life on other planets. 5. *Interrelationships* between the members of the solar system may lead to a discussion of gravity. 6. *Variety* in size, time of rotation, time of revolution, and distances from the sun may be studied. 7. *Energy* from the sun may be included, or it may be given major emphasis. Whether children's concepts grow in these basic science patterns will depend on the ways in which you develop the materials. It is possible to study the solar system or the universe without children's ever being helped to think about the sun as our source of energy, or the interrelationships between members of the universe, or any of the other patterns. But discussions which clarify the basic science patterns would provide new meanings and enrichment beyond that found in many treatments of the subject.

Perhaps you who teach in the primary grades are thinking, "That is fine for children who have some skill in independent reading, but what about my little ones?" Suppose you wish to give young children some experiences that will help to broaden their concepts of energy. This is one of the very large patterns, and you will need to consider the areas in which you wish to work. You may plan for the whole class to have experiences in one area, such as weather, light, or sound, or you may wish to include work in the two areas of machines and magnets. For the remainder of the year's work you may provide experiences in one or more of the other patterns. In any case, in the primary grades you should be working at an experiential level. This is a level where you provide direct experiences so that each child will have as much physical contact with a phenomenon as possible. You provide for verbal expression, but you do not work for complete understanding.

Now let us make some specific applications of this concept of experiential learning in work with young children. Suppose you want to work in ways that will allow each child to expand his concepts of energy. You select the area of machines and will work to give children experiences with their own muscle energy in the use of an inclined plane and a lever. A long board with one end resting over the edge of the sandbox and the other on the floor or ground will be a good inclined plane, or ramp. Here the children learn through experience that it is easier to roll their truckloads of sand up a ramp and dump them into the sandbox than it is to lift each truckload of sand up to the top of the sandbox and dump it. Some of the children may find experimentally that they can slide some heavy things up the ramp which they cannot lift to the top of the ramp. Some young children will use correct terms such as ramp or inclined plane while others will simply call it a board.

In this manipulation of materials the children are each given an opportunity to learn through experiences two ways to do a thing. They will find that one way is easier than the other and that the easy way takes less of their muscle energy. This may be enough for now. At this level it is not likely that any of the children would find it helpful to know how to work problems using the inclined plane. Such understanding can come later. You have provided experiences which have helped each child to build his concepts of his own muscle energy.

You might follow a similar type of procedure for learning about the lever. A long board used with a heavy block of wood or other suitable object as the pivot point, or fulcrum, may be used to lift a stack of books, the teacher, the teacher's desk, or other heavy objects. One second-grade teacher introduced the study of machines by asking if anyone in class could lift her. They then worked with the lever until even the smallest child in class could lift her. If you have seesaws either outdoors or indoors that have movable boards, you may want to let your children find out experientially how they must fix the board if a fifty-pound child and a seventy-five-pound child are to seesaw. If the boards are fastened to the pivot point, the children will learn to move toward the pivot or away from it in order to seesaw successfully with lighter or heavier partners. Experiences with the lever will also add to the children's concepts of energy and the use of their own muscle energy.

In the study of magnets you may provide for individual exploration first and follow this with classwork. You might start by giving each child a magnet and suggesting to him that he see what he can do with it. Small magnets will work just as well for this as large ones and are much less expensive. Each child will have an opportunity to try out his ideas independently. By watching the children, you will get some clues to which children have had some experiences with handling materials and with finding out for themselves. You may have a few children who at first will just stand or sit and hold their magnets. As soon as these children see what others are doing, they are likely to imitate them. You may follow this free exploration period by a sharing time when the children tell and also demonstrate what they have found out about their magnets. This might end your work with magnets or you may wish to develop a reading chart using the information gained. If there are interested and capable youngsters who want to try out some other things with their magnets, they should be encouraged to do so and be given time for such additional exploration. In a study of this kind, children have an experience with a force which can be used to help produce an electric current. Thus you are building toward concepts of energy on an experiential level. You provide for individuals by not requiring all the children to do the same things.

In each case the individualized activity may be followed by class discussion. Such discussions will give you an opportunity to see which children may have developed some misconceptions during their manipulative experiences. Being aware of these, you can plan additional experiences that will help to clarify points of confusion. Discussions will also help children to verbalize their experiences. Children who are reluctant to talk can often be helped if given an opportunity to talk about something that they have just done. The exchange of ideas is also very valuable. Learning to listen to another's ideas is not always easy for young children, but it is an important objective toward which to work.

You may also make an experience chart for each of your activities. Or you may wish to suggest that each child record his experiences in words or in an art medium, or in both. Making and keeping experience charts will help you to follow the growth of your group. It will also help you to know whether you are providing enough scope and depth in your planned science work. Individual records are most valuable in showing the kind and degree of progress a child is making.

Entire Class with Provision for Unrelated Special Interest

Independent work unrelated to classwork in science probably functions most easily and satisfactorily in classrooms where time is set aside each day or week for every child to pursue work of his own choice. This is a time for each child to work on something that he enjoys doing. It is a busy time but also a relaxed time, free from tensions.

Children who have special interests in the area of science may choose this time to work independently or to join with others in small groups. This special interest may be an outgrowth of a stimulus from a television program, something the child has read, something in his Scout work, or perhaps discussion with others or observation of their work. For example, a child whose older brother has made an electric motor may also wish to have one. He has been able to interest several of his classmates in building electric motors. Together they have collected diagrams, directions, and materials to work with. Each child decides which motor he wishes to make and all begin to work. When one has trouble, the others help. In the end each will have his own motor. From such an experience some of the children may go on to design their own motors.

An individual child or a group of children may be interested in plants and how they reproduce. Some of their work may be with seed germination, propagation from cuttings, roots, bulbs, corms, tubers, and rhizomes, and some of it may deal with budding and grafting. As a result of their work they may ask to supply and care for plants in the room. Or in some cases they can be given space to work in a flower bed near their classroom.

Still other individuals or groups might work to build birdhouses, a house for a pet soon to be acquired, animal-feeding stations, their own weather instruments, or a crane with a system of pulleys. Some children may wish to read stories or books of their choice during independent-work times. Books about the lives of some of our great scientists, such as Koch, Pasteur, Einstein, Curie, and Salk, are interesting to many children. Other children are more interested in books about animals, plants, microbes, electricity, or atomic energy. Children interested in the same topic might read independently and then share with each other the things they liked most in their books.

The kinds of things that might be done will vary greatly. Not all children will deal with science topics. But those with special interests in science will have an opportunity to study in the area of their choice. A child working in this kind of program has no set limit on scope, depth, or the number of weeks he works on a given topic. The nature of the projects is limited only by the interests of the children and the practical problem of space and materials.

This kind of program has much to offer if you and your boys and girls can improvise and adapt available materials to fit your needs and can accumulate printed materials that cover a wide range of topics. Children with widely different interests and ability can work in a way that is satisfying to each. In this there need be no comparison of ability. It is often true in such work that a child who is slow in most academic work, as well as a child who is accelerated, may have a hobby or a skill that will be of interest to others. Here he can earn the respect and admiration of some of his classmates. This is also a time when one child will be able to help another develop skill or interest in the things he enjoys. For example, the interest of one or two in building telegraph sounders and receivers may spread to include most of the members of the class.

One teacher who worked in this way always had a project of her own to work on when she was not needed by one of the students. This helped her to illustrate that people, regardless of age, profit by having hobbies and time to work on them. Teachers are human, but we sometimes give little indication to our students that this is true. Children gain much by this kind of sharing with their teacher.

Individualized Work with No Organized Classwork

A science program in which each child in the classroom does individual work gives the greatest possible opportunities for individual growth. It is a kind of program that many teachers are reluctant to try. And I know of no well-developed plans or procedures that can be handed from one to another. Perhaps this is as it should be, for teachers are individuals and should be encouraged to take ideas from many sources. These ideas should be studied, and those which contain parts that can be incorporated into a teacher's way of thinking and working should be adopted. It may be of interest to know that many teachers who have tried working this way find that they are not enthusiastic about returning to total-class instruction. While there are no exact patterns to follow, there are some guidelines that others have found useful.

Because of the limited space and resources in most classrooms, it might be desirable to limit the area of choice for any given period of time. For example, you and your children may have decided that they would like to have experiences in the areas of plants, animals, electricity, and weather. You find that the children have had some experiences in all of these areas except electricity. This may mean that you will do classwork in electricity to help build a vocabulary with meaning and to give a foundation. You will follow this with work on an individual basis. Plants, animals, and weather you will try on an individualized basis because these are areas in which your children have had some basic work, they are very broad areas and you could not begin to cover all that is important, all children are not equally interested in all parts of any of the areas, and there are enough resource materials available for independent work.

Once you and your boys and girls have decided on an area and the individualized plan of study, you will need to discuss some ways of working. There will need to be limits. One of the first of these might be on the selection of a topic for study. If you have chosen the area of plants, then each child would select some phase of plant life he was interested in studying. Topics included might be germination of seeds, the effects which sunlight, water, and temperature have on plants, plant growth in different kinds of soil mixtures, methods of reproduction in plants, budding and grafting of fruit and nut trees, and many others. You may wish to explore the use of some of the basic science patterns. For example, you might use such topics as *changes* which result from the budding or grafting of fruit or nut trees, seasonal *adaptations* of plants and protective *adaptations* of some plants, *interrelationships* between sunlight, water, temperature, and plants, *variety* of ways in which plants reproduce, *variation* in the percentage of seed germinating under different conditions, and *variation* in soil composition and its relation to the growth of different plants. The advantage of these topics is that they not only lead to learning facts but encourage putting those facts together to see relationships.

Several children may select the same phase of plant life for study. In this case they can be encouraged to use different plants and to work independently but during the study to exchange ideas and sources of information and at the end of the study to compare their findings. Children who like to read may be expected to find many of their own reference materials. Those not so skilled in reading may be stimulated by their interest in what they are doing and read more. At first they may need help in finding reading materials. For a slow reader, it is often tiring and discouraging to search through several sources of material. Helping these children to locate materials will allow them to put their efforts into reading. Working in this way, you can gradually help them to gain skill in finding materials; that is, as you help them to locate materials, you are teaching them to work more independently. For some children this is a very slow process.

Other limits will be concerned with ways of working in the room. These should be set up cooperatively so that the need for the limits is understood and accepted. An important point is that the work being done by one child must not be such that it prevents his neighbors from doing their work. If possible there should be some suggestions as to times and ways for children to communicate with classmates. Informal discussions between members of the group can be a very valuable means of learning to communicate ideas. They may also be used to help children learn to challenge ideas and to accept challenge of their ideas.

You will probably find it desirable to arrange some signal that tells you when a child wants help. A return signal that says to him you will come to him as soon as possible is also needed. Well-adjusted children can be encouraged to go on with something else while they wait for you. One set of signals that usually works well is for the child to raise his hand when he wants help. He says nothing but keeps his hand up until the teacher looks his way and nods. The child then lowers his hand and works on something he can do until the teacher arrives.

Limits governing when a child may leave his desk depend in part on the nature of the work being done and the space that is available for working elsewhere. Your rules for cleanup may need to be modified from time to time so that they will be appropriate to the materials being used.

You will probably want to keep records of the work being done by each child. This will enable you to check occasionally to see that opportunities for growth in each of the seven basic science patterns are present. Your record of the large areas studied during the year will enable you to provide scope in your program. Although it is possible to provide for growth of concepts in several, sometimes all, of the basic science patterns during a study of one area, you will have a stronger program if during the year you provide for work in both the biological sciences and the physical sciences.

In keeping individual records of children's work, some teachers have found that a small notebook with a page for each child is useful in making quick, daily notes. This need not take long. If the working time is long enough, a note on the work of each child each day is desirable. However, this is not always practicable. A note at least every other day for each child will enable you to keep a pretty close check on the progress each is making. These notes can later be used to write more complete records. You may also wish to encourage each child to keep a daily record of what he has done. This would include an account of his reading, any experiments that he has carried on, and any illustrations or models he has made. It might also include field trips and observations made when going to and from school. If you wish to emphasize reading, an individual chart of reading progress can be kept by each child. Many teachers feel that for maximum growth a child's competition should be with himself. Each child may be asked to answer in his own daily record such questions as: Am I improving? Did I do better today than I did yesterday or last week? Am I growing in independence?

Findings may be shared informally from day to day. This kind of sharing is between children, and the teacher has a part only as a listener unless invited to participate. With some children this works well, and you may feel that there is no need for a formal sharing period. Informal sharing is learning in a natural way and is much less time-consuming and more rewarding than formal sharing. You may, however, want your children to have experiences of the more formal type. You may arrange a time schedule so that each has a few minutes to tell about his work.

Evaluation of individual experiences, like most kinds of evaluation, should be based on what the individual has done and not on comparison with what others have done. Children should be helped to evaluate their own work. As they look through their records with you, they should be helped to see both their strengths and their weaknesses. You may wish to give written factual tests. If so, and the same test is taken by everyone, you will need to be careful to include only general information which all would have had a chance to learn. Actually, a factual test would have to be made for each of the large topics if one wished to test for details. But if your major concern is for growth of your boys and girls toward logical thinking, independence in research, and methods of work, then you will be less concerned about the specific, detailed content each has learned.

May you have the courage to try letting your children pursue independent interests and the endurance to keep at it until you have some of the satisfactions that come from knowing and working with your boys and girls as individuals.

Records and Evaluation

Reference has been made to records and evaluation under the preceding suggestions for individualized work. Much of this applies to any way of teaching. But when all work is individual, daily or every-other-day records seem to be almost a necessity. In other methods of working, longer intervals of time may occur between entries in the individual records.

A very valuable kind of record for showing individual growth is one which is made of any class or small-group discussion. Such records can most easily be secured by the use of one of the many kinds of recording machines. However, some teachers are able to work with their children in such a way that they can record statements made by each child during a discussion. Records of this type should include the date and the name of the speaker. If possible, discussions should be recorded every two or three weeks during the year. A study of such records will give definite evidence of children's growth or lack of growth in such traits as logical thinking and expression of ideas, consideration of evidence, ability to listen to the contributions of others, accuracy of statements, inclusion of the source or sources of information, willingness to change ideas when the evidence presented is accurate and understandable, and consideration of all available information before formulating generalizations or conclusions.

From such records one can study some of the changes taking place in a given individual. For example, in September and October all Vic's statements were very dogmatic. But on November 20, Vic made one statement using "perhaps" and one using "maybe." For several months he continued to use both dogmatic and relative statements. By May the number of dogmatic statements had definitely decreased. Evidence of this kind of growth is difficult to obtain in any other way than from dated records of the statements made over a given period of time.

By studying records made during a period of months, it is possible to check the effectiveness of one's teaching with respect to the total group and also the individual. Since records of discussions show both correct and incorrect interpretations, they are valuable indicators of the kinds of experiences that are functioning and the kinds of additional experiences that it may be desirable to provide.

Individual file folders where children can place written work and art work become a valuable form of record highly useful in evaluation. Art work is especially useful in showing an individual's understanding and interpretation of what he has read or observed. Some children who are able to repeat the wording of the book or the teacher may show by their art work that real understanding has not taken place. Drawings and models give clues to the kinds of reinforcing experiences that might be needed.

Another help in evaluating behavior is to observe children on field trips. One can quickly begin to form an opinion of the effectiveness of one's efforts to teach respect and concern for all parts of the environment. Children who destroy as they observe and study need many kinds of experiences which will help to give them a feeling of responsibility, of being caretakers of their environment.

In evaluating manipulative experiences, one may be concerned with keeping records that will show whether or not children are improving in their planning and carrying out of experiences. Do they understand what they are doing well enough to substitute materials for those called for? Do they complete the experience as written and then begin to make changes and to test other ideas? Are they developing an increasing awareness of safety precautions? Are they less awkward in handling materials? Are they aware that doing a thing once does not prove anything? Do they repeat experiences? Do they check to see what results others carrying out the same experience have recorded? As you work with children you will find other points to add to such a listing on which you will base your evaluation of work.

Pencil-and-paper tests serve a useful purpose in measuring content which can be verbalized. But they do not give an accurate picture of, or even reliable clues to, the changes in behavior brought about in the individual. Such tests have a part in the total evaluation of the pupil's progress in science but they should not be given major emphasis.

Evaluation of the truly worthwhile parts of our science teaching is difficult because changes in behavior come slowly. But these changes are important and therefore worth working and waiting for.

Teaching Materials

Teaching materials should be gathered from all available sources. What you gather should be determined by the kinds of experiences you wish to provide for your boys and girls. Therefore, no list of equipment which could be given here or in any other book will satisfy your needs. First make your plans for the areas in which you wish to provide experiences. Then begin to make your equipment lists, book lists, audio-visual lists, and so forth.

If you are starting in an area new to you, look through some of the children's books and methods books for teachers which deal with this area. From these you will get ideas about what you wish to do, the equipment you will need, and the kinds of other teaching aids you will want to collect. Your children can help you with this kind of survey. Many children can bring in books and other materials to share with their classmates. Often you and your children can make needed equipment. Perhaps you plan to teach in an area that you have taught for several years at about the same grade level. If so, you probably have accumulated many materials that you share with the children. You can often buy some materials at a reduced price at salvage centers. Local five-and-ten-cent stores and hardware stores will be good sources of some of the equipment you will want. Those materials that must be ordered from supply houses are usually less expensive when selected according to your needs than when bought as part of the preassembled package.

Films, filmstrips, and pictures will be valuable in helping you to provide a wide variety of experiences for your boys and girls. Many of the books that you will use have lists of visual aids that make the text more meaningful. Libraries usually have listings of available visual aids. Many school systems provide some visual-aid materials that can be used in the classroom. By using this kind of resource material you can provide some experience with far-away places, dangerous or inaccessible places, growth processes in plants which cannot be observed in detail, underwater scenes, and much more. You may be limited by available funds in your use of rented audio-visual aids. Things that will tend to "stretch" a budget may help. Look for free aids. Some of these are excellent, and the advertising, if any, is usually unobjectionable. Try to select those visual aids that deal with phenomena with which you and your children cannot have firsthand experiences. Often parents or friends who make a hobby of photography are happy to share their pictures with the children.

One or more good books on methods of teaching science will be of value to you. Some of these books suggest methods of working with children and provide a good, readable section on each of many subject-matter areas which will help to refresh or to build your background of understanding. They also provide lists of other books you may turn to for additional help, and lists of audio-visual aids. The teacher's manuals which accompany most of the children's science texts often list additional reference books for teachers and for children. And they usually give lists of audio-visual aids that would be helpful in the teaching of each chapter. The many popular books about science will be of much value to you. Your librarian will be a valuable resource person for both you and your children.

In Conclusion

Provision can be made for individual differences by helping children pursue special interests that grow out of classwork, by working with them on an interest unrelated to classwork, or by working with each child individually, without having classwork. Whatever plan is followed should allow for working in ways that will help each child:

to observe and to record accurately, to gain information from a variety of sources, to examine all available evidence, to manipulate materials to test hypotheses, to consider all available information before formulating generalizations, to communicate ideas, and to listen with an open mind;

to develop new concepts and to reorganize old ones in the seven basic patterns of the universe: time, space, change, adaptation, interrelationships, variety, and energy;

to work with acquired information and understandings until they cause changes in his behavior;

to develop to the maximum his potential ability in science.

GENERAL REFERENCES

Blough, Glenn O., and Albert J. Hugget, *Elementary-School Science and How to Teach It.* New York: The Dryden Press, Inc., 1951.

Burnett, R. Will, *Teaching Science in the Elementary School.* New York: Rinehart & Company, Inc., 1953.

Craig, Gerald S., *Science for the Elementary-School Teacher.* Boston: Ginn & Company, 1958.

Freeman, K., T. I. Dowling, Nan Lacy, and J. S. Tippett, *Helping Children Understand Science.* Philadelphia: John C. Winston Company, 1954.

Hubler, Clark, *Working with Children in Science.* Boston: Houghton Mifflin Company, 1957.

Sheckles, Mary, *Building Children's Science Concepts: Experiences with Rocks, Soil, Air, and Water.* New York: Bureau of Publications, Teachers College, Columbia University, 1958.

NOTE

[1] For additional information on this framework, see Mary Sheckles, *Building Children's Science Concepts: Experiences with Rocks, Soil, Air, and Water* (New York: Bureau of Publications, Teachers College, Columbia University, 1958), pp. 6-19.

10

Arithmetic

ROBERT L. MORTON

INDIVIDUAL DIFFERENCES AMONG CHILDREN SHOW up strikingly in arithmetic. What some can learn with ease, others learn with difficulty, and still others do not seem to learn at all.

Our schools may be conveniently classified into four groups so far as what they do about individual differences in arithmetic is concerned: those in which all pupils follow the same program and undertake the same assignments at all times; those in which the pupils are divided into more or less permanent groups on the basis of ability and achievement; those which retard some slow learners and accelerate some fast learners; and those which follow a comparatively new plan called "Grouping in Depth." This plan will be described in detail on the succeeding pages.

204

Grouping in Depth

Those who follow the "grouping-in-depth" plan recognize at the outset that the pupils in any classroom are distributed over a wide range of ability and aptitude for arithmetic. But, while acknowledging that some pupils can go much farther than others, they accept the responsibility of providing that all pupils go as far as they can. All pupils, including the slower learners, must be helped to grasp the fundamentals of arithmetic and to achieve useful elementary skills. Many, including average learners, should be helped to exceed the goal of minimum essentials. And a few, the more able, should be stimulated and helped to reach much higher levels of understanding and achievement.

Any teacher who plans a program which is designed to provide for individual differences is faced with the very practical problem of dividing the available time and providing instruction which will give the maximum help and guidance to all of the thirty or more pupils in a classroom. To do this, the teacher must have or devise instructional materials which make specific provision for the needs of the slower learners, the average learners, and those who excel.

The plan here described provides that the entire class take up each new topic at the same time. As a new topic is presented, the teacher, of course, may vary the plan of instruction according to the abilities of the pupils. Some pupils need more experience with concrete and semiconcrete materials than do others. The teacher shrewdly decides when any pupil is ready to move from the concrete to the semiconcrete, and from the semiconcrete to the abstract. Some pupils, the faster learners, go quickly from the concrete to the abstract. Others require more time to make this important transition. A few may require much time. But no one can be said to have really learned arithmetic until he has taken this step.

The teacher also recognizes that certain devices which are

sometimes called "crutches" may, for a time, provide real help to slower learners and, to a lesser extent, to average learners, but that the more able pupils can speedily learn to dispense with such aids. Thus, when learning to change minuends in subtraction examples, a process which is sometimes called "borrowing," many pupils use the device shown here. Recognizing that they cannot subtract 8 ones from 4 ones, they use one of the 6 tens. This ten is equal to 10 ones. To show that the 10 ones and the 4 ones together make 14 ones, they cross out the 4 and write 14, usually in smaller figures, above it. Then to show that one of the 6 tens has been used and that only 5 tens are left, they cross out the 6 and write a 5 above it. The 5 should be slightly separated from the 14. This device seems to help some pupils to see that 6 tens and 4 ones may also be written as 5 tens and 14 ones. Because pupils differ greatly in the extent to which they need the help of this device, and because pupils should be encouraged to discontinue the use of the device as soon as possible, it seems best not to print the device in a textbook or workbook but to let the teacher introduce it if this seems necessary and decide how extensively it should be used by each of the pupils.

$$\begin{array}{r} 5\ \ 14 \\ \cancel{6}\cancel{4} \\ \underline{3\ 8} \end{array}$$

Another illustration of differentiation between ability levels is found in the extent to which the pupils are required or encouraged to write out all of the steps in working certain types of examples. For instance, short division is a useful skill and should be introduced at about the fifth-grade level. But short division is considerably more difficult than long division. We show 526 divided by 8, using the long division form and then the short division form. If this example is worked by short division, the pupil must subtract an invisible 48 from a visible 52, must think, "How many 8's are there in 46?" when only the 6 of the 46 is visible, and then must subtract an invisible 40 from a partially visible 46. This is so difficult that the slower learners may well be excused from short division.

$$\begin{array}{r} 65\text{R}6 \\ 8\overline{)526} \\ \underline{48} \\ 46 \\ \underline{40} \\ 6 \end{array} \qquad \begin{array}{r} 65\text{R}6 \\ 8\overline{)526} \end{array}$$

It is too difficult for them, and, of course, they can get along without it.

Many other opportunities to differentiate between ability levels will occur to the teacher as the various topics and phases of topics are developed. Consider, for example, the addition of $2\frac{3}{4}$ and $3\frac{1}{2}$. We show three forms for the work. Form A is the form which all pupils see at first when this type of example is presented and is the form which the slower learners may well continue to use indefinitely. Form B omits one step. Even average learners can, with encouragement from the teacher after Form A has been thoroughly mastered, see at once that the sum, $5\frac{5}{4}$, is equal to $6\frac{1}{4}$ and write it immediately as shown. Form C is

$$
\begin{array}{ccc}
\text{A} & \text{B} & \text{C} \\
2\frac{3}{4} = 2\frac{3}{4} & 2\frac{3}{4} = 2\frac{3}{4} & 2\frac{3}{4} \\
\underline{3\frac{1}{2} = 3\frac{2}{4}} & \underline{3\frac{1}{2} = 3\frac{2}{4}} & \underline{3\frac{1}{2}} \\
5\frac{5}{4} = 6\frac{1}{4} & 6\frac{1}{4} & 6\frac{1}{4}
\end{array}
$$

for the more able group. They do all of the work "mentally" after the example is written, and write the sum without writing out any of the intermediate steps. The teacher who encourages those who can to take such short cuts will discover that the challenge appeals to many of them and that they gain real satisfaction from such a superior performance. Many other types of examples in fractions provide similar opportunities for differentiation.

After a unit of work has been completed, a carefully prepared diagnostic test is given. This test should indicate precisely where the deficiencies of individual pupils lie. The items of the test should be keyed to the pages in the textbook on which specific topics and phases of topics were developed. After the test has been scored, the teacher has information which can be used for temporarily dividing the class into three groups.

The three groups are as follows:

1. Those who need another chance to learn; these are the slower learners.

2. Those who have mastered the topic fairly well but who can profit from some extra practice and supplementary exercises. These exercises should be designed to extend and deepen understanding for average learners.

3. Those who excel. These pupils should have new and more-difficult materials which are designed to stimulate and challenge, materials which will add further insight and result in a higher level of skill.

It is rarely if ever true that a pupil who is revealed to be a slow learner on one test will be classified as one who excels on another test. However, it not infrequently happens that pupils move back and forth between the slow and the average groups or between the average and the superior groups. The decision as to the group to which a pupil belongs after each test is, of course, left to the teacher.

The following sections present further details as to what may be done for slower learners and for average pupils after each test and, in greater detail, suggestions for caring for the needs of those who excel.

The Slower Learners

We have referred to slower learners as those who need another chance to learn. The mere provision of drill for those who do poorly on a test is probably the worst treatment that can be devised. Practice, or drill, should follow understanding, not precede it. The purpose of drill is to fix what has been learned so that the fact or skill will be available when needed.

If a pupil is unable to work a certain type of example after he has had one chance to learn it, say an addition example that requires carrying to tens' place, we should not assume that he has made no progress whatever toward the mastery of the required skill. But we do know that he has not proceeded to the point of reasonable mastery. Clearly, in the case illustrated, the addition, including the necessary higher-decade addition, has been done correctly but

$$\begin{array}{r} 48 \\ 16 \\ 39 \\ \hline 823 \end{array}$$

the 2 tens in the sum of the first column were not combined with the tens which appear in the second column. This pupil should go back to the page or pages in the textbook on which carrying to tens' place was developed. With any necessary help from the teacher, he should restudy the development there and follow again the steps in the model examples. He may need to see the process illustrated again with concrete materials, such as coins (pennies and dimes), or splints and bundles of splints.

When it seems that the process of carrying to tens' place, and the reason for it, is understood, drill should be provided. The same examples which have been used previously may be used again or different examples may be prepared by the teacher. Some textbooks provide additional practice exercises in the back of the book for this purpose. The examples in the textbook probably have been prepared with great care by an expert. To prepare a new set is very tedious and time-consuming.

Not just any examples will do. The mere fact that they are similar in appearance to those in the textbook does not mean that they have been properly prepared. A set of examples each of which contains three two-figure numbers should be constructed so as to give a wide variety of practice on basic facts and on higher-decade facts. It should require that the pupil carry 1 or 2 in mixed fashion, and, to keep the pupils on their toes, it should include a few examples in which no carrying is required.

The test which sent a part of the pupils back to earlier pages may have revealed that some pupils needed to restudy only a few topics or phases of topics while others needed to restudy several. There should be no such thing as forming a group consisting of those who did poorly on the test and then giving all of the members of the group the same prescription. The reteaching should be individualized. To be sure, two or more who need to be retaught carrying in addition may be retaught together to save time, and any others whose needs are similar may be retaught together. But to force all who have serious deficiencies to cover again the elements which represent the entire needs of the group is to waste time and effort and to cause a loss of interest.

No one can tell the teacher in advance how long this period of restudy and practice should last. The time required will vary with the pupils and the topic under consideration. When, in the judgment of the teacher, the pupils are ready for it, they should be given another diagnostic test. This test should not be identical with the one previously taken but it should parallel it very closely. The purpose, of course, is to discover how effective the reteaching and restudy have been. Usually, if carefully planned and skillfully executed, the plan described here produces very satisfactory results.

Most textbooks contain diagnostic tests which may be used after the completion of major units of the work. However, textbooks cannot be expected to provide the parallel follow-up tests which ordinarily are used by only a minor fraction of the class. Such tests should appear in the teacher's edition. If they are not provided there or elsewhere by the publisher of the textbook, they must be prepared by the teacher. Of course, the preparation of such tests requires much skill and great care.

Summarizing, those who have not completed a major unit of work satisfactorily go back to the indicated pages in the textbook and restudy the development there. This individualized remedial experience is followed by practice. Then a second diagnostic test, very similar to the first one, is taken. The second test is designed to measure the further progress which has been made.

The Average Learners

While the slower learners are trying again to master the elements which they failed to get, and the superior pupils are occupied with exercises which will be described later, some worthwhile provision must be made for the average learners.

As every teacher knows, the average learner is one who has

mastered a unit of work fairly well but not perfectly. His weaknesses are not so serious that he should go back to many of the pages on which the basic ideas were developed. But he may need to restudy the development and the model examples on some of those pages. Furthermore, he can profit from some experience with supplementary exercises that are designed to extend and deepen understanding and to provide further practice.

The abilities of average learners, like those of the other two groups, spread over a considerable range. The range is probably not as wide as it is with the slower group and with the more able group but it is wide enough to reveal individual differences within the group. There is no sharp line of demarcation between the average group and the slower learners or between the average group and those who excel. This means that some members of the average group will be given treatment which is similar to that given to the better members of the slower group while others will be provided with experiences which are not much different from those provided for some of the members of the more able group.

We have referred to extra practice materials which may be found in the back of the textbook, or which the teacher may prepare, in our discussion of the needs of the slower learners. Some of those materials may also be used by average pupils. The teacher may well decide to use certain selected portions of such materials according to the individual needs of the pupils.

When, in the judgment of the teacher, the pupils have studied and practiced sufficiently to overcome their individual difficulties, they are ready for the supplementary exercise to which reference has been made. Such an exercise may be provided in the teacher's edition of the pupils' textbook. If not, it may be prepared by the teacher.

This supplementary exercise should be designed to enrich understanding and to increase skill. It may include slightly different slants on some of the ideas in the recently completed unit of work. It may be done independently by the average learners since it will contain no new learning steps.

The following is taken from a supplementary exercise which was used after the completion of an introductory unit on fractions. This exercise was used in Grade Five.

1. Draw a line 2 inches long. Draw a line one-fourth as long as the 2-inch line. Draw another line one-eighth as long as the 2-inch line. How long is each line?
2. If each piece is one-eighth of a pie, how many pieces can Ida get from 2 pies?
3. Which part would you rather have:
   a. $\frac{1}{6}$ or $\frac{1}{4}$ of a melon?
   b. $\frac{1}{3}$ or $\frac{1}{8}$ of a cake?
   c. $\frac{1}{2}$ or $\frac{3}{4}$ of a dollar?
   d. $\frac{1}{4}$ or $\frac{1}{5}$ of a candy bar?
   e. $\frac{3}{4}$ or $\frac{5}{8}$ of an apple?
4. Four of the following fractions are equal in value. Write these four fractions.

$$\frac{3}{9} \quad \frac{7}{12} \quad \frac{2}{6} \quad \frac{7}{15} \quad \frac{8}{10} \quad \frac{1}{3} \quad \frac{4}{5} \quad \frac{4}{12}$$

Those Who Excel

A gifted child who quickly masters some mathematical idea or the technique of some process should not be forced to continue working at that level but should move on to a higher and more challenging level. This will kindle further interest in arithmetic as mathematics and lead to a sense of satisfaction instead of one of frustration. The school program should stimulate rather than hinder the intellectual growth and development of gifted children.

The special arithmetic materials which are provided for those who excel should conform to the following standards.

1. The materials should be specially planned for the superior group. They should not be merely more of the same thing. They should be related to what others have

but should require a higher level of thinking and performance. They should not consist of what others will
have when in the next school grade. Grouping in depth
is not mere acceleration so far as the superior members
of the class are concerned.

2. The concept should be *thrill,* not *drill.* The materials
should be new and challenging.

3. The materials should add to insight and understanding.
All pupils should understand what they are doing as they
learn arithmetic but there are degrees of understanding.
Gifted pupils should rise to higher levels of comprehension
than can be expected of others. It is a mistake to expect
every pupil to understand fully all that is involved in every
elementary mathematical situation or operation but gifted
pupils can go farther than can the others; they can rise
to higher levels of comprehension.

4. The materials should be useful and of permanent value.
Puzzle problems, trick exercises, and the like belong in
the area of mathematical recreations. Most crossnumber
puzzles, which resemble crossword puzzles, belong in the
same category. There is no objection to the use of such
items by those who enjoy them but the supplementary
arithmetic program for those who excel should be composed of useful rather than useless materials.

5. The materials should be prepared so as to make provision
for individual differences, which exist even among those
who excel. Gifted children are not all equally gifted. In
fact, the abilities of the gifted spread over a rather wide
range. This means that not all of those who excel should
be expected to do all of the exercises which are provided
for that group. Each of these pupils should be encouraged
to go as far as he can but the teacher should recognize
that they cannot all go equally far.

6. Emphasis should be placed on so-called "mental arithmetic." Of course, all arithmetic is mental but this term

is used here to indicate that superior pupils should do more of their arithmetic "in their heads" and should depend less on the use of pencil and paper.

It is not suggested that all six of the standards which have been stated should apply to every special exercise which is prepared for those who excel. However, the total group of such exercises should reflect all six of the standards and no exercise should fail to reflect one or more of the standards.

The exercises which follow are a few of many which have been used in schools. These exercises are mere samples and are presented as illustrations of some of the kinds which may be used advantageously and not as an outline of a complete program. These exercises are presented on a grade-by-grade basis although it will be obvious that many of them can be used in the next lower or the next higher grade. It will also be obvious that several of them can be modified slightly to make them more difficult, and thus they will be appropriate for a higher grade level.

Grade Three. All third-grade pupils learn to supply answers for addition and subtraction facts by responding to such items as the following: $\begin{array}{r} 2 \\ +4 \\ \hline ? \end{array}$ $\begin{array}{r} 7 \\ -3 \\ \hline ? \end{array}$. Variations for those who excel include the following: $\begin{array}{r} 2 \\ +? \\ \hline 6 \end{array}$ $\begin{array}{r} 7 \\ -? \\ \hline 4 \end{array}$. Later, a similar plan may be used with addition and subtraction examples in which two-figure numbers appear.

All third-grade pupils learn about place value in numbers. They learn about ones' place, tens' place, and hundreds' place. They learn that the number 246, for example, means 2 hundreds, 4 tens, and 6 ones. Now, those who excel may also see that 246 means 24 tens and 6 ones; or 2 hundreds, and 46 ones; or 246 ones. Likewise, the money number $2.46 means 2 dollars, 4 dimes, and 6 cents or pennies. It may also mean

24 dimes and 6 pennies; or 2 dollars and 46 pennies; or 246 pennies.

The more able third-grade pupils learn to add or subtract certain two-figure numbers by adding or subtracting both columns simultaneously, rather than one column at a time. This is easiest for two-figure numbers ending in zero. For example, when they see $+\underline{40}^{20}$, or $20 + 40$, they think at once, "20 and 40 are 60." They do not think of writing a 0 in ones' place in the sum and then adding 2 and 4. Likewise, when they see $-\underline{40}^{60}$, they think at once, "40 from 60 is 20."

Later, they react in a similar way to such examples as $+\underline{30}^{42}$ and $+\underline{32}^{40}$. They think at once, "42 and 30 are 72" and "40 and 32 are 72." This is not easy when first attempted, even for those who excel. However, many of the more able pupils get on to what is required rather quickly. For them, seeing the sum of 42 and 30 is almost as easy as seeing the sum of 4 and 3. Likewise, when they see such subtraction examples as $-\underline{40}^{62}$ and $-\underline{42}^{62}$, they learn to think simply, "40 from 62 is 22" and "42 from 62 is 20."

After a few of the easier multiplication and division facts have been learned, such exercises as the following may be used.

"You know that $6 \div 2 = 3$. What is $60 \div 2$? $600 \div 2$?"

Our final illustration is a good example of how third-grade pupils can be led to exercise their ingenuity and do original thinking in a quantitative situation:

"You can pay for a 15-cent toy with a dime and a nickel or with a dime and five pennies. There are four other ways to pay for a 15-cent toy. What are they? Draw pictures of the coins to show each of the four ways." Pictures may be supplied to the pupils to illustrate the two ways which are stated.

It should be added that the teacher who undertakes to make exercises similar to the last one must be careful to avoid making them too difficult. For example, there are thirteen ways to pay for a toy costing 25 cents. Thinking of all of these ways is too difficult for pupils in the lower grades, even for those who excel. There are nine ways to pay for a toy costing 20 cents. It seems best to restrict such exercises to articles costing less than 20 cents. This means that the number of ways to pay for the article will never be greater than six.

Grade Four. The reader is reminded that items which are appropriate for Grade Three may also be appropriate for Grade Four. At least, it is true that items similar to those used in Grade Three can be used in Grade Four. Ordinarily, there should be a slight increase in difficulty.

Furthermore, the skills which we are trying to develop are cumulative. Of course, they will not be cumulative if they are not maintained. The exercises planned for each grade level, then, should be designed so as to maintain skills already developed and also to raise these skills to higher levels. For example, the more able pupils in Grade Four should continue to add two columns at a time if no carrying is involved, and should gradually increase the length of the columns. A few may be able to find the sum for the example shown here, in this manner. They would make two steps out of the last addition. These pupils would respond as follows: "23 and 30 are 53; and 10 are 63; and 20 are 83; and 4 are 87." Note that the 24 is added by adding the 20 first and then the 4. The sum, 87, is written from left to right, not in the usual manner of right to left.

$$\begin{array}{r} 23 \\ 30 \\ 10 \\ \underline{24} \end{array}$$

Two three-figure numbers are handled in a similar way. Thus, the pupil writes the sums for these examples at once, from left to right. A quick look tells him that no carrying is required in these examples and that it is not necessary for him to begin at the right and find the sum column by column.

$$\begin{array}{r} 640 \\ \underline{200} \end{array} \qquad \begin{array}{r} 700 \\ \underline{250} \end{array}$$

Subtraction examples are to be handled in the same way if no minuend changes are necessary. Thus, if the first example above were a subtraction example, the pupil would write the remainder, 440, at once, from left to right.

Fourth-grade pupils learn to distinguish at a glance between examples which they can handle in this manner and those which should be worked step by step in the usual manner, from right to left. The example shown here, for instance, should be worked in the conventional way, whether it is an addition example or a subtraction example.

$$\begin{array}{r} 396 \\ 247 \\ \hline \end{array}$$

There should be considerable experience in rounding numbers, especially numbers which represent prices, as a first step in estimating answers. Suppose, for example, that one article costs $7.10 and another $5.95. Since these amounts are approximately $7 and $6 respectively, the pupils learn to see at once that the sum is about $13. Also, they should not be surprised to find that the difference is only a little more than $1.

$$\begin{array}{r} \$7.10 \\ 5.95 \\ \hline \end{array}$$

Later they will learn to make the necessary adjustments mentally and write the sum $13.05, or the difference, $1.15, at once, from left to right.

The skill which we are describing is a useful one. It often happens that one would like to know the sum of two or more numbers, or the difference between two numbers, without writing either the numbers or the answer. In a store, for example, prices are displayed and we wish to find the total cost of two or more items but do not find it convenient to copy the numbers. Those who are highly competent in arithmetic can do this for almost any prices. Of course, at fourth-grade level, we present only the easier examples.

Multiplication and division examples, similar to those suggested for Grade Three, can also be used in Grade Four.

Fourth-grade pupils who excel can learn ingenious ways to find answers even though the arithmetic involved may seem at first to be something which they have not yet been taught.

For example, Will knows that rolls of film cost $.41 each

and that $2.05 was spent. He wants to know how many rolls were bought. Naturally, he would at once think of dividing $2.05 by $.41 but he has had no experience in dividing by two-figure numbers. (That will come in Grade Five.) There are two ways to solve this problem besides dividing $2.05 by $.41.

Will can think: If I divide $2.05 by the number of rolls of film, the answer will be $.41. By what number should I divide $2.05 to get $.41? Ignoring the dollar sign and the point, he sees that if he divides 20 and 5 by 5, the quotient figures would be 4 and 1. Then the number of rolls of film is 5. As a check, he multiplies $.41 by 5.

$$\begin{array}{r} \$.41 \\ \hline ?)\$2.05 \end{array}$$

Or, Will can think: If I multiply $.41 by the number of rolls of film, the answer will be $2.05. By what number should I multiply $.41 to get $2.05? He sees that if he multiplies the 1 and the 4 of $.41 by 5, the product will be $2.05.

$$\begin{array}{r} \$\ .41 \\ \times\ \ \ ? \\ \hline \$2.05 \end{array}$$

Such exercises help develop the ability to see a problem situation from two or more points of view. This is a useful skill in many of the problem situations which occur in the everyday experiences of life.

Many interesting problems can be built around the calendar. One, which has been found appropriate for Grade Four, may be described as follows. We write the names of the months in a column and after each the number of days. Then we divide the number of days in each month by 7 to discover how many weeks and how many extra days there are in that month. We discover that the number of weeks is always 4 and that the number of extra days is 0, 2, or 3. (It is assumed that the year is not a leap year.) Then we add. We get a total of 365 days, 48 weeks, and 29 extra days. We divide the 29 extra days by 7 and get 4 more weeks with 1 day left over. Adding the 4 weeks and 1 day to the 48 weeks, we find that there are 52 weeks and 1 day in a year. In a leap year, of course, there are 52 weeks and 2 days. The work appears as follows:

Jan.	$31 \div 7 =$	4 weeks $+$	3 days
Feb.	$28 \div 7 =$	4 weeks $+$	0 days
Mar.	$31 \div 7 =$	4 weeks $+$	3 days
Apr.	$30 \div 7 =$	4 weeks $+$	2 days
May	$31 \div 7 =$	4 weeks $+$	3 days
June	$30 \div 7 =$	4 weeks $+$	2 days
July	$31 \div 7 =$	4 weeks $+$	3 days
Aug.	$31 \div 7 =$	4 weeks $+$	3 days
Sept.	$30 \div 7 =$	4 weeks $+$	2 days
Oct.	$31 \div 7 =$	4 weeks $+$	3 days
Nov.	$30 \div 7 =$	4 weeks $+$	2 days
Dec.	$31 \div 7 =$	4 weeks $+$	3 days
Total	365 $=$	48 weeks $+$	29 days
	$29 \div 7 =$	4 weeks $+$	1 day
		52 weeks $+$	1 day

Finally, we divide 365 by 7 and again get 52 with a remainder of 1.

Grade Five. In addition to exercises which have been suggested for Grade Four and others similar to them, but more difficult, certain exercises seem to be especially appropriate for Grade Five. We must remember that as gifted children mature, they experience a greater growth in mental age in a year's time than do average children. A child with an IQ of 125, for example, presumably experiences an increase in mental age of 15 months (1.25×12) in a year, whereas a child with an IQ of 100 presumably experiences an increase in mental age of 12 months in a year. This means that gifted children move farther and farther ahead of average children as the years go by.

Exercises dealing with money can be constructed to test the ingenuity of these pupils. The following are samples.

1. What is the smallest possible number of ten-dollar bills and one-dollar bills that will make $364? (answer: 40; 36 tens and 4 ones)
2. A man cashed a check for $225 and received 16 bills. What were they? (answer: 11 twenties and 5 ones)

3. A man cashed a check for $225 and received 12 bills. What were they? (answer: 1 fifty, 8 twenties, and 3 fives)

It should be noted that the pupils may supply more than one answer for such a problem. We have given the most obvious answer for Problem 2 but the following answers are just as good although not so obvious: 1 fifty, 8 twenties, 2 fives, 5 ones; 2 fifties, 3 twenties, 6 tens, 5 ones. Another answer for Problem 3 is: 2 fifties, 5 twenties, 5 fives. Of course, any correct answer is acceptable. Any pupil should be complimented if he is able to devise more than one correct answer.

We have said that special exercises provided for those who excel should develop useful skills. The foregoing exercises with money are less useful than some but they place such a premium on ingenuity and quick perception of number sizes and relationships that their net contribution is worthwhile. Some pupils find such exercises very intriguing but no pupil should be forced to work on them if they do not interest him.

The more able fifth-grade pupils not only round numbers as a means of estimating answers but also proceed to make the necessary adjustments in order to obtain exact answers. Illustrations follow.

1. Add 19 to 54 by adding 20 and subtracting 1. Thus $54 + 19 = 54 + 20 - 1 = 74 - 1 = 73$.

2. Add such popular price amounts as $5.95 and $3.98 by adding $6.00 and $4.00 and then subtracting $5¢ + 2¢$. Thus, $5.95 + $3.98 = $10.00 - $.07 = $9.93.

3. Find the amount of change due from a 20-dollar bill after making a purchase of $12.95 by subtracting $13.00 from $20.00 and then adding 5¢. Thus, $20.00 - $12.95 = $7.00 + $.05 = $7.05.

4. Find the cost of 3 items at $2.95 each by multiplying $3.00 by 3 and then subtracting 15¢ ($3 \times 5¢$). Thus, $3 \times $2.95 = $9.00 - $.15 = $8.85.

5. Multiply 45¢ by 6 by multiplying 40¢ by 6 and 5¢ by 6 and then adding. Thus, $6 \times $.45 = 6 \times $.40 + 6 \times $.05 =$

$2.40 + $.30 = $2.70. Or, find the product by multiplying 50¢ by 6 and then subtracting 6×5¢.

Gifted fifth-grade pupils learn to generalize certain relations existing in division examples. Illustrations follow.

1. If you double the dividend but do not change the divisor, what happens to the size of the quotient?
2. If you double the divisor but do not change the dividend, what happens to the size of the quotient?
3. If you double both the dividend and the divisor, what happens to the size of the quotient?

Similar questions can refer to making the dividend or the divisor or both three times as large or one-half as large, and so forth.

Some superior children find such questions very difficult at first. It should be suggested that they experiment with specific numbers if necessary. Of course, they are not working out mathematical proofs of the relationships stated; they are merely forming empirical conclusions as to their correctness.

Short cuts which can be used in working certain types of examples in fractions have been mentioned on an earlier page. Some of these are very appropriate for Grade Five. They will be discussed for both Grade Five and Grade Six in the suggestions for Grade Six which follow.

Grade Six. On an earlier page, we used the addition example $2\frac{3}{4}$ $3\frac{1}{2}$ to illustrate the different levels of attainment that might be reached by the slower learners, the average learners, and those who excel. We suggested that the more able pupils could develop the ability to do all of the computation steps mentally and would write only the sum in final form and write it from left to right. Such pupils would mentally change $\frac{1}{2}$ to $\frac{2}{4}$ but would not write the $\frac{2}{4}$. They would add $\frac{3}{4}$ and $\frac{2}{4}$, think of the sum $\frac{5}{4}$ as $1\frac{1}{4}$, and quickly see that the final answer is $6\frac{1}{4}$. This example and others like it have been used successfully in Grade Five.

This short cut should first be undertaken with examples requiring the addition (or subtraction) of like fractions. So far as addition is concerned, these fall into the following groups.

1. Those whose sums require no reduction. Example A below is an illustration.
2. Those whose sums have fractions which must be reduced to lower terms. Example B is an illustration.
3. Those whose sums contain improper fractions which cannot be reduced to lower terms but which must be changed to mixed numbers or whole numbers. Examples C and D are illustrations. The sum for Example C is a mixed number while the sum for Example D is a whole number.
4. Those whose sums contain improper fractions which can be reduced to lower terms as well as changed to mixed numbers. Example E is an illustration.

A	B	C	D	E
$3\frac{1}{3}$	$2\frac{1}{4}$	$7\frac{3}{5}$	$4\frac{1}{2}$	$1\frac{7}{8}$
$4\frac{1}{3}$	$3\frac{1}{4}$	$1\frac{4}{5}$	$3\frac{1}{2}$	$2\frac{3}{8}$
$7\frac{2}{3}$	$5\frac{1}{2}$	$9\frac{2}{5}$	8	$4\frac{1}{4}$

Of course, Example A does not represent a step-up at all. It is included merely to illustrate the first of a series of learning steps. As previously indicated, average learners should learn to do mentally the easy reduction step required by Example B. The better members of the average group may also learn to do Example C and Example D. Example E illustrates the step forward which may be expected from those who excel. It is appropriate for Grade Five.

The simplest examples containing unlike fractions are those in which one of the denominators is the least common denominator. Our example $\frac{2\frac{3}{4}}{3\frac{1}{2}}$ is one of these. An easier example of this type is $\frac{2\frac{1}{4}}{3\frac{1}{2}}$. It is easier because the sum of the fractions is a proper fraction. In neither of these does the fraction part of the sum have to be reduced to lower terms. Examples F, G, H, and I below illustrate four types which should be used. It will be seen that Example F requires no reduction, Example G requires reduction to lower terms, Example H requires changing to a mixed number, and Example I requires reduction to lower terms and changing to a mixed number.

F	G	H	I
$3\frac{1}{8}$	$1\frac{1}{3}$	$5\frac{7}{8}$	$2\frac{5}{6}$
$1\frac{1}{4}$	$4\frac{1}{6}$	$2\frac{3}{4}$	$4\frac{1}{2}$
$4\frac{3}{8}$	$5\frac{1}{2}$	$8\frac{5}{8}$	$7\frac{1}{3}$

All of the foregoing examples are suitable for Grade Five. Those which follow are, in general, more difficult. The teacher may decide that some of them can be used in Grade Five and others in Grade Six or Grade Seven. What can be done satisfactorily depends upon the ability of the pupils and the progress they have made.

As least common denominators become larger, the examples become more difficult. This is true whether the least common denominator is the product of the given denominators or a number smaller than their product.

Halves and thirds present little difficulty. The only possible fraction combinations are $\frac{1}{2} + \frac{1}{3}$ and $\frac{1}{2} + \frac{2}{3}$. In the first case, the sum is a proper fraction and in the second an improper fraction. These can easily be used in Grades Five and Six.

The following examples contain all possible combinations of thirds and fourths, fourths and sixths, and sixths and eighths. In the second and third of these three groups, it will be seen that the least common denominator is a number smaller than the product of the given denominators. It is understood that no examples should contain reducible fractions. Such an example as $3\frac{2}{4}$ over $2\frac{2}{3}$ is unreal. If it appeared in a real-life experience it would appear as $3\frac{1}{2}$ over $2\frac{2}{3}$. Therefore, when we refer to "all possible combinations of thirds and fourths," we refer to $\frac{1}{3} + \frac{1}{4}$, $\frac{1}{3} + \frac{3}{4}$, $\frac{2}{3} + \frac{1}{4}$, and $\frac{2}{3} + \frac{3}{4}$.

	a	b	c	d
1.	$1\frac{1}{3}$	$3\frac{1}{3}$	$2\frac{2}{3}$	$4\frac{2}{3}$
	$2\frac{1}{4}$	$2\frac{3}{4}$	$1\frac{1}{4}$	$2\frac{3}{4}$
	$3\frac{7}{12}$	$6\frac{1}{12}$	$3\frac{11}{12}$	$7\frac{5}{12}$
2.	$2\frac{1}{4}$	$5\frac{1}{4}$	$1\frac{3}{4}$	$3\frac{3}{4}$
	$1\frac{1}{6}$	$2\frac{5}{6}$	$2\frac{1}{6}$	$3\frac{5}{6}$
	$3\frac{5}{12}$	$8\frac{1}{12}$	$3\frac{11}{12}$	$7\frac{7}{12}$
3.	$3\frac{1}{6}$	$5\frac{1}{6}$	$4\frac{1}{6}$	$6\frac{1}{6}$
	$1\frac{3}{8}$	$2\frac{3}{8}$	$3\frac{5}{8}$	$4\frac{7}{8}$
	$4\frac{7}{24}$	$7\frac{13}{24}$	$7\frac{19}{24}$	$11\frac{1}{24}$
4.	$1\frac{5}{6}$	$2\frac{5}{6}$	$1\frac{5}{6}$	$3\frac{5}{6}$
	$1\frac{1}{8}$	$1\frac{3}{8}$	$2\frac{5}{8}$	$3\frac{7}{8}$
	$2\frac{23}{24}$	$4\frac{5}{24}$	$4\frac{11}{24}$	$7\frac{17}{24}$

Probably, the examples in Rows 1 and 2 can be used satisfactorily in Grade Six. In each row, Examples b and d are more difficult than Examples a and c because the former yield improper fractions in the sums. The most able sixth-grade pupils probably can do all of the examples in Row 3 mentally. Only one, 3d, yields an improper fraction and this fraction, $\frac{25}{24}$, is not very hard to change to a mixed number. A few of the pupils may do Example 4a without much difficulty but the remaining three examples in Row 4 probably should not be undertaken at this grade level.

We are not taking the space to present similar details for subtraction. The types of examples resemble those already presented for addition. The most difficult examples, obviously, are those in which the fraction in the subtrahend is larger than the fraction in the minuend, especially when the least common denominator is fairly large. None of these should be assigned for Grade Five; a few may be assigned for Grade Six. Examples in which no minuend changes are required may be assigned for both Grade Five and Grade Six.

Certain exercises which are designed to develop a better understanding of large numbers are appropriate for Grade Six. Having read that a certain airplane costs $1,500,000, the pupils built up some understanding of what a large amount this is by answering such questions as the following.

1. A certain car costs $2500. What would 100 of these cars cost? $250,000 is what part of $1,000,000?
2. How much would 200 of these cars cost? $500,000 is what part of $1,000,000?
3. How much would 300 of these cars cost? $750,000 is what part of $1,000,000?
4. How much would 400 of these cars cost? Since 400 of these cars would cost $1,000,000, how many could be bought for $1,500,000, the price of one of these airplanes?

Many useful and interesting exercises can be made from calendar dates. Illustrations follow.

1. What date is 4 weeks after April 15? (Let the pupils use the calendar for April and May, if necessary.)
2. What date is 5 weeks after May 15? (Let the pupils use the calendar for May, but not the calendar for June.)
3. What date is 7 weeks after June 15? (Let the pupils use the June calendar but not that for July or August.)

The pupils will count forward by 7's. This is easy except when one goes over the end of the month. To do such an exercise satisfactorily, the pupils must recall immediately the number of days in the month and not through such a roundabout method as reciting a rhyme, "Thirty days hath September," and so forth. To get the date which is 1 week after April 29, they should quickly think: "1 day left in April; 6 more days needed to make a week; May 6."

Valuable exercises for the more able sixth-grade pupils may be prepared by using the scale of a map and having them calculate distances between points. They measure the distances on the map as accurately as they can and then multiply the number of miles represented by 1 inch by the number of inches. Because measurements are never exact, their answers will differ, but slight differences are to be expected. They can begin to understand a very important point, namely, that all measurements are approximate.

Grade Seven. The more able pupils at this grade level can develop skill in adding two columns simultaneously, as it were. In finding the sum for the example at the right, these pupils learn to respond as follows: "29, 49, 59, 63, 83, 91." Adding 20 to 29 "all at once" was in the program for these pupils when in Grade Three. Now they add 14 to 49 by adding the 10 first and then the 4. Likewise, they add 28 to 63 by adding the 20 first and then the 8. Adding upward as a check, these pupils think: "28, 38, 42, 62, 82, 91."

$$\begin{array}{r} 29 \\ 20 \\ 14 \\ 28 \\ \underline{91} \end{array}$$

The ability to add two-digit numbers in this manner is not only interesting because it is challenging but it is also useful. If we want to know the sum but cannot, or should not, write it, the usual way of adding may not be satisfactory. We sometimes find that we have forgotten the ones' figure in the sum by the time we find the sum for the tens' column.

Such examples become a little more difficult if the sum is more than 100. In this example, adding downward, the pupil thinks: "37, 77, 86, 106, 111, 121, 129." With a little practice, though, the more able seventh-grade pupils take such examples in stride.

$$\begin{array}{r} 37 \\ 49 \\ 25 \\ \underline{18} \end{array}$$

These pupils may also learn the well-known short cut for multiplying by 50 and 25. To multiply by 50, they multiply by 100 and then divide by 2. Thus, $50 \times 68 = 6800 \div 2 = 3400$. To multiply by 25, they multiply by 100 and then divide by 4. Thus, $25 \times 68 = 6800 \div 4 = 1700$. At first, the multiplicands should be even numbers; it is a little easier to multiply even numbers than odd numbers in this way because it is easier to divide an even number by 2 or 4 than to divide an odd number by 2 or 4. But odd numbers should also be used as multiplicands. Examples: $50 \times 37 = 3700 \div 2 = 1850$; $25 \times 37 = 3700 \div 4 = 925$.

The more able seventh-grade pupils can rise to higher levels of judgment in estimating quotient figures than can be expected of all pupils. In estimating the number of 48's in 297, for instance, most well-taught pupils would round 48 to 50 and estimate the quotient figure by thinking: "How many 5's are there in 29?" They would try 5 and have to make a correction after multiplying and subtracting. But those who excel can learn to think: "There are almost six 5's in 29; 48 is less than 50, so I'll try 6."

$$\begin{array}{r} 6 \\ 48\overline{)297} \\ 288 \\ \hline 9 \end{array}$$

Another new wrinkle in estimating quotient figures may be illustrated by the example at the right. Ordinarily, $6004\overline{)30000}$ when the divisor is a four-digit number, we round it to the nearest thousand, ignoring the third and fourth digits entirely. It is easily seen that 30,000 is equal to exactly 5 times 6000 but since the divisor is a little more than 6000, the quotient must be less than 5; it must be 4.

More light can be thrown on the "invert and multiply" rule in division of fractions for the more able seventh-grade pupils. We illustrate with the example: $4 \div \frac{2}{3} = ?$ Of course, we interpret this example according to the measurement idea of division. This example asks the question: "How many $\frac{2}{3}$'s are there in 4?"

First we draw 4 rectangles, as illustrated below. We divide each rectangle into thirds and shade two-thirds of each rectangle. We have four $\frac{2}{3}$'s plus four extra $\frac{1}{3}$'s. The four extra $\frac{1}{3}$'s make two more $\frac{2}{3}$'s. Then the number of $\frac{2}{3}$'s in 4 is $4 + 2$, or 6.

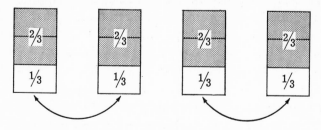

Now we take a different approach. We ask: "How many $\frac{1}{3}$'s are there in 4?" Since there are three $\frac{1}{3}$'s in 1, there must be four times as many in 4. Then the number of $\frac{1}{3}$'s in 4 is 4×3. Since $\frac{2}{3}$ is twice as much as $\frac{1}{3}$, there must be one-half as many $\frac{2}{3}$'s in 4 as there are $\frac{1}{3}$'s in 4. There are 4×3, or 12, $\frac{1}{3}$'s in 4. Then the number of $\frac{2}{3}$'s in 4 is one-half of 12, or 12 divided by 2, or 6. This agrees with what we discovered from the diagram. We took two steps:

First step   Second step

$4 \times 3 = 12$ $12 \div 2 = 6$

We can write these two steps together this way: $4 \div \frac{2}{3} = \dfrac{4 \times 3}{2} = 6$. Compare this with the "invert and multiply" rule: $4 \div \frac{2}{3} = 4 \times \frac{3}{2} = \dfrac{4 \times 3}{2} = 6$. It will be seen that what we have done is exactly the same as what we do when we use the "invert and multiply" rule.

Seventh-grade pupils who excel find it interesting to explore the mysteries of average rates. Suppose, for example, that two towns are 240 miles apart. We drive one-half of this distance at 40 miles per hour and then, on a turnpike, we drive the remaining one-half at 60 miles per hour. What is our average speed for the entire trip?

Most people think that the average of these two rates is simply $\dfrac{40 + 60}{2}$, or 50 miles per hour. It is easily shown, however, that this is not the case. Since we drove 120 miles at 40 miles per hour, the time required for the first half of the trip was 3 hours. Likewise, the time required for the second half of the trip was 2 hours. Then the entire trip of 240 miles was made at an average rate of 48 miles per hour, since $240 \div 5 = 48$. To find the average of two or more rates, then, we divide the total distance by the total time. We cannot apply to rates the conventional idea of an average. Later, when they study mathematics in college, these pupils may learn that the ordinary average is called the *arithmetic mean* and that the average of two or more rates is called the *harmonic mean*. At that time, they will learn another way to calculate an average rate.

Grade Eight. Further interesting ideas about averages may well be explored by the more able eighth-grade pupils. Here are the scores of 10 pupils on a test. The average is exactly 7. In the next column, we have set down the difference between each score and the average, using plus signs for those who are above the average and minus signs for those who are below the average. The sum of the plus differences is 7 and the sum of the minus differences is also 7 (or, rather, —7). This is a check on the

Scores	Differences
8	+1
6	−1
10	+3
7	0
9	+2
6	−1
8	+1
5	−2
6	−1
5	−2
10)70	0
7	

accuracy of our work. The sum of the differences from the average is always zero. In this case, $+7 - 7 = 0$.

If the division does not come out even and we round the average to the nearest whole number, the sum of the plus differences will not be exactly equal to the sum of the minus differences. The average of these seven scores, to the nearest whole number, is 86. The exact average is $85\frac{5}{7}$, or $\frac{2}{7}$ less than 86. Then the sum of the plus and minus differences should be —2, as indeed it is. The sum should be —2 because we

Scores	Differences
86	0
91	5
79	−7
83	−3
95	9
80	−6
86	0
7)600	−2
86	

used 2 extra points to make the average 86. If the sum of the scores had been 602, the average would have been exactly 86.

A short method for finding an average may now be introduced. We guess the average. In this case, suppose that we guess that the average is 8. Then we look at each score, note the difference between it and the guessed average, and mentally sum these differences as we go along. Beginning at the top of the column, we think, "minus 1" because the score 7 is 1 less than the guessed average, 8. Moving to the next score, we think, "plus 1" because the +2 which we get by comparing 10 with 8 combined with the —1 we already had makes

7
10
8
9
12
6
11
8

a total, so far, of +1. We look at the third score, 8, and again we think, "plus 1" because the difference between this score and the guessed average is zero. Proceeding, we look at the 9 and think, "plus 2." We look at the 12 and think, "plus 6." Then, for the last three scores, we think, "plus 4, plus 7, plus 7." This means that the sum of the plus differences is 7 greater than the sum of the minus differences. There are 8 scores, so we must spread the plus 7 over the 8 scores. The exact average, then, is $8 + \frac{7}{8}$, or $8\frac{7}{8}$.

If we had guessed that the average is 9, we would have moved down the column thinking, "minus 2, minus 1, minus 2, minus 2, plus 1, minus 2, zero, minus 1." The exact average, then is $9 - \frac{1}{8}$, or $8\frac{7}{8}$, as before.

Pupils develop considerable skill in finding averages by this method provided that the scores do not spread over a wide range. If the scores are widely spread, it is better to find the average by the ordinary method.

All pupils learn that multiplication is a short cut for addition. Eighth-grade pupils who excel may now see that we could find how much forty-two 57's are by addition, as shown in Example B. We know that ten 57's are 570. We write 570 four times to show forty 57's. Then we write 57 two times and add to find forty-two 57's. Multiplication is again seen as a short cut for addition.

A	B
57	570
42	570
114	570
228	570
2394	57
	57
	2394

Next, we show that division is a short cut for subtraction. To find how many 57's there are in 2394 by subtraction, we first subtract ten times 57 (570) as often as we can. (We would subtract 100×57 if it were possible to do so.) Then we subtract 57 as often as we can. In all, we subtracted 10×57 four times and 57 two times. In all, we subtract forty-two 57's. We found that there are forty-two 57's in 2394.

Fractions as small as sixty-fourths and their decimal equivalents are often used in ma-

$$
\begin{array}{r}
42 \\
57)\overline{2394} \\
228 \\
\hline
114 \\
114 \\
\hline
\end{array}
$$

2394
−570
1824
−570
1254
−570
684
−570
114
−57
57
−57

chine shops. Here we show the decimal equivalents of each of the sixty-fourths from $\frac{1}{64}$ to $\frac{8}{64}$, or $\frac{1}{8}$. The pupils devise various ways to find the decimal equivalent of $\frac{9}{64}$. It is $\frac{1}{8} + \frac{1}{64}$, or .125 + .015625, or .140625. It is also $\frac{7}{64} + \frac{1}{32}$, or $\frac{3}{32}$ + $\frac{3}{64}$, or $\frac{5}{64} + \frac{1}{16}$, or $9 \times \frac{1}{64}$, or $3 \times \frac{3}{64}$. Many similar exercises can be devised to find the decimal equivalent of $\frac{5}{32}$ ($\frac{10}{64}$), or any other number of sixty-fourths.

The subject of *tolerance* in measurements may be introduced. The pupils already know that no measurements are exact. For example, a bolt is to be 4.125 inches long and a tolerance of .012 inch is allowed. This means that any length from 4.113 inches to 4.137 inches is acceptable. We sometimes write $4.125'' \pm .012''$ to express the length desired and the tolerance allowed. We read this latter expression as follows: "4.125 inches plus or minus .012 inch."

$$\frac{1}{64} = .015625$$

$$\frac{1}{32} = .03125$$

$$\frac{3}{64} = .046875$$

$$\frac{1}{16} = .0625$$

$$\frac{5}{64} = 0.78125$$

$$\frac{3}{32} = .09375$$

$$\frac{7}{64} = .109375$$

$$\frac{1}{8} = .125$$

The 6% 60-day method of computing interest was at one time popular. One found the interest on a sum of money for 60 days at 6% by simply moving the decimal point two places to the left. Thus, the interest on $428.85 for 60 days at 6% is $4.2885, or $4.29. Since 60 days are one-sixth of a year, the rate for 60 days should be one-sixth of the rate for a year, or $\frac{1}{6}$ of 6%, or 1%. This method has declined in popularity because an interest rate of 6% is seldom found. When we move the decimal point two places to the left, we divide the principal by 100; that is, we find 1% of it.

The more able eighth-grade pupils may be interested in a 4% 90-day method and in a 3% 120-day method. Moving the decimal point in the principal two places to the left will give the interest for 90 days at 4% or for 120 days at 3%. The reason is similar to the one stated above for the 6% 60-day method.

Here is an interesting exercise to use in connection with the study of solids. A 3-inch cube is painted red and then cut into 1-inch cubes. How many of the 27 1-inch cubes have 3 red faces?

2 red faces? 1 red face? no red face? The accuracy of the answers can be checked by seeing if their sum is 27.

Those who find this exercise too difficult might work on a similar exercise involving a 2-inch cube. A drawing should lead them to see that all 8 of the 1-inch cubes in this case would have 3 red faces. In the case of the 3-inch cube, there are, of course, 8 smaller cubes with 3 red faces, 12 with 2 red faces, 6 with 1 red face, and 1 with no red face.

A more difficult exercise is one involving a 4-inch cube. In this case, there are, as always, 8 smaller cubes having 3 red faces (one for each corner), 24 having 2 red faces, 24 having 1 red face, and 8 having no red face. The total this time, of course, is 64.

There is another interesting check. In the case of the 4-inch cube, the 8 smaller cubes having 3 red faces would have a total of 24 square inches of painted surface. Likewise, the 24 having 2 red faces would have 48 square inches of painted surface, and the 24 having 1 red face would have 24 square inches. This makes a total of 96 square inches of painted surface. The total surface area of a 4-inch cube is, of course, $6 \times 4 \times 4$, or 96 square inches.

The better eighth-grade pupils should understand thoroughly the subject of relative differences as opposed to absolute differences. For example, Andy is 12 years of age and his grandfather is 60. Six years from now, Andy will be 18, and his grandfather will be 66. In that 6-year interval Andy's age will increase 50% but his grandfather's age will increase only 10%. Absolutely, the two increases are the same, of course; but, relatively, the increase in Andy's age is much greater than the increase in his grandfather's age, in fact, five times as great. And, incidentally, we can expect the change in Andy in that 6-year period to be much greater than the change in his grandfather.

If the price of a certain car is increased $50, we think of this as a small increase. That is, the increase is small relative to the original price of the car. But if the price of a vacuum sweeper is increased $50, we think of this as a large increase. It is large relative to the original price of the sweeper.

Concluding Statement

An effort has been made to describe briefly the grouping-in-depth plan for providing for individual differences among children as they are revealed in arithmetic. The suggestions offered for those who excel appear in more detail than for the average learners and the slower learners. The reason is the fact that those who excel are frequently the most seriously neglected pupils in a class. But even for those who excel, the suggestions made are brief and sketchy. It is hoped, though, that they will be useful and that they will suggest to the teacher other and related ideas.

The grouping-in-depth plan will not dispose of all of the teacher's problems. There will still be perplexing cases that require individual diagnosis and specialized treatment. It is believed, however, that no other plan so far proposed and tested comes as near to answering the teacher's question, "What can I do to provide for individual differences in arithmetic?"

11

Records, evaluation, and reports

NORMA E. CUTTS *and*
NICHOLAS MOSELEY

EVERYTHING YOU DO IN KEEPING RECORDS, EVALU-
ating progress, and making reports centers on your pupils as
individuals. You may and should use the various processes to
help you become a better teacher, but your primary purpose is
to help each pupil become a better person. Your opinions, of
course, will be helpful to later teachers, the child's parents, and,
above all, the child himself in planning his education and in the
choice of a career. But, because the elementary-school record is
rarely decisive in determining admission to college, you have
considerable leeway in such matters as marks and ratings. You
are relatively free to exercise your judgment about what to enter
in a child's record or to report to his parents. You may even be
able to experiment with the forms which records and reports
should take.

Streamlining Records

In theory, cumulative records are one of the most valuable instruments of evaluation and guidance.[1] Examination of hundreds of records convinces us that they are truly so *if* the records are well devised, fully kept, and conscientiously used. But we see schools where, despite good forms, the only entries are the results of one or two standardized achievement tests and group intelligence tests. In a six-room school we found one teacher meticulously making every required entry and, of his own volition, writing a brief report about each pupil which described interviews with parents, unusual incidents in the year, and the pupil's response to various methods of instruction. Another teacher's only entries were adverse comments on the characters of twelve of his twenty-six students; for example, "Watch this boy—he will steal your eyeteeth."

Cooperation is the key to good records. If you and all the other teachers in your school will discuss very frankly how you have used the available information and what information you have needed but not found, you will gain a new insight into record keeping and realize that it is worth the effort. You may also be able to eliminate some items and see how time can be saved in making entries under others. Your school administrators will welcome your conclusions.

A series of faculty meetings can well be devoted to a detailed evaluation of record forms. Each teacher should have a copy of the present official form and of another record form whose merit has been recognized, for example, that developed by the Educational Records Bureau.[2] Take up each item, beginning with those common to both forms. Have each teacher tell when and why he last used or wished he had had the information called for. Reference to specific pupils is essential if the discussion is to be so vivid and so convincing that you will always make the entry in question.

If none of you has ever used or seriously wanted the information called for, the item should be eliminated unless it is required by law or can be elaborated in a way that will make it useful. An opportunity for elimination may be found in the long list of character traits which many records contain and which each teacher is expected to check plus or minus.[3] If you discover that the opinions thus indicated for some of the traits have never helped any of you in working with a child, you can agree that you will all omit checking these particular traits in the future. You may also discover that you have not been using information about absences in prior years. A record of absences is probably a legal requirement. If the reason for the absence is entered, the record becomes more valuable. Consider the relative significance of a single day missed because of a cold and a day's truancy, of a three-month stay in a foster home in another town and a three-month trip to Europe.

Exceptional Facts

If you study record forms in the light of their use in specific cases, you will probably find that certain entries are much alike for all but one or two pupils in a class. For example, many forms have the item "Language spoken in the home." This is usually English. There is no point in taking time to write "English" on every child's form. But when a foreign language is spoken, the fact ought to be a matter of record because it might explain a difficulty or be useful in guidance or help the teacher locate a resource person.

There is much to recommend a policy of entering only exceptional facts, especially if unusual talents, accomplishments, and experiences are included in the exceptional. The entries may be made in the spaces provided on the form, for example under "Home influences," or on separate sheets of paper. Noting merely the exceptional is a great time saver. Moreover, because there are few entries, these carry more weight. They are not lost like needles in a haystack.

The same considerations apply to the keeping of anecdotal

records. The principal purpose of the anecdotal record is to provide data on personality development and behavioral changes.[4] We have no doubt that it does this better than any other means at your disposal. (See Chapter 2, pages 19-20.) But keeping anecdotal records for thirty pupils takes fifteen or more minutes a day, plus the time required to write periodic summaries. Moreover, both the records and the summaries tend to become so stereotyped as to be almost impersonal. On the other hand, objective descriptions of a series of unusual incidents offer important evidence of abilities or disabilities.

Many exceptional facts that a teacher or counselor or outside expert ought to know if a child is to be helped are confidential in nature. For example, facts about illegitimacy or parental difficulties should be available for professional use but safeguarded from the child or the curious gossiper of any age. Moreover, when a child has, for example, stolen something or been involved in sex play, there is no need for later teachers to know this unless the child shows a tendency to repeat the behavior. But if he does repeat, the earlier incidents are important. The solution of this problem is to have the principal keep records of such nature in a locked file in his office. When he thinks it necessary, he and the child's teacher go over the record at the beginning of the year so that the teacher can try to keep the child out of temptation. Usually the child is not a habitual offender, and the record will remain undisturbed until he leaves the school, and then be destroyed.

The ordinary record should be readily available to the classroom teacher, preferably in his own desk. The impulse to look up something in the record is often as momentary as it is sound. If the teacher has to wait until after school and then disturb the principal, the record generally goes unconsulted.

A Time Saver

Most record forms call for the information contained in reports sent parents. If only marks are included, copying them does not take long. But when written comments are used in place of or in addition to the marks, copying these may take quite an amount of time. This can be saved by making a carbon copy. A little extra pressure produces a legible copy of even a cardboard report, and carbon paper is cheap. Carbon copies of reports of health examinations, letters to parents, and the principal's notes of his interviews with parents are also often helpful. When parents return a report with written comments of their own that might help later teachers understand the child, it can be substituted for the carbon copy.

Continual Evaluation

You evaluate each pupil's status at the beginning of the year when you study his record. During the year you evaluate the progress he is making, and at the end of the year, the results he has achieved. In one sense of the word, "to express numerically," you evaluate any paper to which you give a mark. You evaluate not only a child's achievements in subject matter but the child as a personality. Expressions of opinion—"A nice youngster," "He tries hard," "Not very well adjusted"—are evaluations. And whenever you help a pupil consider his goals and his progress toward them, you are asking him to evaluate himself.

Taking this broad view of evaluation prevents a common mistake—the postponement of evaluation until the end of a unit, a term, or the year, when it is too late for you and your pupils to improve plans and increase effort. Evaluation should be a continuing process aimed at disclosing how a student has progressed in the past, what progress he is making, where he now stands, and what progress he should make in the future.

The Pupil's Part

When a pupil understands and accepts an objective, whether it is to do better in a subject, change an attitude, or do well in his part of a project, he profits from evaluating his own progress. In fact, evaluation of one's own progress is one of the best forms of motivation.

Most children need assistance in making realistic plans and in gauging their progress honestly. You can help a child by asking him questions that lead him to relate the here and now to the future and the past: What do you want to do when you grow up? Will you need to read to do that? Better than you do now? How long did it take you to read the last story? Is this story as good? Does it have more words you do not know? How are you finding out what they mean? How long do you think it will take you to read this story?

When pupils are old enough to write down their plans and to keep records of progress, there are many advantages in having them do so. Both you and they save time, and the written documents make convincing evidence for evaluation. Records for some subjects, such as spelling and arithmetic, may well be in the form of graphs of the number of correct responses made. Pupils enjoy keeping these, and an ascending line has a motivating force all its own. When the objective is a change in behavior, factual descriptions of the behavior to be avoided and that to be cultivated can be written down and the pupil encouraged to enter the dates on which he behaved one way or the other. He may even rate the behavior noted as severe or mild, excellent or fair. Another device is to have a pupil keep a diary. This may recount incidents bearing on one or several objectives, including subject-matter achievement, effort, and attitudes.

Group Judgments

Children, like their elders, are constantly evaluating each other. If you keep a rough record of the children's reactions to each other, you can tell whether a given child is improving or damaging his status with the group. Class choices of children for committees, for offices, for sides in a game, and for duties such as welcoming visitors give you good clues. When the activity involves reading or bookkeeping or public speaking, the children may pick a pupil you had not thought the best, and they may be right. You'll probably rotate offices and duties so that a few "born leaders" will not monopolize them, but if you allow free nomination you'll soon know the children's opinions of each other and whether or not these are changing. A child is aware of the opinions of his classmates, and he is extremely eager to stand well with them. If you have a record of incidents, you need not hesitate to discuss these with him. Then, if you listen, he'll evaluate his own actions and tell you how he should behave.

Rates of Progress

What to expect of an individual child is a perennial problem in evaluation. So many things beyond his control—intelligence, physical and mental health, family background—affect both his capacity to learn and his motivation that you may unwittingly set impossible goals and, when he fails to achieve them, evaluate him as a failure. The situation is the same whether the goal is academic or social. Even when your study of a child has given you much detailed information, you may be puzzled about how fast and how far he should go in any given time.

Other things being equal—which they never are—you obviously do not expect a slow child to progress as rapidly as a bright child. Here the IQ and the MA are rough but useful indicators. If the work to be done in a month or a year is about right for a child with an IQ of 100, a child with an IQ of 85 would theoretically be able to do 85 per cent of it, and one with an IQ of 125 a quarter more. However, the cumulative effects of slowness and brightness complicate matters. A child who does only 85 per cent of the work of each year is soon way behind.

The equation $CA \times IQ = MA$, when IQ is treated as a percentage, gives you an approximate MA. (There are some variations at different age levels. You can easily find a theoretically accurate MA from the tables in the test manual or in a book on tests and measurements.) A slow child's work may be judged satisfactory if he is doing as well as the average child whose chronological age matches the mental age of the child in question. For example, a child whose CA is 10 years (120 months) and whose IQ is 85 has an MA of 102 months, or 8 years 6 months. The average child who is chronologically 8 years 6 months old is in third or fourth grade. If the 10-year-old with an IQ of 85 is doing third- or fourth-grade work satisfactorily, you should not expect more of him even if he is in Grade V with most of his age mates.

The bright child, even if he has studied books ahead of his actual grade placement, will probably not work up to his "MA grade placement" because he lacks the necessary experience and social development. However, he ought to be well in advance of his CA.

When you add differences in background and adjustment to differences in intelligence, you can see that few, if any, children can be expected to learn exactly what a course of study prescribes for a certain month or to advance exactly one grade each ten months in their scores on standardized tests. The best you can do is to take each child where you find him and set up with him some immediate objectives that are challenging but appear to be within his capacity, and also some tentative long-range objectives. Show him how to evaluate his progress day by day, and evaluate it with him from time to time. Joint evaluation is especially advisable whenever, according to the schedule, he should have attained an immediate objective. Then you and he can readjust his program in conformity with your combined judgment of what is possible and desirable.

Determining what is reasonable progress toward better adjustment is more difficult still. Changes in behavior are almost always slow. When a child is deeply disturbed by some unaltering factor in his environment, he may feel compelled to continue behaving in undesirable ways. But if you accept him as he is, he may find in school a security that he treasures and may strive very hard to do what he knows he should. When you judge that he is succeeding, your praise will add to his security and enhance his desire to do better.

Achievement Tests

Many teachers and administrators think of standardized achievement tests as synonymous with evaluation. They take the grade norms as objectives (and sometimes the content of the test as a curriculum guide!) and are satisfied if the grade average shows an advance of the proper number of months since the last test was given. We have known cases where the tests were corrected by machine and the classroom teacher never saw the answers made by his pupils and did not even know each pupil's battery median. All the advantages of the test for evaluating individual progress and guiding individual pupils were lost. In contrast, the following cases show how sensitive teachers used standardized tests to help two pupils.

Jane Andrews, a second-grader, was 6 years 10 months old in October; her IQ was 120 (on an individual Binet test) and her MA, 8 years 2 months. She is a happy, attractive child from a good home. Along with the rest of her class she took the Stanford Achievement Test, Primary Battery, Form K, in October, and Form L in April. The national norms for a second grade are 2.1 in October and 2.7 in April. Jane's scores gave the following results:

	CA	Par. Mean.	Word Mean.	Av. Read.	Spell.	Arith. Reas.	Arith. Comp.	Av. Arith.	Bat. Med.
Oct.	6.10	2.4	2.1	2.3	1.6	1.9	2.5	2.2	2.1
Apr.	7.4	3.6	3.2	3.4	3.5	2.9	2.6	2.8	3.2
Gain	0.6	1.2	1.1	1.1	1.9	1.0	.1	.6	1.1

Already in October near grade level or above it in everything except spelling, Jane in six months made more than a full year's progress in everything except arithmetic. Her MA in April was about 8 years 9 months. If she had been chronologically this age, her scores, according to the test manual, should have been at the grade level 3.7. Her actual scores are about halfway between her real grade level and her MA grade level. The big advance in spelling reflects the hard work Jane and her teacher did on that subject. They had talked over the relatively low rating and set out to improve it. Jane worked hard on arithmetic, too, and was disappointed in her score. An examination of her answers showed that she had done correctly all the examples of the type contained in the book she had been using but had not gone beyond these. Her present teacher, her next year's teacher, and Jane have talked over the situation and made plans for Jane to try to travel faster and further in arithmetic next year. All agree that she can and should bring this up to the level of her other subjects.

Bruce Adams, a fourth-grade boy, was 9 years 7 months old in October, one of the oldest boys in his class. The cumulative record of test results shows that Bruce has never been quite up to grade. He had been given an Otis Quick-Scoring Mental Ability Test, Alpha A, when he was 8 years 7 months old. The IQ obtained at that time was 92, at the lower end of the average range and in line with his somewhat slow progress. His scores on a Stanford Achievement Test given in October showed him about six months behind the norms for the grade in most subjects, three years behind in Language, and at grade level only in Arithmetic Reasoning. His teacher felt that he was not making much progress and gave him another form of the Stanford Achievement Test in February. This showed an actual decline in Paragraph Meaning (from 3.8 to 3.4), and, though he had made some improvement in other subjects and good progress in Language (from 1.2 to 2.1), he was not up to grade level in any except Arithmetic Reasoning.

The teacher asked for a conference with Bruce's parents. They said frankly that they had almost no time for Bruce. He was born in their late thirties when they had not expected more children. His brother and sister are much older than he, and no one in the home was making any point of talking with

Bruce or sharing his activities. The parents agreed to arrange for a physical examination. This was given and disclosed no organic defects.

Bruce responded to the teacher's evident interest in him and not only tried to do better work but began to spend more time reading, because, as he told his teacher, "You read a lot." By April, when his CA was 10.1 and his MA approximately 9.3, test results showed that he had gained decidedly, especially in Language (from 2.1 to 3.8) and in Arithmetic Reasoning (from 4.4 to 5.3). He's up to grade level only in arithmetic. But, according to the Stanford Achievement Test Manual's table of "Age-Grade" couplets, his battery-median score is exactly what it would be if his CA matched his MA, and, except for the good score in Arithmetic Reasoning, the scores on the subtests vary very little from what would be expected.

Bruce is being promoted to Grade V, partly because of his age. The fifth-grade teacher is aware of his difficulties and of his need for affection and will continue to give him personal attention. He and his present teacher have made a list of library books that he would like to read this summer. The books are mainly easy ones about mechanical things. The teacher hopes they will show Bruce, who now thinks he wants to be an engineer, that there are interesting openings in mechanical work, which he might enter if he later finds that he cannot qualify for a college course in engineering.

Teacher-Made Tests

Whenever you ask a pupil a question or assign a set of arithmetic examples to be done or require a report, you are testing him. Moreover, a series of such informal tests offers excellent evidence for evaluating progress. But frequently you want to find out not how well a pupil is learning but what he has learned. And you want to find out specifically whether he has learned what you think he should have learned in your class—which may be quite different from the content on which any standardized test is based. At other times you'll want to see how well he can organize his knowledge or use it creatively as he works on a new problem. In these situations a test which you make out yourself will probably serve your purposes better than any standardized test would. Moreover, you can make as many tests as you wish and give them whenever you need to evaluate the progress of a pupil or your class as a whole, or when you need fresh information to reorganize groups or to plan units.

Another advantage of the teacher-made test is that you can adjust it to the levels of the pupils who are taking it and to the period which has elapsed since the last test. You can make separate short tests for different groups of pupils or make the test long enough to cover the range of abilities present. Frequently you can devise short tests that can be corrected very quickly, perhaps by the pupils themselves.

The methods of making objective tests and of preparing questions for the essay type of test, as well as ways of deciding which type is best for a given purpose, have been discussed by several authorities.[5] Here we have room for only a very brief consideration of the relative merits of the two types.

When you are mainly interested in the pupils' knowledge of content, an objective test, probably of the multiple-choice variety, is usually best. Formulating good questions takes time, but this is balanced by the ease of correcting and scoring. Each pupil should have a test blank, and this requires that the test be mimeographed or otherwise reduplicated.

When you wish to test the pupils' abilities to organize and apply knowledge, essay questions are preferable to objective tests. The essay question should be carefully formulated to serve your purpose, but it is relatively easy to work out, and the questions can be given to the class orally or written on the board. The answers represent the thinking of the pupil, not merely recognition of a fact—or a good guess. The drawbacks are the time required to read the answers and the difficulty of grading the answers in any way that lets you evaluate the relative achievement of all the members of your class. But if your purpose is to help individuals, the grading problem does not affect the value of the essay type of test.

The Purpose of Report Cards

Parents say, "We have a right to know how our child is doing in school." This is certainly correct, as far as it goes. The trouble is that parents ought to know not only how a child is doing, but also why he is doing well or poorly, how they can help him do still better, and how they can use their knowledge to guide the child into making realistic plans for his future education and a realistic choice of vocation. The sole purpose of a report is to help the parents work with the child.

When teachers, parents, and children keep this purpose firmly in mind, they can use almost any form of report as a constructive instrument of guidance. When the report is regarded by the teacher as merely another chore, by the child as a threat, and by the parents as a source of shame or pride, it may do more harm than good.

The Pupil and His Report

The first step in changing report cards from an emotionally charged recurrent crisis to a cooperative effort to improve each child's work and attitudes is to have a class discussion on the purpose, problems, and form of reporting. How well this works is shown by a child's paper from a set written for us by a summer-school class on "How I Feel When I Take My Report Card Home." The pupil writes:

My teacher last year was very understanding. She tried to make report cards a happy time. No one was afraid. And she always put a comment which enlightened the hearts of her children (pupils). So you see I have nothing to be unhappy about. I except the joys and sorrows of report cards. And take life as it comes.

Children have good ideas of their own about report cards—after all, they are the ones most concerned. If you can bring these ideas out in class, the chances are that they will be discussed at home too, and thus aid in creating a good mental set. For example, on the controversial question of cash rewards, one pupil writes:

I really don't think paying children a certain amount of money for every A is right because a child ought to be willing to work without getting paid for it. My and several of my friends' parents offered to pay us but we thought it wasn't right.

About marks, a child writes:

We have only one easy marker in our school, and it's pretty hard for the children in her room to go on to the next grade and pass from an A to a C though they may be trying harder.

Another pupil writes:

A report card is not something that the teachers try to scare you into doing more work, but to show your parents how you are doing in school. When my mother sees my report card she says that it is very good but says that I should do a little extra work in the subjects that were not as well done as other subjects. Usually my father enjoys seeing my report card. He says he's got something to be proud of and gives me a few problems in spelling and arithmetic and we discuss the news which has to do with Social Studies.

A personal talk with each pupil about his report is very worth while. Even a very brief conference gives you time to be sure he understands the meaning of the report and to make more suggestions than you could in pages of comments. The child's talk with you is a sort of rehearsal of what should happen at home. Give him a chance to express his opinions. If he has not done as well as he might in any subject, lead him to see how knowing more about that subject will help him in the future. A conscious connection of learning with use is a much better form of motivation than a mere desire to raise a mark. Plan with him how, between now and the next reporting date, he is going to keep up what the report says he does well and bring up what it says needs improvement. His specific suggestions as to what he can do at home and in school are much more efficacious than a vague generalization such as, "I ought to study harder."

A good method, especially in Grades IV-VI, is to have each child, before he confers with you, write a report himself. Have the pupils use the same form which goes to the parents. You can use this self-report as the basis of your conference. When a pupil overrates or underrates himself he gives you an excellent opportunity for guidance. In general, you'll find that most children are very frank and surprisingly correct in their statements. Here are some quotations from bright sixth-graders.

I've not done my best in any subject. I did not put my mind to it and fooled around too much.

Studying South America in Social Studies is new to me because I was studying Europe in the school I came from. Otherwise I've done all right in all subjects.

I have been working very hard to stay at the top of my class. Science is my hardest subject, and so I should spend more time studying it. I hope next year's science will be more interesting and that we will have more experiments.

At first I didn't work hard because I thought it would be easy. Then I realized it wasn't easy so I have been working harder.

Arithmetic has been quite easy but I have been careless. Social Studies has been a lot harder than I have been used to and I have done very well.

If you are free to experiment, you may wish to try using the reports which pupils write as the actual report to the home. You can add your own comments and thus let the parents know that you are not avoiding responsibility and that you do take a personal interest in the child. Both you and the pupil should include any suggestions for work at home and other kinds of out-of-school activities that might help his development. If each pupil uses a sheet of carbon paper, he can prepare his report in duplicate and take both sheets home. The parents can add their comments on one sheet and return it for the cumulative record, keeping the other.

Your talks with the individual pupil and the remarks which he volunteers in the class discussion will give you some inkling of how his parents are likely to react to his report card. If you suspect that a child will be undeservedly punished or unduly praised, make every effort to forestall such consequences. Even if the report form does not provide space for comment, you can write a note or telephone to the parent or seek an interview. Foresight and action on your part are particularly desirable when a slow child has tried hard but must be given low marks. Too often the home situation is like that of the pupil who wrote: "My mother knows just what will happen if my father sees my report. Sometimes I'm likely to get a beating." The usual result of such punishment is not improved work but a hatred of school.

Numerical and Letter Grades

Almost all parents prefer numerical or letter grades to any other form of report. But teachers are aware that a child who has been trying hard and still receives a low mark may quit trying. They also know that the bright child who automatically receives an A may be developing poor work habits and becoming dangerously overconfident. Various solutions to the marking problem have been suggested, including two marks in each subject, one based on straight achievement and the other on achievement in relation to effort and ability. Parents find this confusing. A single set based on effort and ability is dangerous, because the child and his parents may be seriously misled—for example, into giving up the idea of college for a lazy bright child or into encouraging professional ambition in a hard-working slow child.

When marks are given, even in the elementary school, the best practice seems to be to base them on straight achievement and to include opposite each mark comments on effort and progress. A three-point scale is easier to use than a four-point, and a four-point easier than a five-point. Parents who dislike H for honors, S for satisfactory, and U for unsatisfactory might accept the more traditional A, C, and D. Many schools have found that parents do not complain when a four-point scale, A, B, C, D, is used and the letters are explained as very good, good, fair, and poor. The letters E and F are to be avoided.

Parents sometimes interpret an E as "excellent" and an F as either "fair" or "failing."   •

A written comment opposite each mark increases the effectiveness of the report. One pupil writes: "Actually, I think there should be more room on our report card for the teacher's comments." Written comments impress parents more than check marks. "Tries hard" and "Improving" cushion the effect of a D for a slow child and win extra praise for the bright child's A. "Should do still better" requires an explanation from the child who has an A or B, and if you and he have agreed that he really should do better he is quite likely to be honest with his parents. The discrepancy between the mark and the comment may lead the parent to come to school and talk with you.

Ratings

Authorities disagree on the value of including ratings of traits on reports to parents.[6] Accurate ratings are notoriously difficult to make, even when the rater knows the person being rated as well as a teacher knows his pupils. On the one hand there are the human tendency to be lenient and the halo effect, on the other hand, the influence of prejudice and, perhaps unconscious, antagonism. Moreover, the cause of a difficulty which results in an unfavorable rating (for example, of honesty or control of temper or behavior) is quite likely to be found in the home. An unfavorable rating may cause parents to punish a child and thus aggravate his difficulties. It quite certainly strains home-school relations. But ratings offer a quick way for teachers to express their opinions of a pupil's strengths and weaknesses, and these opinions may be important evidence for sound personal, educational, and vocational guidance.

There are several ways to improve ratings. The traits—or habits and attitudes—to be rated should be few. Teachers should agree on descriptive statements of behavior which calls for satisfactory or unsatisfactory rating on each trait. Objective anecdotal records make the best basis for accurate judgment.

Whenever possible, several teachers should rate the same child at the same time. When a rating is unfavorable, every effort should be made to agree with the child and parents on a constructive continuing program for improvement.

The Parents' Part

Parents are so interested in report cards that it is generally easy to attract a good number of them to a meeting on the subject. Certainly any school system that is revising the form of its card should give the parents a part in the process.[7] If the parents will agree that the report ought to be a foundation for cooperative action by parents, child, and teacher, they might well adopt a procedure like the one advocated above for teachers working on records; a careful consideration of each possible item, with a review of how parents have actually used similar information to help their children, would be very revealing. The parents might even decide that the time teachers spend in making out reports had better be devoted to holding conferences with the parents and child.

In any case, you will find group conferences with the parents of your pupils useful for explaining the form of report you are using and for showing the parents some of the things they should and should not do when and after a child brings his card home. General discussion about report cards will lead parents to see the merit of ideas that they might not accept as suggestions from you. Topics for discussion include the purpose of the report cards, the role of parental praise, cash rewards, punishment, the desirability of homework, and the use of report cards in guidance. The problem of marks in relation to ability and effort is sure to come up, but if you are lucky you can play it down until you're sure the group is working well together.

The general meeting might well be followed by brief private conferences with each parent in which, out of your knowledge of the child and of the home situation, you can make specific suggestions about ways the parent can help. Be sure to emphasize the child's good points and show how these can be developed. For example, suggest that a good reader be encouraged to use the public library, a budding scientist to expand his collection, and a mechanic to set up a "shop" of his own. If a child needs help in a subject, explain the importance of a regular schedule and a quiet place for homework and how the parent can assist. Remember that if a young child reads to a parent for fifteen minutes each night, the parent gives him more individual attention in a week than you can in a month.

In talking with parents, you will find it very useful to show them successive samples of their child's work and to have at hand any records that he has kept for you. The concrete evidence that a child is very bright, or hard-working, or in need of help, is often the only means of convincing the parent that your evaluation is correct. Sometimes you will want to cite the results of standardized tests, but you'll be wise to use very general terms, like "bright," "average," and "did less well than most."

When you think that a report may be misunderstood at home and you cannot arrange for an interview with the parent in school time, consider the desirability of visiting the home in the evening, when you can talk with the father, the mother, and the child together. Not many teachers do this, but every teacher we know who has tried it is enthusiastic about the results. There is no surer way of showing your eagerness to help and of securing constructive cooperation.

NOTES

[1] Ruth Strang. *The Role of the Teacher in Personnel Work,* 4th ed. (New York: Bureau of Publications, Teachers College, Columbia University, 1953), pp. 393-409.

[2] *Cumulative Record Form for Independent Schools,* Educational Records Bureau, 21 Audubon Ave., New York 32, N.Y.

[3] John W. M. Rothney, *Evaluating and Reporting Pupil Progress,* What Research Says Series, No. 7 (Washington, D.C.: National Education Association, 1955), pp. 5-6.

[4] Arthur E. Traxler, *The Nature and Use of Anecdotal Records,* Educational

Records Supplementary Bulletin D, rev. (New York: Educational Records Bureau, 1949), p. 34.

[5] Robert L. Thorndike and Elizabeth Hagen, *Measurement and Evaluation in Psychology and Education* (New York: John Wiley & Sons, Inc., 1953), pp. 26-49.

[6] Dorothy Barclay, "Report Cards," *The New York Times Magazine*, October 12, 1958, pp. 56, 58.

[7] Rothney, *Evaluating and Reporting Pupil Progress*, pp. 16, 21; Thorndike and Hagen, *Measurement and Evaluation in Psychology and Education*, pp. 366-77; Traxler, *The Nature and Use of Anecdotal Records*, pp. 29-31.

12

Self-realization

NORMA E. CUTTS *and*
NICHOLAS MOSELEY

THE PREVIOUS CHAPTERS OF THIS BOOK HAVE considered how you as a teacher can determine a child's needs and help him develop his abilities. Special attention has been given to ways by which you can make sure that he will be well grounded in the principal subjects of the elementary-school curriculum and that he learns as much of each as he is able. This final chapter discusses how you can help the child become a well-adjusted, integrated person who fulfills his own best self. It applies and extends many principles implicit in the earlier part of the book.

The Teacher as a Friend

Your study of a child's record and achievement is barren if he does not come to regard you as a friend. If he finds you are a person to whom he likes to talk, he will reveal to you his true feelings in a way that breathes life into the facts accumulated in his folder. When he knows from experience that you always stand ready to help him, he will turn to you for guidance. He will want to do well because this is one way of pleasing you, of paying the debt he owes for your interest. He will, probably unconsciously, begin to imitate you, to try to be the kind of person you seem to him to be.

A great deal has been written about the kind of personality a teacher should have. Unfortunately, or fortunately, none of us can remold ourselves to a set of specifications. Changes in personality are very difficult to achieve. We cannot even control our feelings, but we can control our actions.

You may not like every child in your room. You may actually dislike those whose attitudes and behavior trouble you and the other children. But you can treat every child as a friend. You can listen when he talks. You can respect his ideas. You can recognize his good points and express your approval of those. You can be alert to his needs, material and more especially emotional, and quickly try to help him satisfy them.

Emotional Needs

All human beings need love, security, recognition, and new experiences, and we need to find them in all phases of our existence, in the home and in our work, in our inner life—our thoughts about ourselves—and in our association with other people. The vast majority of children have loving parents, feel secure in their home lives, and win recognition from parents and relatives. Children must, however, have their needs satisfied in school as well as in the home. Entering school is usually the child's first move away from the family toward the independence he must achieve within a few short years if he is to become a good parent himself. If he finds school a warm friendly place as he goes up through the elementary grades, he will gain self-confidence. If he is treated coldly in school, if he feels insecure and disliked, he may want to retreat. He may never become courageous enough to attain maturity. You should, therefore, consider your attitudes and your methods with a view to their emotional impact on your pupils.

The Happy Room

Take a look about your room. Is it as cheerful a place as you can make it?

Children, like adults, are susceptible to their physical surroundings. They respond gaily to brightness. You probably cannot repaint your room, but you can emblazon the walls with richly colored reproductions of famous pictures and a changing panorama of children's drawings. You can keep vases full of flowers or of red and yellow autumn leaves or of yellow marsh grasses. You can cover the library table with books and magazines open to display illustrations. You can, if you are a woman, dress decoratively, and, if you are a man, select your ties with care.

A well-arranged room invites children to new experiences. An abundant variety of books, exhibits of apparatus and collections, readily accessible art materials and musical instruments, and bulletin boards with clippings of current events stir the children's interests and make them eager to learn.

Your own temperament, or, rather, the way you yourself behave, sets the emotional tone of your room. If, when a child comes into the room, you smile at him, greet him by name, and exchange comments about the blizzard, he senses your personal interest. He feels that you like him and that he amounts to something in your eyes. When you can, share a joke and laugh with him, especially if the joke is on you. During the day, and day after day, try to keep in a good humor with individual pupils, with the class as a whole, and with yourself. But be quick to sense the children's moods, including the not-uncommon one of wanting to finish a job. And when you see that a child is having difficulty of any kind, think what you can do to help. If a child is becoming desperate because he can't get the answer to a problem, be ready at the right moment to show him what he is doing wrong. And you may earn everlasting gratitude by coming to the rescue with a piece of Kleenex when you see a child snuffling a nose drip.

Toward Self-Discipline

Only if you are a good disciplinarian will you and your pupils feel secure in the kind of room we have been describing. And only if they learn to discipline themselves will they be able to carry on the type of responsible independent work upon which provisions for individual differences depend. Paradoxically, self-discipline begins in firm consistent discipline by parents and teachers. Children who are well disciplined see that if they work for what they want they are more likely to get it than if they grab.

Essential to good discipline in the classroom is the teacher's ability to command the undivided attention of the group and their complete cooperation in carrying out a request. Moreover, each pupil and the group as a whole must know that misbehavior will not be tolerated. A child who fears he might go too far in trying out his independence may not be willing to go far enough.

In a room where children are responsible for their own behavior, the pupils keep themselves busy. A child who finishes what he is doing has in mind what he ought to do next, and proceeds to do it on his own initiative without dawdling or dreaming or plaguing his neighbor with questions or playing ticktacktoe. There is a good deal of movement as children go to shelves to look up references or fetch materials, but, as they come and go, the children do not interfere with each other's work. There is no idle questioning, no pushing a book from another's desk, and no tripping up of passers-by. Most of the time the children are free to talk to each other, subject always to the rule that there is no wanton interference with work. The rule does not preclude informal conversations between children about what they are doing. Committees and groups working together discuss and debate quietly. There is no angry shouting and no furtive whispering. Scheduled shifts from one subject to another and preparation for recess and dismissal are managed by the children themselves with a minimum of delay. When a visitor comes into the room, most of the children look up and smile at him, but there is no real interruption of work. If a child is serving as the official greeter of the day, he welcomes the stranger and asks if he wishes to speak to the teacher or if there is something special he wants to see or if he has just come to visit. In short, the children are interested in their work, cheerful, and courteous.

If you have trouble maintaining this type of informal order—as do many beginning teachers and teachers who have never before tried to be informal—here are a few rules of thumb that experienced teachers have found helpful.

Cultivate the art of giving directions. Wait until you have everyone's attention. Speak at your normal speed, not loudly but in a deep tone. Be positive—"Do this" is more effective than "Don't do that." Be sure you have been understood. Give the class an opportunity to ask questions and make suggestions.

Remember that children are trying out their ways of behaving. They naturally tend to see how far they can go. If they are used to being regimented by a martinet, they find general disorder an exciting adventure, even though they really prefer order. Therefore in the beginning it is wise to exercise firm control over the class. Stand where you can see the whole room, or circulate about it. Check the first sign of deliberate disorder or deliberate challenge to your authority. Usually the pupil will not continue if he knows you are aware that he was about to misbehave. Often all you need do is to smile at him or call him by name. But you should know what punishments you can use and be determined to use them if necessary.

When you think punishment is called for, act promptly. Don't waste time in warnings or scoldings or threats. Try to make the punishment fit the crime. Isolate the child who attacks others. Deprive a child of a privilege or possession which he abuses. If the offense was deliberate, make a child do over anything he has done wrong, clean up a mess, and repair or replace damaged property. But when you see that a mishap was really accidental, pitch in and help rectify matters.

Be consistent in what you forbid. If you permit disorder one day and are strict the next, the children do not know what to expect. They are tempted to take a chance. And they feel insecure.

Keep rules and regulations to the minimum necessary for the safe and efficient management of the room. Be sure the children understand the reason for every rule and sincerely agree that it is wise. Have them discuss the rules from time to time to see if any should be added or eliminated.

In brief, be friendly, firm, and consistent.

First Aid—The Withdrawing Child

If your classroom is a happy, secure place where the children feel free to talk together about their work, you ought to be concerned about a child who does not take an active part in the life of the room, one who is a chronic daydreamer or very timid or very shy. Daydreaming, timidity, and shyness are not in themselves bad. The daydreamer may be thinking great thoughts that someday he will really carry out in action. The timid person may be wisely cautious. The shy one may be the best of all friends, the friend who listens and never imposes. But a person may live so intensely and continuously in his dream world that he loses touch with reality, may be so fearful that he never dares depart from a fixed routine, so shy that he cannot consort with his fellows.

Excessive withdrawal is such an unfavorable symptom that one of your most important duties is to notice it and to take remedial action. Research has demonstrated that many, perhaps most, withdrawing children escape any special attention from their teachers. The quiet, shy dreamer is lost sight of in the busy crowd of his fellows. Teachers, questioned about mental patients of the withdrawing type whom they have had in class a few years previously, often fail to remember their names or recognize their pictures. One of the best arguments for deliberate and systematic observation of each pupil in your class is that you cannot be sure to discover the withdrawing child in any other way.

You can help the child with a tendency to withdraw if you slowly but surely build up his participation in the activities of the classroom. He should not be thrust suddenly into the limelight—he would be frightened and retreat still further. Make opportunities to talk with him alone. Try to discover his interests and give him a chance to work at these independently. Then try placing him with a small group who share an interest with him, and note if any friendly exchange develops. Praise him privately when you know he has contributed to a group's effort. When he shows that he is emerging from his shell, extend and expand his opportunities for more general participation in the projects and the games of the other children. But do not force matters. For example, give him a walk-on part in a play before you ask him to speak any lines. Wait until the child is thoroughly at home in one type of activity before you suggest another. In the meantime he may surprise you by losing his fears and self-consciousness and matter-of-factly doing everything the other children do.

When, despite your friendly attentions and encouragement, a child seems to be withdrawing further into himself or when he has great swings in mood, being overaggressive at one time and excessively withdrawing at another, do your best to see that he gets expert help either at a child-guidance clinic or from a psychiatrist in private practice. Early diagnosis and prompt, continuing care are even more important in the treatment of a mental illness than they are in treatment of a physical illness.

The Overaggressive Child

No matter how friendly a person you are and how good a disciplinarian, you will from time to time have an overaggressive child in your room—a child who simply won't stay in his seat, who constantly attacks other children and their possessions, and who impertinently defies your directions. You must somehow control a child of this type if the other pupils are to concentrate on their work. Control is particularly necessary if you are trying to help individual children. You can't very well work with a small group or a single child if there is a chronic aggressor in the room who breaks out every time your back is turned.

When you first discover that you have a pupil who will not cooperate, you will be tempted to punish each succeeding incident of misbehavior ever more severely. If he answers you back or if he attacks you physically, you may find it almost impossible to control your own angry reaction. Try to remember that the purpose of punishment is prevention. When a child repeats behavior for which he has been punished, the punishment has obviously failed. There is a slim chance that the punishment was not severe enough, but there is a greater chance that it aggravated the cause of the trouble.

Isolation is the best immediate action in the case of a child who continues to attack others. Getting the child out of the room—usually to the principal's office—gives you and the class some peace. It may also give the child a chance to regain his self-control, which he may be sorry to have lost.

Because a child does not really like the antagonism which his aggression causes, you may be able to prevent some incidents. Keeping a young child near you may give him the support he needs. An older child often knows how he feels just before he becomes unbearably restless. If he can recognize the symptoms, you may be able to trust him to leave the room of his own accord—perhaps to go out and run around the playground—and not come back until he is sure he can settle down.

The long-range treatment of overactivity—and of any aberrant behavior—starts with trying to find the cause. The first step is a thorough physical examination by a doctor who understands the behavior problem. Overactivity is sometimes caused by a brain injury or the aftereffects of an illness, for example scarlet fever. These causes are difficult to diagnose, because there is no outward bodily sign of the difficulty. If the cause is physical, the behavior is compulsive, literally beyond the child's control. His best hope is hospitalization.

Usually the overaggressive child is suffering from some form of frustration. Often a need for love, security, recognition, or new experiences has not been satisfied, and, though he may not know this, his attacks are attempts to gain what he lacks. For example, the "attention seeker," so well known in the lower grades, is very probably a child who has not earned recognition for anything done well but has found out that bad behavior compels the teacher and his classmates to notice him. Similarly, a child who feels unloved and insecure, perhaps because he comes from a cracked or broken home, may try to establish himself in the esteem of his fellows by outdoing them all in misbehavior. And almost every child enjoys as a new experience any challenge of authority. An attack on another child has the added excitement that most men find in combat. A child who has idle time on his hands, who is not busy and interested, may have a double thrill, first in concocting a plan of misbehavior and then in carrying it out.

Even when you do not know which of a child's needs are unsatisfied at home, you can try very hard to see that they are all satisfied in school. Befriend him despite his behavior. Search for something he does well that you can sincerely approve, and be generous with your praise. Plan ahead with him so that he feels sure of your continued interest. Help him make friends and find a secure place in the group. Direct his energies to worthwhile new experiences. Be sure he is kept busy with work that he can do and is interested in doing. This multiple effort on your part may bring complete recovery to the child and give him the emotional strength to overcome continuing bad conditions in his home.

Adapting Work to Ability

Schoolwork that is too hard for a child may cause either withdrawal or overaggression. The child who withdraws may simply quit trying and idle away his time until he is old enough to leave school, or he may retreat into a world of fantasy where he sees himself as the successful leader. The child who responds to failure aggressively is in better shape. He feels humiliated by his failure and sets out to prove that there are some things he can do that the other children can't or won't. If you lead him to direct the energy he expends in misbehavior into constructive work adapted to his ability and give him recognition for any progress he makes, he will cease to be a behavior problem. If he continues to fail, he may join a gang of delinquents, try to win their approval by dangerous escapades, and grow up to be a criminal.

All the effort you expend to provide for individual differences, to discover each child's abilities, needs, and interests and to plan his work in accord with these, will be repaid if you save a single child from eventual mental illness or delinquency.

Of course, work should be adapted to the abilities, needs, and interests of every child in your room, and not merely to the slow, nor yet the slow at one extreme and the gifted at the other. Your purpose is to help each of your pupils realize his own best self. This does not entail a complete program of individual instruction. There are minimum essentials in all the subjects of the elementary curriculum that practically all children can master. But the individual child should be encouraged to go as far as he can beyond the minimum and to see how he can apply all that he learns to the development of his emerging interests.

Guidance

Educational and, to some extent, vocational guidance may well begin as soon as a teacher is able to gauge the abilities of a child. The notion that guidance is not a function of the elementary school ignores the facts of education. The elementary school is the place where a child learns the fundamentals on which all later learning rests. More important, he learns here the attitudes toward education, the habits of study, and the habits of mind which will probably determine his future efforts to improve himself. Early guidance conduces to his best development in all of these respects.

Much has been said recently about the large number of boys and girls who fail to go to college though they are bright enough to profit from a college education. The surest way to correct this situation is for elementary-school teachers to plant the idea of college in the minds of bright children and their parents. This can be done in conferences with the child and his parents, in comments on report cards, and in class discussions. When a child has an interest, whether it is missiles or music, that can be best developed by higher education, the sooner he realizes this the better.

Good vocational guidance observes the principle that the final choice must rest with the individual. All that counselors can do is to help a person see the possible openings and to correlate his characteristics with those of people who have succeeded or failed in a given line of work or profession. If you follow this principle, you need have no hesitation in encouraging suitable ambitions in your young pupils. Many of the best teachers in our schools today made up their minds when they were children in the first or second grade that they wanted to be teachers and never wavered. Many leaders in other fields are, like Albert Schweitzer, carrying out plans they began to form in elementary school. Less-intellectual ambitions are equally worthy, provided only that they offer the child concerned full opportunity to use what abilities he has. An early ambition that gives way to another, or to a succession, not only does no harm but is in itself valuable because it gives the child a focal point for his efforts, an acknowledged reason for learning. So do all you can to discover and encourage a pupil's present interests and to help him develop new ones. When you see his parents, suggest that he be given space and equipment so that he can work at a hobby out of school. Let him work at it independently in school, or as part of a project to which he can make a special contribution, and give him a chance to explain it to the class. Put him in touch with friendly adults who are working in his field and will be willing to talk with him and show him what they are doing. And set him a good example by cultivating a hobby of your own. A vital interest is the key to good adjustment, for you as well as for him.

Motivation

One inevitably comes back to the fact that the more a child tries to learn the more he can learn. Therefore the major part of your work as a teacher concerns motivation. And because of the individual differences in children's abilities, interests, and goals, your efforts to be sure that each pupil is well motivated must take these differences into account.

The desire to learn is deeply rooted in all human beings. It is manifested in many ways. Endless curiosity prompts constant exploration through manipulation, looking, wandering, and wondering. The verbal "Why?" "Why?" "Why?" develops into hypothetical thoughts and mental trial and error, but the impulse to ask "What do you call it" "What's its proper name?" is never stilled.

Imitation is an early and continuing method of learning. Children naturally imitate first their parents and then teachers and other admired adults. They struggle to measure up to the expectations of their group of friends, as later they will try to conform to the mores of society. The fundamental need for recognition drives the child to achieve what parents, teachers, and the group expect, and to achieve both quickly and greatly in the effort to merit great praise. Quite early each child begins to adopt values and ideals. The desire to be like his mother, father, or teacher shifts to a desire to resemble an image for which he himself poses before his mind's eye. The features of loved adults are still present, but heroes from real life, from history, from fiction have added to its stature. To fulfill this ideal the child *imagines* himself achieving honored goals in admirable ways and then strives to make his dreams come true.

If you keep these three points in mind—that a child wants to learn, that he imitates, and that he can rise above imitation —you will gain insight into your role as a teacher. In brief, you channel his efforts to learn so that he is directed to goals you believe to be worth while, you set him a good example by your evident enthusiasm for the values which the goals represent—an enthusiasm that you express when you praise him for progress—and you help him set up new and challenging goals for himself.

The adaptation of work to ability is as important in good motivation as it is in avoidance of frustration. No matter how much a child—or adult—wants to achieve a goal, his strength of purpose will lag if he feels he is not making progress toward it. On the other hand, nothing succeeds like success. Practically, this means that you should know each child's level of ability and achievement, start him on work you are sure he can do, and gradually increase the difficulty of the work so that he is constantly challenged to do better and can see for himself that he is making progress. Progress is possible only when the objectives, immediate and remote, are realistic, that is, within attainment by the child. When a considerable period must elapse before an objective can be reached, a record that the child can keep for himself is an excellent means of sustaining motivation. But, because there are usually plateaus when little progress in learning is evident, it is important to praise continued effort as well as marked achievement. Then the child will understand that persistence earns recognition, and he will try harder and harder. Of course, the principles of starting a child within his range and of continually challenging him to progress apply not only to a slow child but to every child, each at his own particular level.

Expectation of use creates a good mental set for learning and promotes retention. A simple example is the way you listen to the name when you are introduced to a teacher new to your school and the ease with which you remember it. If you know each child's current interests and his goals, you can help him see the usefulness of learning and remembering the subject matter which he studies in school.

New and exciting experiences, like any situation that stirs the emotions, compel an attention that results in quick learning and generally in long retention. Often a movie, a book, a field trip, or the visit of a stranger will key up a whole class. But, because of differences in background and in what they have read, some children will already know, and so be bored by, materials which excite others. On this account, the classroom with a rich variety of equipment and of books which offer individual pupils fresh approaches to topics they have already covered, is far more efficacious than the one where only standard texts are available.

Good morale in the whole group has a direct effect on the learning and the adjustment of each member. Good morale thrives in a happy room and on common purposes, group self-confidence justified by achievement, and high standards. The group expects each individual to do his best to live up to its standards. It recognizes individual effort and achievement. The leader—you, as the teacher—sets standards, helps organize efforts, and praises accomplishment. When a child is not accepted by the group, you try to show him how he can contribute to the common goals and you arrange for members of the group to support his efforts.

Responsibility and Self-Realization

The well-adjusted, mature person feels secure in his human relationships and in his economic position. He knows what he wants to do with his life and what he must do if he is to fulfill his wishes. He is confident of success because his past experiences have given him a fair estimate of his own abilities. He persists in the face of difficulties, but he does not attempt the impossible. He manages his own affairs and makes his own decisions without undue worry and without seeking help or advice that he does not need. He conforms to the accepted standards of his community without losing his independence of opinion or action. His contributions to the group are in line with his abilities and may be greatest when they are original and unexpected. He enjoys working and playing with his family and his friends.

The elementary school is a principal training ground for maturity. If your pupils are to profit as much as they can, each must have opportunities to:

Win your approval and that of the group.

Succeed in his schoolwork by exerting persistent effort.

Evaluate his own progress and achievement.

Plan part of his own work and share with his classmates in planning work, play, and class management.

Work independently on projects of his own in connection both with his schoolwork and with his own special interests.

Contribute the results of independent effort and study to the projects of the group.

GENERAL REFERENCES

Cutts, Norma E., and Nicholas Moseley, *Practical School Discipline and Mental Hygiene*. Boston: Houghton Mifflin Company, 1941.

———, *Teaching the Disorderly Pupil in Elementary and Secondary School*. New York: Longmans, Green and Co., 1957.

Index

A

Ability:
  arithmetic, 205-207
  art, 98-99
  ascertaining, 13-32
  music, 105, 109-10, 124-25
  social studies, 153-54
  See also Achievement; Intelligence
Ability grouping. *See* Grouping
Acceleration, 74-76
Achievement:
  ascertaining, 15-32
  changes in, 3, 17, 54-57, 208
  and grouping, 37-39
  patterns of, 18
  range in, 2-3, 37-38, 55
  See also Evaluation; Records; Tests
Adjustment of child, 2, 15-16, 24, 26,
    31, 49, 124-25, 155, 241-42, 254-68
Age of admission to school, 63-65
Aggression, 261-63
Arithmetic, 57, 204-33
Art, 36, 57, 61-63, 79-103, 135
Audio-visual aids:
  art, 91, 102

Audio-visual aids (*cont.*):
  future, 51-52
  language arts, 56, 132, 134-35
  music, 106, 119, 126
  science, 192, 201
  social studies, 171
Automation, 51-52
Average pupils, 7, 37-38, 60-61, 175,
    205-208, 210-12 (*see also* Identi-
    fication; Intelligence; IQ; Men-
    tal age; Range; Tests)

B

Basal texts. *See* Texts
Books for children, 42, 56, 133-34, 165-
  66, 176-77, 192-93
Boys, interests of, 92-93, 114, 182
Bright child:
  acceleration of, 74
  arithmetic, 205-208, 213-33
  assignment to groups, 37-38, 174
  and basal texts, 41-43
  characteristics of, 11, 47-48
  evaluating achievement of, 240-42
  as helper, 51
  methods adapted to, 47-48

Bright child (*cont.*):
  out-of-school instruction for, 63
  science, 181
  social studies, 174
  See also Gifted child; Identification;
    Intelligence; IQ; Mental age;
    Range; Tests
Bruene, Elizabeth, 55

C

Center of interest, as topic, 141-42, 148
Class:
  discussions, 56, 93, 97-98, 135, 142-43,
    170, 187-91
  size, 70
  taught as whole, 5, 45, 157, 174, 186-
    91, 205
  See also Grouping
Classroom:
  equipment, 106, 133-34, 256
  tone, 256-57, 267
  See also Audio-visual aids; Books;
    Materials
College, age of admission to, 75-76
Conferences:
  case, 16
  with parents, 16, 31-32, 67, 108, 243-
    44, 251-52
  with pupils, 6-7, 16, 24-25, 26, 108,
    174, 247-49
  with teachers, 16, 18-19, 108
Crafts, 94-95, 99, 101
Creativity:
  art, 79-80, 87, 94, 97-98, 100
  language arts, 130, 137, 142, 145-48
  music, 124-25
Curriculum:
  adapted to abilities, 48, 59, 263
  arithmetic, 205
  and automation, 52
  following the, 5, 205
  language arts, 130, 132-33
  music, 106-107
  science, 180, 184-86, 187
  and texts, 41
  types of, 46
  See also Scheduling

D

Deafness, 17, 19, 31
Delinquency, 66-67

Depth of learning, 181, 205
Development:
  art, 80
  differences in, 2, 15-16, 109, 180-81
  language arts, 132, 136-37, 140
  music, 109, 110, 122, 123
  rate of, 180-81
  social, 15-16, 24, 49, 155
Diagnostic tests. *See* Tests, diagnostic
Diary of behavior, 20, 31 (*see also* Rec-
    ords, anecdotal)
Differences. *See* Identification; Range
Discipline, 257-58
Dolch, Edward William, 138
Dramatics, 46, 95, 135, 144
Drill, 39, 49, 141, 208-10, 213
Durrell, Donald D., 40

E

Educational Records Bureau, 235
Emotional adjustment, 15, 16, 31, 255-
    56
Enrichment. *See* Books; Independent
    work
Evaluation:
  methods of, 50, 238-46
  of pupil by group, 239-40
  pupil's self-, 45, 97, 107, 136, 137-38,
    149, 197, 198-200, 238-39, 241,
    248
  in science, 198-200
  in social studies, 173-74
  teacher's self-, 87, 90, 199
  of units, 49
  See also Records; Tests
Experience chart, 142-43, 191

F

Family background, 15-16, 18, 108, 154-
    55, 181, 236 (*see also* Parents)
Field trips, 199
Files. *See* Records
Films, 91, 102, 126, 201 (*see also* Audio-
    visual aids)
Fitzgerald, James A., 139
Forcing, 81-83, 93
Fundamentals, 6, 49, 80, 138-40, 205,
    263

G

Games, 52-53
Gifted child, 98-99 (see also Bright child)
Girls, interests of, 92-93, 182
Goals. See Objectives
Goltry, T. Keith, 139
Goodenough, Florence, 88
Graded study guides, 162-65
Grouping:
  by ability, 2-3, 35, 36-40, 60, 71-74, 181
  in arithmetic, 204, 206-208, 211
  cross-ability, 156-59
  in depth, 204-33
  entire-class, 5, 45, 157, 174, 186-91, 205
  in language arts, 140, 142-44, 145
  in science, 187-88, 192-93
  in social studies, 156-59
Guidance, 15-16, 246, 264-65
Guidance in the Curriculum, 25

H

Halo effect, 21
Handwriting, 136, 139
Havighurst, Robert J., 52-53
Health:
  mental, 15-16, 124-25, 254-68
  physical, 15-16, 31, 36, 108
Home. See Family background; Parents
Homework, 53-54, 251, 252
Horn, Ernest, 139

I

Identification of differences, 13-33, 71-73, 108-10, 153-56, 207-208 (see also Achievement; Evaluation; Intelligence; Tests)
Independent work, 42, 43, 49-50, 187-88, 191-98
Integration of subjects, 45, 62, 132, 142
Intelligence, 2, 28-29, 64, 109, 153, 157, 167, 240-44
Interest:
  center of, 141-42, 148
  centers of, in room, 106, 133-34, 148
Interests, 39, 45, 50, 92-93, 167-69, 182, 187-88, 192

IQ, 2, 28-29, 240-44 (see also Intelligence; Mental age; Tests)

J

Jones, W. Franklin, 139

L

Language arts, 54, 56, 128-51 (see also Reading)
Library, 56, 134 (see also Books; Reference materials)
Listening, 117-20, 135, 141, 159-60
Lowenfeld, Viktor, 5-6, 44, 80, 85-86, 96

M

McHugh, Walter J., 169
McKee, Paul, 140
Marks, 237-38, 249-50
Materials:
  arithmetic, 209, 211, 212-14
  art, 84-85, 90, 91, 99, 101
  language arts, 132-38
  music, 106, 126
  reference, 135-36, 154, 165-66, 195
  science, 187-88, 189-91, 200-201
  social studies, 165-66, 169-70
  See also Audio-visual aids; Books; Texts
Maturity, 20, 181
Mental age, 28-29, 64, 240-44
Mental health, 15-16, 124-25, 254-68
Methods, 34-57
Minimum essentials, 49, 138-40, 205, 263
Modeling, 82, 94-97
Morton, Robert Lee, 44
Motivation:
  art, 85-87, 93, 99
  language arts, 141-42, 145-49
  major factor in learning, 15-16, 265-67
  music, 114, 124-25
  and report cards, 247
  in unit, 170-71
Music, 36, 57, 61-62, 104-27

N

Needs, 15-16, 255-56, 267 (see also Adjustment of child)

Newland, T. Ernest, 139
North, Robert D., 30

O

Objectives:
arithmetic, 205
music, 104-105, 118
pupil's, 146, 148, 238-39, 241, 266
science, 182-84, 202
social studies, 173
Oral reports, 46, 48, 132, 140-41, 169, 172, 197
Oral work, 16, 20-21 (see also Language arts)
Overage pupil, 66-67

P

Parents:
conferences with, 16, 31-32, 67, 108, 243-44, 251-52
and homework, 54
and music, 114
reports to, 237-38, 246-52
status of, 2
as tutors, 51
See also Family background
Participation, record of pupil's, 19-21, 198
Physical development, 15-16, 109
Physical education, 61
Planning by pupils, 107, 239 (see also Evaluation, pupil's self-; Units)
Pooley, Robert C., 139
Practice, 137 (see also Drill)
Pressey, S. L. and L. C., 139
Primary unit, 65
Projects. See Independent work
Promotion, 65-67
Psychological examination, 30-31, 64
Pupil specialties, 168-69
Pupil teams, 40, 162-66
Purpose. See Objectives
Pursuit of Excellence, The: Education and the Future of America, 10

R

Radio. See Audio-visual aids
Range of differences, 1-3, 72-73, 208, 211, 213

Ratings of traits, 236, 250-51
Reading:
and age of admission, 64
music, 119-20
in primary unit, 65
science, 193, 195
social studies, 153-54, 162-66
summer, 54-57
See also Books; Language arts
Recommended Records and Books for the School Curriculum, 120
Recordings. See Audio-visual aids
Records:
anecdotal, 20, 31, 108, 174, 236-37, 250
cumulative, of art work, 100; contents of, 29, 235-37; kept by child, 24, 146, 147; kept by teacher, 235-38; of music work, 108; for parents, 252; of reading, 146; recordings as, 198-99; samples of work filed with, 22, 50, 100, 108, 135, 199; of science work, 191, 196-97, 198-200; and teacher's self-evaluation, 199; use of, 14, 17-18, 29, 236, 237-38
Reference materials, 135-36, 154, 165-66, 195 (see also Books; Library)
Release from school for special instruction, 63
Remedial teaching, 51, 67-69
Report cards, 237-38, 246-52
Reports, oral, 46, 48, 132, 140-41, 169, 172, 197
Retardation, 65-67, 68
Rinsland, Henry D., 139
Rockefeller Report on Education, 10
Rolliston, Donald H., 139

S

Scheduling, 35-36, 61, 62, 68, 107, 131-32, 192
Science, 36, 55, 57, 179-203
Self-confidence, 84, 98, 124-25
Self-criticism. See Evaluation, pupil's self-
Singing, 110-17
Slow learner:
books for, 56, 159-60
characteristics of, 47-48, 153-54, 167
gains by, 11, 181, 240-42

Slow learner (*cont.*):
  and grouping, 36-39, 154-59, 205, 207-10
  methods for, 47-48, 159, 162-63
  remedial teaching and, 67-69
  retardation of, 65-68
  teacher of, 60
  and texts, 41, 42-43, 133, 159
  tutoring of, 50-51
  See also Identification; Intelligence; IQ; Mental age; Range; Tests
Social development, 15-16, 24, 49, 155
Social situation, 128-30, 142
Social studies, 57, 152-78
Sociometric techniques, 24
Specialists, 16, 30-31, 61-62, 262
Spelling, 54, 56, 135-36, 139 (*see also* Language arts)
Stammering, 116
Standards, 49, 80, 131, 138-40, 205, 263
STEP tests, 173
Subject preferences, 155-56
Summer activities, 54-57, 76-77
Superior learner. *See* Bright child
Supplementary materials. *See* Books; Materials; Reference materials

T

Talks with pupil. *See* Conferences
Teacher:
  and administrators, 59-60
  assignment of, 60-63
  assistants, 22, 69-70
  attitudes of, 4-10, 14-15, 254-55, 256-57
  hobbies of, 100, 193
  remedial, 51, 67-69
  and separate subjects, 61, 105-106, 129, 132, 136, 184-85, 201-202
  teams, 62

Tests:
  achievement, 27-30, 154, 197, 200, 242-44
  diagnostic, 28, 31, 50, 209-10
  essay type, 245-46
  and grouping, 37-39
  intelligence, 28, 64, 240-41
  interpreting, 18, 27-30
  teacher-made, 173, 197, 245-46
  variation in scores, 27-29, 73
  vocabulary, 161-62
  See also Evaluation; Identification
Texts, basal:
  language arts, 133, 138-39
  music, 106
  social studies, 159-60, 162-66
  use of, 41-44, 46, 152-53, 171
Thinking, 166-68
Traits, ratings of, 236, 250-51
Traxler, Arthur E., 30
Tutoring, 50-51, 67-69
TV. *See* Audio-visual aids

U

Units, 45-47, 142, 169-73, 184-86

V

Vocabulary, 133, 135-36, 138-39, 145, 153-54, 160-63

W

Withdrawal, 259-60
Wood, Ben D., 30
Workbooks, 44-45, 133, 137, 141, 206
Wrightstone, J. Wayne, 47-48, 66

Y

Yale-Fairfield Study, 69-70